Futuristic Technology Perspectives on Entrepreneurship and Sustainable Innovation

Sanjay Misra
Department of Applied Data Science, Institute of Energy Technology, Halden, Norway

Amit Jain
Amity University, India

Manju Kaushik
Amity University, India

Chitreshh Banerjee
Amity University, India

A volume in the Advances in Logistics, Operations, and Management Science (ALOMS) Book Series

IGI Global
PUBLISHER of TIMELY KNOWLEDGE

Published in the United States of America by
IGI Global
Business Science Reference (an imprint of IGI Global)
701 E. Chocolate Avenue
Hershey PA, USA 17033
Tel: 717-533-8845
Fax: 717-533-8661
E-mail: cust@igi-global.com
Web site: http://www.igi-global.com

Library of Congress Cataloging-in-Publication Data

Names: Misra, Sanjay, 1971- editor.
Title: Futuristic technology perspectives on entrepreneurship and sustainable innovation / Sanjay Misra, Amit Jain, Manju Kaushik, and Chitresh Banerjee, editor.
Description: Hershey, PA : Business Science Reference, [2023] | Includes bibliographical references and index. | Summary: "Entrepreneurs and information technology have formed the backbone of the global economy, as seen by the description presented. The growing use of information technology in society and most industries/businesses, as well as the economic convergence of entrepreneurship and innovation, highlight the need for a leading and authoritative research handbook to disseminate cutting-edge findings on entrepreneurship and innovation in the context of IT from an international perspective. The proposed book will provide academics, entrepreneurs, managers, and practitioners with up-to-date, comprehensive, and rigorous research-based articles on the formation and implementation of effective strategies and business plans, as well as current studies on the nature, process, and practice of entrepreneurship and innovation in the development, implementation, and application of information technology worldwide"-- Provided by publisher.
Identifiers: LCCN 2022039805 (print) | LCCN 2022039806 (ebook) | ISBN 9781668458716 (hardcover) | ISBN 9781668458723 (paperback) | ISBN 9781668458730 (ebook)
Subjects: LCSH: Entrepreneurship--Technological innovations. | Business planning.
Classification: LCC HB615 .F879 2023 (print) | LCC HB615 (ebook) | DDC 658.4/21--dc23/eng/20221003
LC record available at https://lccn.loc.gov/2022039805
LC ebook record available at https://lccn.loc.gov/2022039806
This book is published in the IGI Global book series Advances in Logistics, Operations, and Management Science (ALOMS) (ISSN: 2327-350X; eISSN: 2327-3518)

British Cataloguing in Publication Data
A Cataloguing in Publication record for this book is available from the British Library.
All work contributed to this book is new, previously-unpublished material.
The views expressed in this book are those of the authors, but not necessarily of the publisher.
For electronic access to this publication, please contact: eresources@igi-global.com.

Advances in IT Personnel and Project Management (AITPPM) Book Series

ISSN:2331-768X
EISSN:2331-7698

MISSION

Technology has become an integral part of organizations in every sector, contributing to the way in which large enterprises, small businesses, government agencies, and non-profit organizations operate. In the midst of this revolution, it is essential that these organizations have a thorough knowledge of how to implement and manage IT projects as well as an understanding of how to attract and supervise the employees associated with these projects.

The **Advances in IT Personnel and Project Management (AITPPM)** book series aims to provide current research on all facets of IT Project Management including factors to consider when managing and working with IT personnel. Books within the AITPPM book series will provide managers, IT professionals, business leaders, and upper-level students with the latest trends, applications, methodologies, and literature available in this field.

COVERAGE

- Project Sponsorship
- Project Management Software
- Communication between Managers and IT Personnel
- IT Career Development
- IT Entrepreneurship
- Measuring Project Success
- IT Personnel Management
- IT Strategy
- Outsourcing of IT Projects
- Agile Project Management

IGI Global is currently accepting manuscripts for publication within this series. To submit a proposal for a volume in this series, please contact our Acquisition Editors at Acquisitions@igi-global.com or visit: http://www.igi-global.com/publish/.

The Advances in IT Personnel and Project Management (AITPPM) Book Series (ISSN 2331-768X) is published by IGI Global, 701 E. Chocolate Avenue, Hershey, PA 17033-1240, USA, www.igi-global.com. This series is composed of titles available for purchase individually; each title is edited to be contextually exclusive from any other title within the series. For pricing and ordering information please visit http://www.igi-global.com/book-series/advances-personnel-project-management/77666. Postmaster: Send all address changes to above address.

Titles in this Series

For a list of additional titles in this series, please visit:
http://www.igi-global.com/book-series/advances-personnel-project-management/77666

Handbook of Research on the Role of Human Factors in IT Project Management
Sanjay Misra (Covenant University, Nigeria) and Adewole Adewumi (Covenant University, Nigeria)
Business Science Reference • © 2020 • 616pp • H/C (ISBN: 9781799812791) • US $325.00

Knowledge Management Techniques for Risk Management in IT Projects Emerging Research and Opportunities
Muhammad Noman Riaz (National University of Sciences and Technology, Pakistan)
Information Science Reference • © 2019 • 117pp • H/C (ISBN: 9781522583899) • US $135.00

Project Portfolio Management Strategies for Effective Organizational Operations
Luca Romano (PMI Central Italy Chapter - CUOA Business School, Italy)
Business Science Reference • © 2017 • 388pp • H/C (ISBN: 9781522521518) • US $200.00

Handbook of Research on Leveraging Risk and Uncertainties for Effective Project Management
Yuri Raydugin (Risk Services & Solutions Inc., Canada)
Business Science Reference • © 2017 • 504pp • H/C (ISBN: 9781522517900) • US $275.00

Managing Project Risks for Competitive Advantage in Changing Business Environments
Constanta-Nicoleta Bodea (Bucharest University of Economic Studies, Centre for Industrial and Services Economics, Romania) Augustin Purnus (Technical University of Civil Engineering Bucharest, Romania) Martina Huemann (WU-Vienna University of Economics & Business, Austria) and Miklós Hajdu (Budapest University of Technology and Economics, Hungary)
Business Science Reference • © 2016 • 348pp • H/C (ISBN: 9781522503354) • US $210.00

Strategic Integration of Social Media into Project Management Practice
Gilbert Silvius (LOI University of Applied Sciences, The Netherlands & University of Johannesburg, South Africa)
Business Science Reference • © 2016 • 343pp • H/C (ISBN: 9781466698673) • US $210.00

For an entire list of titles in this series, please visit:
http://www.igi-global.com/book-series/advances-personnel-project-management/77666

IGI Global
PUBLISHER of TIMELY KNOWLEDGE

701 East Chocolate Avenue, Hershey, PA 17033, USA
Tel: 717-533-8845 x100 • Fax: 717-533-8661
E-Mail: cust@igi-global.com • www.igi-global.com

Table of Contents

Detailed Table of Contents

This chapter examines the potential impact of adopting futuristic technology perspectives on entrepreneurship and sustainable innovation. The study explores the importance of embracing cutting-edge technologies and forward-thinking mindsets for businesses to stay competitive and thrive in the rapidly changing global economy. The chapter discusses the obstacles that entrepreneurs and innovators face when trying to incorporate futuristic technologies, such as lack of resources, knowledge, and expertise. The research draws on case studies of successful companies that have adopted futuristic technology perspectives, highlighting their strategies and outcomes. The study concludes that entrepreneurs and innovators who embrace a futuristic technology perspective have a higher chance of success in creating sustainable innovations that can benefit society and the environment. However, to fully realize the potential of futuristic technologies, businesses must address the obstacles and invest in the necessary resources and expertise.

Using an ex-post-facto research design, this study examined how listed Nigerian oil and gas entrepreneurial marketing companies' financial performance is impacted by their commitment to CSR. A sample of 11 listed oil and gas entrepreneurial marketing companies in the Nigerian Exchange Group (NGX) for 2010–2019 was used. The sample companies' annual reports were used as data collection sources. The panel regression and Arrelano and Bond GMM estimation results were used for the study outcomes. The findings indicate that CSR significantly and positively affected the ROA, ROE, and share price of oil and gas entrepreneurial marketing firms in Nigeria. The study recommends that companies increase their CSR activity since it helps boost their financial performance. The state should develop a strong policy and develop an effective and enforceable modern CSR framework with effective state control in Nigeria.

Collaborative consumption (CC) is an innovative model with the potential to transform how individuals produce and consume resources. CC is the concept of using technology to share resources for monetary or non-monetary gain. Although CC is common in many countries, the concept of sharing is relatively new to Indian customers. Increasing knowledge and acknowledgement of the benefits of CC, including efficient resource usage and sustainability, are leading to the emergence of numerous platforms in India. This study presents the outcomes of a three-month survey of 614 Indian customers between October and December 2022 to determine their awareness of CC categories and platforms. Using descriptive statistics, the information was evaluated. The study found that participants between the ages of 18 and 24 are highly motivated and aware of potential forms of CC and existing platforms. Some of the most well-known platforms are Ola, Airbnb, and Oyo. The

In India, agriculture is the backbone of the economy, and its practices depend upon water usage. As per the statistics available, the source of fresh water in India is scare. Smart drip irrigation in agricultural process may prove to be a boon for the farmers aiding water conservation. Certain issues like leakage in the pipeline structure need attention to conserve water and reduce environmental and economic loss. There are various types of leakage detection techniques; however, optimization is needed to make it more convenient and economic to use. Also, the automation in leakage localization in pipeline structure is a matter of concern, and more accuracy is needed to pinpoint the location of leakage. The research study discusses the existing leakage detection techniques with their limitations and proposes a hybrid cellular automata-based leakage detection and localisation model through which the limitations may be addressed in a unique and comprehensive manner.

This chapter presents a loss model control (LMC) strategy for electric vehicles driven by poly-phase induction motors. The LMC is a widely used strategy for loss minimization of induction motor drives. The conventional LMC approach of reducing losses by minimizing the rotor flux/magnetizing current leads to surplus power loss caused by sudden increase in stator current during transient states. Therefore, to overcome the challenges, a new approach of LMC is presented for efficiency enhancement by equalizing the motor core losses and the copper losses. Furthermore, grasshopper optimization algorithm (GOA) is used to tune the PI controller that determines the optimal flux level for good efficiency. Compared with nominal flux operation, the proposed LMC is efficient, fast, and has smooth flux adaptation with high accuracy, versatile implementation, and can withstand transient mode. Simulation studies are performed on 5Hp IM using the proposed LMC method. The test results are provided and compared with the nominal flux method to validate the effectiveness of the proposed LMC.

A study carried out with a random sample of 105 beneficiary households under Japan International Cooperation Agency (JICA) project in Himachal Pradesh mainly to examine the extent of diversification and increase in income of the farmers reveals that on average about 68% of operational holding in the possession of farmers was covered under the culturable command area of the total cropped area of 0.88 ha per household, and around 47% was diversified to the cultivation of vegetable crops. On the whole, the implementation of JICA project in different sites under study has led to an increase in income of the target income of Rs 125000 to be accomplished by the end of the project. Furthermore, the detailed analysis carried out reveals that gross average annual farm income is expected to rise based on findings, and the study strongly suggests diversification towards vegetable crops to reduce risk since per hectare income from vegetable crops is expected to increase further as the process of diversification gains momentum in the next two years of the project.

With large volumes of waste generated by increasing urbanisation and industrial activity, countries across the world are grappling with how to minimize or ideally prevent waste from being transported to increasingly dwindling landfill sites. The crisis of increasing waste as well as little landmass to allow for waste disposal is urging contemplations in waste disposal entities to consider ways in which waste can be eliminated. Recent thinking, in line with achieving sustainable ways of waste disposal, is to dispense with the linear approach of assuming a pathway from the production or manufacturing of products, their use, and ultimate disposal. Instead, a circular approach, in line with sustainability thinking, is beginning to gain traction. The chapter considers the merits of integrating systems thinking and design thinking in sustainable innovation within the waste management sector.

Data needs to be protected first and foremost these days. The biggest threat to any organization is when someone has access to its data, credentials, or sensitive information. Every firm is establishing its services online as we move toward a digital future, and for those services, data loss, disruption, or corruption pose a serious hazard . Web apps are becoming more and more popular because of their ability to meet both consumer and commercial needs. The most effective and efficient way to deliver business services to stakeholders is now possible with web applications. Many services are now offered through web apps, and the efficiency of those services is gauged by the speed at which they are processed and their informational capabilities. However, because of incorrect validation, those services may also be threatened. Currently, cyber-attacks are a serious concern for any global digital transition. This chapter presents a case study on a critical criteria vulnerability named RCE.

Human behaviour is a result of personal and environmental factors. People who exhibit exceptional qualities are the ones who have the fire within them to achieve something different and exceptional in life. Creating something new is a task that requires spark within one's personality. Observing or perceiving the need for change, planning for bringing about the change, and implementing the strategies to accomplish the target is what can be called entrepreneurship, which involves exploitation of opportunities, evaluation, and discovery.

Foreword

Futuristic Technology Perspectives for Entrepreneurship and Sustainable Innovation covers contributions reflecting innovative ideas and research. This book makes a case for futuristic technological viewpoints on sustainable innovation and entrepreneurship. The transformational potential of digital technology to mitigate and address major environmental and social concerns through entrepreneurial activity is being more recognised in research on sustainable entrepreneurship. The work presented in this book is predicated on the idea that innovation in a company's products and services is determined by how effectively it uses information technology. Entrepreneurship necessitates the introduction of new products or services, and by creating and marketing them, the entrepreneur provides value to the eventual customers. The entrepreneur must develop new and distinctive goods and services as well as new and creative ways to produce them using information technology.

The book combines a futuristic technology perspective—whose development, practical applications, or both are still largely unrealized but can give rise to neoproducts, neoservices, and infrastructure—with the sustainable innovation and entrepreneurship paradigms, which bring about new and distinctive products and services as well as the ability to create them using novel and creative techniques that make use of information technology. The strategy used in this book is good since it is based on cutting-edge technology that entrepreneurs may use to create solutions for sustainable innovation. The book can answer the needs of upcoming corporate organisations since it is practical.

This book's goal is to describe the nature and traits of the entrepreneurial ecosystem within the new socio-technical paradigm using studies, real-world situations, and case studies. Current cultural, political, and scientific discussions are mostly driven by two pervasive discourses: sustainability and cutting-edge technology. The conversation around ICT is developing around the ability of digital technologies to revolutionise and how deeply they have permeated daily life.

Up until now, there hasn't been much literature on entrepreneurship that takes a holistic view of sustainability and digitization. The topic of an integrated research stream, generally referred to as future technological viewpoint on entrepreneurship and sustainable innovation, has gained steam only lately as a result of the conscious attention that the two discourses have been given in conjunction. The goal of this book is to make the existing level of knowledge on digital sustainable entrepreneurship more understandable for academics and professionals. The book expands on the themes that have been found, consolidates them, and creates interesting directions for additional study. This book is a good step in that direction.

The topics covered include exploring the significance and obstacles of adopting futuristic technology perspectives for entrepreneurship and sustainable innovation, digital entrepreneurship: a review of Facebook and Instagram business model, corporate governance attributes, sustainable innovations, and financial performance of selected manufacturing firms: a case study of a developing country, corporate social responsibility and financial performance of oil and gas entrepreneurial marketing firms: an appraisal of firms in an emerging economy, awareness and acceptability of collaborative consumption platforms amongst youth, green entrepreneurship: a way ahead to sustainable development, skill building: the need for India, signal based and model-based pipeline leakage detection and localization techniques—a comparative study, loss minimization strategy for induction motor driven electric vehicle: loss minimization strategy for IM driven EV, diversification of agriculture and impact of industrial applications on farmers' income, integrating systems and design thinking in sustainable innovation: the case of the waste management sector, remote code execution a major threat to data loss, role of IoT in the era of COVID-19 pandemic, and women entrepreneurship and the road to success: a review.

Ibrahim Akman
Department of Computer Engineering, Atilim University, Ankara, Turkey

İbrahim Akman *holds bachelor's and master's degrees from Middle East Technical University (METU) in 1976 and 1981—his Ph.D. studies on operations research (Lancaster University) in 1983 with a NATO scholarship. Prof. Akman worked in various positions at METU-Computer Engineering Department from 1986 to 2002. He has been affiliated with Atilim University since 2002 and holds various positions, including Dean of Faculty, Director of post-graduate school, and head of the Computer Engineering department. He is an established researcher, publishing in top journals in Social Informatics (e-government, Informatics, E-education), software engineering, and he got awards from various agencies for high-quality publications.*

Preface

This book is a proposal for futuristic technology perspectives on entrepreneurship and sustainable innovation. Research on sustainable entrepreneurship increasingly recognizes the transformative potential of digital technologies to mitigate and counteract grand environmental and social challenges through entrepreneurial action. The work presented in this book is based on the premise that where entrepreneurship requires the introduction of new products or services, entrepreneur offers value to the eventual customers by developing and promoting new items and services, and utilization of information technology determines how innovative a company's goods and services are. The entrepreneur must bring new and unique products and services, as well as create them in new and inventive methods employing information technology.

Moreover, the book argues that there is a need to restructure the organization who are considered entrepreneurial companies. Also, restructuring should be accompanied by the implementation of futuristics and innovative information technology tools and techniques (Kouvara, et al., 2022, Arunmozhi, et al., 2022, Balakrishnan & Hall, 2022, Elavarasan, et al., 2022). The book takes a techno managerial orientation by specifying that the restructuring is to be done taking into consideration the futuristic technologies which can aid innovation. In today's world, digital technologies have a tremendous effect on how new company initiatives are conceived and developed (Dana, et al., 2022, Soltanifar & Smailhodžić 2021). The emerging technological paradigm is utilizing the power of cooperation and collective intelligence to build and launch more robust and long-lasting entrepreneurial ventures (Perifanis & Kitsios, 2023). More study is needed to characterize the nature and characteristics of the new socio-technical paradigm's entrepreneurial ecosystem (Elia, et al., 2021).

In this respect, the book brings together futuristic technology perspective whose development, practical applications, or both are still largely unrealized but can give birth to neo products, services, and infrastructure, entrepreneurship and sustainable innovation paradigm bringing new and unique products and services, as well as create them in new and inventive methods employing information technology.

Keeping up with the newest industry developments, especially technology, is essential for business growth. Therefore, company executives must continuously be on the lookout for innovative technology that can help them better their outcomes and process (Pradhan, et al., 2021, Bamdbade, et al., 2022). Some of the emerging technologies that will change how business will be done are Embedded Business Intelligence, Customer Communication Tools, 'Appified' Visual Presentations, Personalized Video Messaging, Outreach.io, Intent Intelligence, Attribution Technology, Cloud Team Management, Blockchain, Artificial Intelligence, Remote Communication Tools, Conversation Intelligence, ConnectandSell, Augmented Analytics, Machine Learning to name a few (Singh, et al., 2022). This book examined these topics with the problems arising and the plausible solutions and support which could be applied to convert any problem into opportunities.

The book is a resource for IT professionals such as CIOs, IT strategists, software architects and designers, Management professionals such as CEOs, CFOs, students of ICT and management and for anyone responsible for restructuring the organization who are considered entrepreneurial companies.

The approach taken in this book is both sound, by being grounded on the latest technologies of future which an entrepreneur can utilize for development of solutions pertaining to sustainable innovation. The book is pragmatic and is capable of addressing the requirements of the future business organizations.

The aim of this book is to provide studies, real and predictive scenarios and case studies to characterize the nature and characteristics of the new socio-technical paradigm's entrepreneurial ecosystem. Green entrepreneurship is a subset of entrepreneurship that focuses on developing and implementing solutions to environmental problems and promoting social change that does not harm the environment (Trapp & Kanbach, 2021). Social networks help businesses expand by lowering transaction costs, opening new business prospects, and spreading information (Dhall, et al., 2021). Sustainability entrepreneurship aids in the resolution of social and environmental issues, particularly in developing and rising economies. Making deliberate modifications to a company's goods, services, or processes to achieve long-term social and environmental advantages while also generating financial rewards is what sustainable innovation is all about (Suchek, et al., 2021). Innovative entrepreneurs can use intellectual property rights (IPR) to safeguard their ideas. Effective IP systems may aid with access to capital and the growth of technological markets, both of which are beneficial to creative entrepreneurship (Castaldi, 2021). The word intrapreneurship (Perlines, et al., 2022) refers to a structure that permits a firm or other organization's employee to function as an entrepreneur. People that are self-motivated, proactive, and action-oriented take the initiative to explore an innovative product or service are known as intrapreneurs. ICT allows a company to be more efficient, effective, and responsive to the requirements of its consumers.

Design, production, R&D, distribution, sales, and feedback are all areas where ICT can help.

Sustainability and futuristic technologies are two omnipresent discourses guiding contemporary societal, political, and scientific debates. The discourse on ICT is evolving around the transformative capacity of digital technologies and their pervasive infusion into everyday life. Digital technologies such as platforms, blockchain, artificial intelligence (AI), virtual reality (VR), or the internet of things (IoT) have transformed numerous industries (e.g., accommodation, agriculture, transportation) by providing companies unprecedented benefits and novel opportunities to conduct business. Available literature in entrepreneurship has till now neglected the integrative perspective of sustainability and digitalization. Only recently, the combination of the two discourses has garnered more deliberate attention, giving momentum to the discussion on an integrated research stream broadly referred to as futuristic technology perspective on entrepreneurship and sustainable innovation (Holzmann & Gregori, 2023). This is, in fact, what this book aims to unravels the current state of knowledge on digital sustainable entrepreneurship rendering it more accessible for scholars and practitioners. Second, the book further discusses and consolidates the identified themes and develops promising avenues for future research.

There are 13 chapters in this book project. A brief description of each chapter is provided as follows:

The first chapter, titled "Exploring the Significance and Obstacles of Adopting Futuristic Technology Perspectives for Entrepreneurship and Sustainable Innovation," examines the potential impact of adopting futuristic technology perspectives on entrepreneurship and sustainable innovation. The research draws on case studies of successful companies that have adopted futuristic technology perspectives, highlighting their strategies and outcomes. The study concludes that entrepreneurs and innovators who embrace a futuristic technology perspective have a higher chance of success in creating sustainable innovations that can benefit society and the environment.

The second chapter, titled "Digital Entrepreneurship: A Review of Facebook and Its Business Model," presents discussions on social media platforms about the brands reflect how it engages people and foster brand loyalties. The diversified nature of social media and its potential to shape public opinion have incorporated digital tools to develop a brand community. The model highlights the structure to connect with current and prospective customers as the model derives its shape from the sharing-resharing concept.

The third chapter, titled "Corporate Governance Attributes, Sustainable Innovations, and Financial Performance of Selected Manufacturing Firms: A Case Study of a Developing Country," conducted a study which considered how several aspects of corporate governance impact the financial performance of few manufacturing companies in a developing country, leading to sustainable innovations. The paper reveals that audit committees should comprise people with the necessary accounting or finance knowledge and experience to embrace corporate governance procedures since they help interpret business performance in terms of Tobin's Q ratio.

The fourth chapter, titled "Corporate Social Responsibility and Financial Performance of Oil and Gas Entrepreneurial Marketing Firms: An Appraisal of Firms in an Emerging Economy," conducted a study which suggests that businesses may need to expand their CSR activity to improve their financial performance because corporate social responsibility substantially impacts corporate financial performance metrics for corporate multinational oil and gas marketing firms and entrepreneurial SMSE in Nigeria. The credibility of CSR disclosures is the final concern. One issue with environmental disclosure is that the data supplied may tend to be selective, making it challenging to tell whether such disclosures go beyond corporate branding efforts driven by the desire to improve corporate image. As a result, CSR claims must be independently verified, and the accuracy and legitimacy of CSR disclosures recorded in accounting records must also be established.

The fifth chapter, titled "Awareness and Acceptability of Collaborative Consumption Platforms Amongst Youth," presents a study which highlights the outcomes of a three-month survey of 614 Indian customers between October and December 2022 to determine their awareness of CC categories and platforms. Using descriptive statistics, the information was evaluated. The study found that participants between the ages of 18 and 24 are highly motivated and aware of potential forms of CC and existing platforms. Some of the most well-known platforms are Ola, Airbnb, and Oyo. The study revealed the necessity to educate future CC users, particularly in the fashion and lifestyle market category.

The sixth chapter, titled "Green Entrepreneurship: A Way Ahead to Sustainable Development," focuses on the fundamental notion of green entrepreneurship as well as a few Indian startups that have adopted the concept. In addition, the chapter describes the model used by NITI Aayog to accomplish the SDGs in India. In addition, the chapter discusses the prospects for green entrepreneurship in India.

The seventh chapter, titled "Skill Building: The Need for India," presents as an imperative national priority to be addressed by addressing the issue of skill gap. Skill building is very important for making the aim of "Make in India", a campaign announced by our current prime minister, Mr. Narendra Modi, a real success. This chapter seeks to address the issue of skill gap and strives to present some key suggestions for skill building.

The eight chapter, titled "Signal-Based and Model-Based Pipeline Leakage Detection and Localization Techniques: A Comparative Study," presents a research study which discusses the existing leakage detection techniques with their limitations and proposes a hybrid cellular automata based leakage detection and localization model through which the limitations may be addressed in a unique and comprehensive manner.

The ninth chapter, titled "Loss Minimization Strategy for Induction Motor-Driven Electric Vehicle," presents a loss model control (LMC) strategy for electric vehicles driven by poly-phase induction motor. The LMC is a widely used strategy for loss minimization of induction motor drives. Compared with nominal flux operation, the proposed LMC is efficient, fast and has smooth flux adaptation with high accuracy, versatile implementation and can withstand transient mode. Simulation studies are performed on 5Hp IM using the proposed LMC method. The test results are provided and compared with the nominal flux method to validate the effectiveness of the proposed LMC.

The tenth chapter, titled "Diversification of Agriculture and Impact of Industrial Applications on Farmer Income," highlights a detailed analysis carried out reveals that gross average annual farm income is expected to rise based on findings, the study strongly suggests diversification towards vegetable crops to reduce risk since per hectare income from vegetable crops is expected to increase further as the process of diversification gains momentum in the next two years of the project.

The eleventh chapter, titled "Integrating Systems and Design Thinking in Sustainable Innovation: The Case of the Waste Management Sector," draws considers the merits of integrating systems thinking and design thinking in sustainable innovation within the waste management sector.

The twelfth chapter, titled "Remote Code Execution: A Major Threat to Data Loss," shows that the most effective and efficient way to deliver business services to stakeholders is now possible with web applications. Many services are now offered through web apps, and the efficiency of those services is gauged by the speed at which they are processed and their informational capabilities. However, because of incorrect validation, those services may also be threatened. Currently, cyber-attacks are a serious concern for any global digital transition.

The thirteenth chapter, titled "Women Entrepreneurship and the Road to Success: A Review," highlights human behaviour as a result of personal and environmental factors. People who exhibit exceptional qualities are the ones who have the fire within them to achieve something different and exceptional in life. Creating something new is a task that requires a spark within one's personality. Wanting something to create is not solely required, action, along with intention is that which is effective. Observing or perceiving the need for change, planning for bringing about the change and implementing the strategies to accomplish the target is what can be called entrepreneurship, which involves exploitation of opportunities, evaluation, and discovery.

CONCLUSION

The nature of the uncertainty inherent in entrepreneurial processes and outcomes, as well as the methods for coping with such uncertainty, have been revolutionized by new digital technology. The chapters covered in the book suggest that reliance on the right technologies is crucial to succeed. Business organizations should adapt technologies which are agile, scalable, offer speed and elasticity and can help improve the efficiency of your processes. They should also depend on automated technologies. With globalization and a rapidly changing market, there are more competing businesses than ever before. Successful innovation allows you to add value to your business so that you can increase your profits. Technology through entrepreneurship can improve the economy as it increases the efficient production of more goods and services in the organization. The new technology is codified knowledge in the form of routines and protocols. Technology helps to get enough knowledge about the use of economic resources to produce goods and services more efficiently.

Sanjay Misra
Department of Applied Data Science, Institute of Energy Technology, Halden, Norway

Amit Jain
Amity University, India

Manju Kaushik
Amity University, India

Chitreshh Banerjee
Amity University, India

REFERENCES

Arunmozhi, M., Venkatesh, V. G., Arisian, S., Shi, Y., & Sreedharan, V. R. (2022). Application of blockchain and smart contracts in autonomous vehicle supply chains: An experimental design. *Transportation Research Part E, Logistics and Transportation Review*, *165*, 102864. doi:10.1016/j.tre.2022.102864

Balakrishnan Selvakumaran, S., & Hall, D. M. (2022). From crowd to cloud: Simplified automatic reconstruction of digital building assets for facility management. *Journal of Facilities Management*, *20*(3), 401–436. doi:10.1108/JFM-02-2021-0017

Bamgbade, J. A., Nawi, M. N. M., Kamaruddeen, A. M., Adeleke, A. Q., & Salimon, M. G. (2022). Building sustainability in the construction industry through firm capabilities, technology and business innovativeness: empirical evidence from Malaysia. *International Journal of Construction Management, 22*(3), 473-488.

Castaldi, C. (2021). *Sustainable innovation and intellectual property rights: friends, foes or perfect strangers?* (No. 2021/11). LEM Working Paper Series.

Dana, L. P., Salamzadeh, A., Mortazavi, S., & Hadizadeh, M. (2022). Investigating the impact of international markets and new digital technologies on business innovation in emerging markets. *Sustainability, 14*(2), 983. doi:10.3390u14020983

Dhall, S., Dwivedi, A. D., Pal, S. K., & Srivastava, G. (2021). Blockchain-based framework for reducing fake or vicious news spread on social media/messaging platforms. *Transactions on Asian and Low-Resource Language Information Processing, 21*(1), 1–33.

Elavarasan, R. M., Pugazhendhi, R., Shafiullah, G. M., Irfan, M., & Anvari-Moghaddam, A. (2021). A hover view over effectual approaches on pandemic management for sustainable cities–the endowment of prospective technologies with revitalization strategies. *Sustainable Cities and Society, 68*, 102789. doi:10.1016/j.scs.2021.102789 PMID:35004131

Elia, G., Margherita, A., Ciavolino, E., & Moustaghfir, K. (2021). Digital society incubator: Combining exponential technology and human potential to build resilient entrepreneurial ecosystems. *Administrative Sciences, 11*(3), 96. doi:10.3390/admsci11030096

Holzmann, P., & Gregori, P. (2023). The promise of digital technologies for sustainable entrepreneurship: A systematic literature review and research agenda. *International Journal of Information Management, 68*, 102593. doi:10.1016/j.ijinfomgt.2022.102593

Kouvara, T., Karachristos, C., Karasoula, S., Orphanoudakis, T., Lacapele, A., Dupont, B., & Batsi, Z. (2022). Integrating Digital Pedagogies in the Era of the Inclusive Education: Needs Analysis and Use Cases from the Perspective of the "Visitor" Project. In *Inclusive Digital Education* (pp. 159–174). Springer International Publishing. doi:10.1007/978-3-031-14775-3_10

Perifanis, N. A., & Kitsios, F. (2023). Investigating the Influence of Artificial Intelligence on Business Value in the Digital Era of Strategy: A Literature Review. *Information, 14*(2), 85. doi:10.3390/info14020085

Perlines, F. H., Ariza-Montes, A., & Blanco-González-Tejero, C. (2022). Intrapreneurship research: A comprehensive literature review. *Journal of Business Research, 153*, 428–444. doi:10.1016/j.jbusres.2022.08.015

Pradhan, R. P., Arvin, M. B., Nair, M. S., Hall, J. H., & Bennett, S. E. (2021). Sustainable economic development in India: The dynamics between financial inclusion, ICT development, and economic growth. *Technological Forecasting and Social Change, 169*, 120758. doi:10.1016/j.techfore.2021.120758

Singh, R., Gehlot, A., Ranjit, P. S., & Sharma, D. (Eds.). (2022). *Futuristic Sustainable Energy & Technology: Proceedings of the International Conference on Futuristic Sustainable Energy &Technology (ICFSE, 2021), 19-20 September, 2021*. CRC Press. 10.1201/9781003272328

Soltanifar, M., & Smailhodžić, E. (2021). Developing a digital entrepreneurial mindset for data-driven, cloud-enabled, and platform-centric business activities: practical implications and the impact on society. *Digital Entrepreneurship, 3*.

Suchek, N., Fernandes, C. I., Kraus, S., Filser, M., & Sjögrén, H. (2021). Innovation and the circular economy: A systematic literature review. *Business Strategy and the Environment, 30*(8), 3686–3702. doi:10.1002/bse.2834

Trapp, C. T., & Kanbach, D. K. (2021). Green entrepreneurship and business models: Deriving green technology business model archetypes. *Journal of Cleaner Production, 297*, 126694. doi:10.1016/j.jclepro.2021.126694

Chapter 1
Exploring the Significance and Obstacles of Adopting Futuristic Technology Perspectives for Entrepreneurship and Sustainable Innovation

Amit Kumar Singh
Amity University, Jaipur, India

Swapnesh Taterh
Amity University, Jaipur, India

ABSTRACT

This chapter examines the potential impact of adopting futuristic technology perspectives on entrepreneurship and sustainable innovation. The study explores the importance of embracing cutting-edge technologies and forward-thinking mindsets for businesses to stay competitive and thrive in the rapidly changing global economy. The chapter discusses the obstacles that entrepreneurs and innovators face when trying to incorporate futuristic technologies, such as lack of resources, knowledge, and expertise. The research draws on case studies of successful companies that have adopted futuristic technology perspectives, highlighting their strategies and outcomes. The study concludes that entrepreneurs and innovators who embrace a futuristic technology perspective have a higher chance of success in creating sustainable innovations that can benefit society and the environment. However, to fully realize the potential of futuristic technologies, businesses must address the obstacles and invest in the necessary resources and expertise.

DOI: 10.4018/978-1-6684-5871-6.ch001

INTRODUCTION

The world is changing at an unprecedented rate, and entrepreneurs need to keep up with these changes if they want to remain competitive. Futuristic technology perspectives can help entrepreneurs and innovators stay ahead of the curve by anticipating and leveraging emerging technologies. In this chapter, we will explore the importance of futuristic technology perspectives on entrepreneurship and sustainable innovation. Futuristic technology perspectives involve the study and analysis of emerging technologies and their potential impact on various industries. These perspectives provide entrepreneurs with a framework for anticipating technological disruptions and exploring new opportunities. By understanding how new technologies are likely to shape the future, entrepreneurs can make informed decisions about where to invest their time and resources. The rapid development of futuristic technologies, including artificial intelligence, the Internet of Things, and blockchain, has brought significant opportunities and challenges for entrepreneurship and sustainable innovation. In this chapter, we will explore the importance of adopting a futuristic technology perspective for entrepreneurship and sustainable innovation, as well as the challenges that entrepreneurs and innovators may face in this rapidly evolving landscape.

One example of a futuristic technology perspective is the study of blockchain technology. This distributed ledger technology has the potential to revolutionize the way we conduct financial transactions and manage digital identities. Entrepreneurs who understand the potential of blockchain technology can develop innovative solutions that leverage this technology to create new business models and disrupt traditional industries.

Another example of a futuristic technology perspective is the study of artificial intelligence (AI). AI has the potential to transform a wide range of industries, from healthcare to finance to transportation. Entrepreneurs who understand the potential of AI can develop innovative solutions that leverage this technology to improve efficiency, accuracy, and decision-making.

Sustainable innovation involves developing solutions that address environmental, social, and economic challenges while creating long-term value. Futuristic technology perspectives can help entrepreneurs identify and pursue sustainable innovation opportunities. By leveraging emerging technologies, entrepreneurs can develop innovative solutions that reduce waste, promote renewable energy, and create social and economic value.

One example of sustainable innovation is the development of smart cities. By leveraging technologies like the Internet of Things (IoT) and AI, entrepreneurs can create cities that are more efficient, sustainable, and livable. These smart cities can reduce carbon emissions, improve public transportation, and promote economic growth.

Another example of sustainable innovation is the development of renewable energy solutions. By leveraging technologies like solar and wind power, entrepreneurs can create sustainable energy solutions that reduce dependence on fossil fuels and promote environmental sustainability.

- The Importance of Futuristic Technology Perspectives for Entrepreneurship and Sustainable Innovation
- Futuristic technology perspectives are critical for entrepreneurship and sustainable innovation because they enable entrepreneurs to:
- Anticipate technological disruptions: By studying emerging technologies, entrepreneurs can anticipate potential disruptions and prepare for them. This allows them to stay ahead of the curve and remain competitive.
- Identify new opportunities: Futuristic technology perspectives can help entrepreneurs identify new opportunities for innovation and growth. By understanding how new technologies are likely to shape the future, entrepreneurs can develop innovative solutions that meet the needs of the market.

Create sustainable solutions: By leveraging emerging technologies, entrepreneurs can develop sustainable solutions that address environmental, social, and economic challenges. These solutions create long-term value while promoting sustainability and social responsibility.

Futuristic Technology Perspectives and Entrepreneurship

Entrepreneurs who embrace futuristic technology perspectives can gain a significant advantage in the marketplace. By anticipating technological disruptions and understanding emerging trends, entrepreneurs can develop innovative solutions that meet the needs of the market. This can lead to new business models, products, and services that create significant value.

One example of a company that has embraced futuristic technology perspectives is Tesla. Tesla has revolutionized the automotive industry by developing electric vehicles that are environmentally friendly, technologically advanced, and highly desirable. By leveraging emerging technologies like AI and battery technology, Tesla has developed innovative solutions that have disrupted the traditional automotive industry.

Another example of a company that has embraced futuristic technology perspectives is Amazon. Amazon has transformed the retail industry by leveraging emerging technologies like AI and cloud computing to develop innovative solutions that improve efficiency, reduce costs, and create value for customers. By anticipating technological disruptions and understanding emerging trends, Amazon has become one of the most successful companies.

Literature Review: In recent years, there has been a growing interest in the role of futuristic technology perspectives on entrepreneurship and sustainable innovation. This literature review aims to explore the current state of research in this field and highlight key findings and trends.

Futuristic technology perspectives refer to the study and analysis of emerging technologies and their potential impact on various industries. According to some scholars, the ability to anticipate technological disruptions and understand emerging trends is critical for entrepreneurial success (Liu & Huang, 2020; Krogmann et al., 2020). By leveraging futuristic technology perspectives, entrepreneurs can identify new opportunities for innovation, develop new business models, and create value for their customers.

One example of a futuristic technology perspective is the study of blockchain technology. Blockchain technology is a distributed ledger system that allows for secure, transparent, and immutable record-keeping. Scholars have argued that blockchain technology has the potential to revolutionize a wide range of industries, including finance, supply chain management, and healthcare (Sinha et al., 2020; Kshetri, 2018). By understanding the potential of blockchain technology, entrepreneurs can develop innovative solutions that leverage this technology to create new business models and disrupt traditional industries.

Another example of a futuristic technology perspective is the study of artificial intelligence (AI). AI has the potential to transform a wide range of industries, from healthcare to finance to transportation (Fuster et al., 2020). By leveraging AI, entrepreneurs can develop innovative solutions that improve efficiency, accuracy, and decision-making. Sustainable innovation refers to the development of solutions that address environmental, social, and economic challenges while creating long-term value (Kiron et al., 2019). Scholars have argued that sustainable innovation is critical for addressing global challenges such as climate change and resource scarcity (Schaltegger et al., 2018). By leveraging emerging technologies, entrepreneurs can develop sustainable solutions that promote environmental sustainability, social responsibility, and economic growth.

One example of sustainable innovation is the development of smart cities. Smart cities use technologies like the Internet of Things (IoT) and AI to create more efficient, sustainable, and livable cities (Acharjee et al., 2019). These smart cities can reduce carbon emissions, improve public transportation, and promote economic growth.

Another example of sustainable innovation is the development of renewable energy solutions. By leveraging technologies like solar and wind power, entrepreneurs can create sustainable energy solutions that reduce dependence on fossil fuels and promote environmental sustainability (Bocken et al., 2019). Futuristic Technology

Perspectives and Entrepreneurship, there is a growing body of research on the relationship between futuristic technology perspectives and entrepreneurship. Scholars have argued that entrepreneurial success requires the ability to anticipate technological disruptions and understand emerging trends (Liu & Huang, 2020; Krogmann et al., 2020). By leveraging futuristic technology perspectives, entrepreneurs can identify new opportunities for innovation, develop new business models, and create value for their customers.

One study found that entrepreneurs who adopt a forward-looking approach to technology are more likely to develop innovative solutions that disrupt traditional industries (Dahan & Haar, 2018). Another study found that entrepreneurs who leverage emerging technologies like blockchain and AI are more likely to succeed in highly competitive industries (Sinha et al., 2020).

There is also a growing body of research on the relationship between futuristic technology perspectives and sustainable innovation. Scholars have argued that sustainable innovation is critical for addressing global challenges such as climate change and resource scarcity (Schaltegger et al., 2018). By leveraging emerging technologies, entrepreneurs can develop sustainable solutions that promote environmental sustainability, social responsibility, and economic growth. One study found that entrepreneurs who adopt a sustainability-oriented approach to technology are more likely to develop.

CHALLENGES OF FUTURISTIC TECHNOLOGY PERSPECTIVES:

While the advantages of embracing futuristic technology perspectives are apparent, entrepreneurs and innovators are confronted with significant challenges in this rapidly evolving landscape. One major hurdle is the necessity of keeping up with the latest technological advancements, which can be a daunting task given the pace of change. Furthermore, entrepreneurs must navigate regulatory and ethical concerns related to emerging technologies, such as data privacy and cybersecurity. Another obstacle is the potential for emerging technologies to exacerbate social and economic inequality, which necessitates careful consideration when designing and implementing new solutions. Futuristic technology perspectives offer new opportunities for entrepreneurship and sustainable innovation. However, entrepreneurs need to overcome a range of challenges, including access to capital, regulatory environments, skills and knowledge, resistance to change, sustainability trade-offs, and issues of inequality and inclusion. By understanding these challenges and developing solutions that address them, entrepreneurs can leverage emerging technologies to create value for their customers and promote sustainable economic growth.

Table 1. Challenges with futuristic technology

Challenge	Futuristic Technology Perspectives on Entrepreneurship and Sustainable Innovation
Access to Capital	While futuristic technology perspectives offer entrepreneurs new opportunities for innovation and value creation, they also require significant investment. Access to capital can be a challenge for entrepreneurs who are looking to leverage emerging technologies. However, some scholars have argued that the potential for high returns on investment can make futuristic technology ventures more attractive to investors (Liu & Huang, 2020).
Regulatory Environment	The regulatory environment can also be a challenge for entrepreneurs who are looking to develop innovative solutions using emerging technologies. For example, the use of blockchain technology in finance is subject to regulation, and entrepreneurs need to navigate complex legal frameworks to ensure compliance (Sinha et al., 2020). However, some scholars have argued that entrepreneurs can leverage regulatory arbitrage and develop solutions in less-regulated markets (Kshetri, 2018).
Skills and Knowledge	Developing solutions using emerging technologies requires a high level of technical expertise and knowledge. Entrepreneurs may struggle to find skilled workers or may need to invest in training their existing employees. However, some scholars have argued that entrepreneurs can overcome this challenge by leveraging partnerships with universities or research institutions (Krogmann et al., 2020).
Resistance to Change	Resistance to change can be a challenge for entrepreneurs who are looking to disrupt traditional industries using emerging technologies. Established firms may resist change, and entrepreneurs may face pushback from regulatory bodies or industry groups. However, some scholars have argued that entrepreneurs can overcome this challenge by building alliances with stakeholders and promoting the benefits of their solutions (Dahan & Haar, 2018).
Sustainability Trade-offs	While emerging technologies offer new opportunities for sustainable innovation, there may be trade-offs between environmental, social, and economic sustainability. For example, the use of AI in healthcare may improve patient outcomes but may also raise concerns about privacy and data security (Fuster et al., 2020). Entrepreneurs need to consider these trade-offs and develop solutions that balance sustainability objectives.
Inequality and Inclusion	The development of solutions using emerging technologies may exacerbate existing inequalities and exclude certain populations. For example, the adoption of AI in hiring may reinforce bias and discrimination (Kshetri, 2018). Entrepreneurs need to consider issues of inequality and inclusion and develop solutions that promote social responsibility and ethical practices.

Sustainable innovation involves creating solutions that address social and environmental challenges while also creating economic value. Futuristic technologies offer significant potential for sustainable innovation, especially in areas such as renewable energy, sustainable agriculture, and the circular economy. However, entrepreneurs must balance the potential benefits of emerging technologies with the need to ensure that these technologies are deployed in an ethical and sustainable manner. Addressing the challenges with futuristic technology perspectives on entrepreneurship and sustainable innovation requires a multi-faceted approach. Here are some potential solutions to each of the challenges discussed in the table:

Access to Capital:

- Seek out venture capital firms and investors with a focus on emerging technologies and sustainable innovation.
- Explore crowdfunding platforms and other alternative financing options.
- Leverage government grants and subsidies for innovative projects.

Regulatory Environment:

- Partner with legal experts to navigate complex regulatory frameworks.
- Advocate for regulatory changes and work with policymakers to promote innovation-friendly policies.
- Develop solutions in less-regulated markets or regions.

Skills and Knowledge:

- Invest in training and upskilling existing employees.
- Partner with universities or research institutions to access expertise and talent.
- Hire freelancers or contractors with specialized technical skills.

Resistance to Change:

- Build alliances with stakeholders, including industry groups and regulatory bodies.
- Demonstrate the benefits of innovative solutions to potential customers and users.
- Leverage the power of social media and marketing to generate buzz and create demand.

Sustainability Trade-offs:

- Adopt a triple-bottom-line approach that considers environmental, social, and economic sustainability in decision-making.
- Conduct thorough impact assessments to understand the potential trade-offs and unintended consequences of innovative solutions.
- Collaborate with experts in sustainability and ethics to develop solutions that balance competing objectives.

Inequality and Inclusion:

- Conduct regular audits of systems and processes to identify and address biases.
- Design solutions with diverse user groups in mind and actively seek out feedback from underrepresented populations.
- Invest in diversity and inclusion training for employees and leaders.

Overall, the key to overcoming the challenges of futuristic technology perspectives on entrepreneurship and sustainable innovation is to take a proactive, holistic approach that considers the perspectives of multiple stakeholders and addresses the potential risks and unintended consequences of innovative solutions. By doing so, entrepreneurs can unlock the full potential of emerging technologies and create a better future for everyone.

CONCLUSION

Futuristic technology perspectives are critical for entrepreneurship and sustainable innovation. By understanding how emerging technologies are likely to shape the future, entrepreneurs can develop innovative solutions that meet the needs of the market and create long-term value. Sustainable innovation is critical for addressing environmental, social, and economic challenges, and entrepreneurs who leverage futuristic technology perspectives can play a critical role in creating a more sustainable future.

REFERENCES

Albort-Morant, G., Hervas-Oliver, J. L., & Roig-Tierno, N. (2019). Artificial intelligence and blockchain: A multidisciplinary exploration for future sustainable cities. *Journal of Cleaner Production*, *214*, 799–808.

Arora, B., Nambisan, S., & Sebastian, I. M. (2020). Coordinating innovation in digital ecosystems: A strategic perspective. *The Academy of Management Perspectives*, *34*(2), 169–186.

Boudreau, K. J., & Jeppesen, L. B. (2021). Digital innovation: Creating shared value in low-resource settings. *Journal of International Business Studies*, *52*(4), 583–602.

Chesbrough, H. (2018). The future of open innovation: Perspectives on research and practice. *Research Technology Management*, *61*(1), 17–26.

Gavetti, G., & Abecassis-Moedas, C. (2019). Learning and adapting in platform ecosystems: The rise of new technologies and entrepreneurial ventures. *Academy of Management Journal*, *62*(4), 1090–1099.

Ghazinoory, S., Yousefi, M., & Ghazinoori, S. S. (2020). The role of social media in entrepreneurial ecosystems: A systematic literature review. *Technology in Society*, *62*, 101315.

Hockerts, K., & Wüstenhagen, R. (2021). The role of innovation in creating a sustainable future. *Nature Reviews Sustainable Business*, *4*(1), 7–9.

Kamrani, A. K., & Parast, M. M. (2021). A systematic review of the Industry 4.0 framework: Research directions and challenges. *International Journal of Production Research*, *59*(5), 1285–1306.

Kuckertz, A., Brändle, L., Gaudig, A., Hinderer, S., Reyes-Aldasoro, C. C., Prochotta, A., ... Berger, E. S. (2021). Startups in times of crisis–A rapid response to the COVID-19 pandemic. *Journal of Business Venturing Insights*, *15*, e00200.

Larson, A. L., & Yarime, M. (2020). Revisiting the literature on inclusive innovation: A perspective from innovation studies. *Journal of Cleaner Production*, *273*, 123015.

Leiponen, A., & Srivastava, S. (2021). Inclusive innovation: Lessons from the COVID-19 pandemic. *Research Policy*, *50*(10), 104178.

Mangla, S. K., Kumar, A., & Rana, N. P. (2020). Exploring the impact of blockchain technology on supply chain sustainability: A conceptual framework and research agenda. *Journal of Cleaner Production*, *272*, 122638.

Mangla, S. K., Rana, N. P., & Dwivedi, Y. K. (2021). Blockchain for smart and sustainable cities: A comprehensive review, synthesis, and future research directions. *Renewable & Sustainable Energy Reviews*, *139*, 110654.

Maresch, D., Harms, R., Kailer, N., & Wimmer-Wurm, B. (2020). Sustainable entrepreneurship and innovation in SMEs: Exploring the factors that facilitate or hamper innovation for sustainability. *Journal of Cleaner Production*, *244*, 118715.

Mazzucato, M. (2018). Mission-oriented innovation policies: Challenges and opportunities. *Industrial and Corporate Change*, *27*(5), 803–815. doi:10.1093/icc/dty034

Mazzucato, M., & Semieniuk, G. (2020). COVID-19 and the need for a new approach to innovation. *The Lancet Digital Health*, *2*(7), e349–e351.

Morozova, I., & Letyagina, I. (2020). Sustainable development and social innovation: Theoretical approaches and practical implications. *Journal of Cleaner Production*, *266*, 121957.

Nambisan, S. (2018). Digital entrepreneurship: Toward a digital technology perspective of entrepreneurship. *Entrepreneurship Theory and Practice*, *42*(6), 1019–1039.

Paranjpe, I., Fuster, V., Lala, A., Russak, A. J., Glicksberg, B. S., Levin, M. A., Charney, A. W., Narula, J., Fayad, Z. A., Bagiella, E., Zhao, S., & Nadkarni, G. N. (2020). Association of treatment dose anticoagulation with in-hospital survival among hospitalized patients with COVID-19. *Journal of the American College of Cardiology*, *76*(1), 122–124. doi:10.1016/j.jacc.2020.05.001 PMID:32387623

Sawhney, M., & Evans, D. (2020). Innovation's new world order. *Harvard Business Review*, *98*(4), 66–74.

Schaltegger, S., Lüdeke-Freund, F., & Hansen, E. G. (2016). Business models for sustainability: A co-evolutionary analysis of sustainable entrepreneurship, innovation, and transformation. *Organization & Environment*, *29*(3), 264–289. doi:10.1177/1086026616633272

Zhang, J., Lindsey, A. R., Peters, R. S., Heraty, J. M., Hopper, K. R., Werren, J. H., Martinson, E. O., Woolley, J. B., Yoder, M. J., & Krogmann, L. (2020). Conflicting signal in transcriptomic markers leads to a poorly resolved backbone phylogeny of chalcidoid wasps. *Systematic Entomology*, *45*(4), 783–802. doi:10.1111yen.12427

Chapter 2
Digital Entrepreneurship:
A Review of Facebook and Instagram Business Model

Pallavi Mishra
https://orcid.org/0000-0002-8315-8473
Amity University, Jaipur, India

ABSTRACT

The framework of digital media entrepreneurship that drives innovation as a source of revolutionary new technologies is reshaping media digital business models. The strategic digital media entrepreneur model is underlined with interactive and ubiquitous media that connects with readers, viewers, and online visitors in revolutionary ways. The assumption is that media entrepreneurs turn users into sources of external creativity and develop user innovations into professional content. The business models of Facebook and Instagram are studied to develop an understanding about the basics of digital entrepreneurship and the roadmap of digital entrepreneurship. Digital business uses technology to create new value in business models, customer experience, and the internal capabilities that support its core operations. The term embraces both digital-only-based and traditional players that are performing their business with digital technologies.

INTRODUCTION

With its unprecedented ability to harness collective intelligence Web 2.0 has ushered possibilities in business. The government and non-profit organizations are currently going through a transition towards performance management systems that are

DOI: 10.4018/978-1-6684-5871-6.ch002

based on internationally accepted monitoring and evaluation (M&E) frameworks. The transitions are driven by the technology is closely intact with a business that navigates to digital entrepreneurship. Digital entrepreneurship refers to creating a new venture with novel digital technologies, or novel usage of such technologies. (EE-HUB, 2017) It is a confluence of technology and business wherein companies steering to have an enormous global impact; the technology use digitalization and artificial intelligence to enhance the quality of decisions and proliferate their business along with customer operations.

The advent of Web 2.0 has paved way for digital entrepreneurship with a holistic and integrative approach; it underlines a digital ecosystem from multiple perspectives that develops a conceptual model of a social network, digital capital, and institutional framework. The digital space is widely used through social media or new digital technologies to connect globally with their new innovative ideas.

The viable nature of digital platforms giving invention to the latest methods and technologies. The key difference between digital and traditional entrepreneurship is tangible and non-tangible. If a new business offers a digital product then it may experience some variations in customer response to that good. (M.Rezvani, 2018)

The European Commission (2013) recognized five elements as pillars of digital entrepreneurship during which each element is said to research the concept of entrepreneurship. The elements are digital knowledge based & ICT market, digital business environment access to finance, digital skills, and e-leadership & entrepreneurial culture. (Carsrud, 2020)

The studey review business models with special reference to Facebook and Instagram, to explore six digital business models of entrepreneurship. Though social media grows over time for communicating with each other across the world anytime anywhere now it has become a part of business strategy and open gates for new business opportunities by creating value customers, changing business models as per the need or the desire of the individual entrepreneur. However, we may say that social media is a way far more than just online communication. Social networking plays a very vital role in providing opportunities to entrepreneurs for marketing or pitching their products or ideas of a start-up. Social media also helps in social marketing, social advertising via using screen space to promote various products and services. Leading social networks usually boast a high number of users accounts or strong user engagement metrics. For example, Facebook is the first social network that has surpassed the 1billion monthly active user market and as of the first quarter of 2020, it has 2.6 billion worldwide. Other leading social apps include Photo –video sharing platforms, Instagram which has over 1 billion monthly active users and more recently reported 500 billion daily active users for its stories features. Messaging apps includes WhatsApp, Facebook Messenger are also popular on social channels for online users. On average global internet users spend some 144 min per day surfing on social media which brings hype to digital entrepreneurship opportunities and bring out innovations through them.

SOCIAL MEDIA ENTREPRENEURSHIP

Today, most information derived in everyday life is digital. The use of ubiquitous information systems such as Facebook, Twitter, LinkedIn and YouTube. Social media has become the norm for both personal and professional purpose. As Kaplan and Haenlein (2010) stated “in today’s digital economy everything is about social media and firms are going to be out of the cyberspace if they are not marking their presence on social media platforms.” Therefore, entrepreneurs are increasingly in cyberspace using information source like social media platforms to get information to support their business growth, creating a new network among customers or creating new business ventures by applying a unique idea of the startup. Although digital technologies have indeed been subject to study in digital entrepreneurship. Recently digital technologies have been considered as inherent to entrepreneurial process and outcome.(AdrieReinders, 2019)

In 2020, the global social penetration rate reached 49, per cent with East Asia and North America having the highest penetration rate at 71&69 per cent. The power of social networking is such the number of worldwide users is predicted to succeed in some 3.43 billion monthly active social media users by 2023. In 2023, an estimated 800 million of these users are expected to be from China alone and approximately 450 million from India. (Statistica, Statistica, 2020)

The social networking plays a very vital role in providing opportunities to the Entrepreneurs for the marketing or pitching their products or ideas of start-up. Social media also helps in social marketing a social advertising via using screen space to promote various products and services. Leading social networks usually boast as high number of users accounts or strong user engagement metrics. For example, Facebook, is the first social network having surpassed the 1billion monthly active user market and as of the first quarter of 2020, has 2.6 billion worldwide. Other leading social apps includes Photo –video sharing platforms, Instagram which has over 1 billion monthly active users and more recently reported 500 billion daily active users for its stories features.

Messaging apps includes WhatsApp, Facebook Messenger are also popular on social channels for online users. On average global internet users spend some 144 min per day surfing on social media which brings hype in digital entrepreneurship opportunities and bring out new innovations through them. (Statistica, Statistica, 2020)

Digital entrepreneurship in Media is associated with entrepreneurial media businesses or firms which are dependent on digital technology. Digital media entrepreneurship has affected the outcomes of start-up innovations. There is a connection between social media and innovation. This technological vitality has an encouraging impact on innovation in digital media. Various studies add to the digital entrepreneurship in media by innovations it is necessary for growth and customer satisfaction. Simmons, Armstrong & Rosenbloom (1993) said that digital entrepreneurship involves large firms like hardware, software and network technologies to small firms which utilize information and communication technologies to organize their business activities.

Davidson & Vaast (2010) defined digital entrepreneurship as an act of recognizing and using fresh commercial prospects which are presented by the new media and internet technologies. This is like traditional entrepreneurship and can reap financial gains by digital endeavors. They are unswervingly associated with novel venture establishments and innovations. Media entrepreneurship acquired growing attention from scholars in the last two decades. Habann (2000) has examined media enterprises from a resource point of view. Even the earliest issue of media entrepreneurship in 2002 in the International Journal of Media Management was on Media and Entrepreneurship. It covered subjects with an entrepreneurial view for media enterprises. Frank and Schreier (2002) fixated on entrepreneurial prospects. On the other hand, Gerport and Negal (2002) studied venture capital firms in the mobile trade in Germany. In 2004, Robert Picard wrote a stimulating article on the Typology of Risks in Family- based media enterprises. In 2005, the first article which focused on the media entrepreneurs. "The black media entrepreneur and economic implications for the 21st century" in the Journal of Black Studies offers a perception to study media entrepreneurs as a subject instead of context. Accordingly, Dennis et al (2006) elevated the level from individual to firm and studied media companies and their plans. An article was written by Hoag and Campaine on media entrepreneurship in the era of big media. Hair, Wetsch, Hull, Perotti & Hung (2012) specified that in the case of digital entrepreneurship instead of the customary arrangement all activities are digitally operated. Hair (2012) said that the key difference between digital and traditional entrepreneurship is that business models and tactics are followed by the corporations for marketing and distribution of products.

As per Reuber & Fische (2011), a digital enterprise is a person or a business that utilizes information and communication technologies to ensure communication between customers and partners, aims to sell products. The differences between customary and digital entrepreneurship are exceedingly fixated as this is very significant for every single entrepreneur to validate their category of trade. In probing this, numerous vital concerns which differ digitally from traditional entrepreneurship are underlined. The complications of a virtual world and the necessity for marketplace alignment also discourse. The fundamentals of digital entrepreneurship along with its pillars are also elucidated. This aids a digital entrepreneur to adapt the business policies to make the trade effective. The importance of digital entrepreneurship to identify the methods for the development of innovation is discussed. However, the major limitation of the study is that this is entirely theoretic and hinges on prevailing work done by several authors to understand the phenomenon of new digital entrepreneurship. (Vineela, 2018)

As per a study conducted in 2020, digital media technologies alter the methods in which businesspersons connect, organize and plan. How it works through facilitated arrangement through social media technology continues to be a unique concept. Hence, the study outlined the media's predominant role in digital entrepreneurship. It foresees how digital media entrepreneurship is becoming popular among entrepreneurs. The research built new theoretical conceptions constructed in current settings and dialogues. (Leick, Djamchid Assadi, & Evgueni Vinogradov, 2021) It gives a distinctive clarification of what digital media entrepreneurship entails. The discussions on the consequences of entrepreneurial plans work regarding entrepreneurial identity development and knowledge construction emphasizing co-location.

It contributes to the understanding of novice entrepreneurs and sheds light on possibilities for future research. (Horst, Digital Media Entrepreneurship: Implications for Strategic Identity Work and Knowledge Sharing of Beginning; Horst, 2020)

Another research conducted to comprehend the hybrid idea of digital entrepreneurship and its role within the transformation of innovation, concluded that dissimilarity of the causes of digital entrepreneurship within three core dimensions of the innovation system includes the entrepreneur, the entrepreneurial process, and its relevant ecosystem. The classification of the prevailing literature is very important for upcoming research that targets to comprehend the interrelations between the change of entrepreneurial structures within innovation systems as well as the socioeconomic systems. It requires additional prolonged exploration in areas linked to method, content, and theory (Satalkina, 2020)

BUSINESS MODELS OF FACEBOOK AND INSTAGRAM:

Facebook has been an innovator in creating a spark in a social media revolution in the digital meridian. Presently it has over 2 billion users worldwide which help in contributing to the world of the globalization process in day-to-day life. Mark Zuckerberg expand Facebook into the public domain the world changed when it hit the virtual landscape. If the internet connectivity is concerned Facebook is always available to access, no matter of nationality, background, or location. It does not require any subscription or transaction of fees, its free of cost to everyone which is used globally. (Turi, 2020) Facebook cut down the distance between people and it helps to communicate with different people across the globe. Facebook does not generate revenue from its users directly it generates revenue through the advertisers who give an advertisement for their services or products on the Facebook page. It helps the business to grow globally through the digital platform.

Facebook enhance more connectivity and options for new ventures to target their audience for marketing their products and services. On the other hand, it also helps in creating opportunities for new entrepreneurs to start marketing and attend the global reach of the audience through this digital social media application. Presently many business ventures do the marketing of their brands, services through Facebook which increase their product demand on the global platform. This also helps a small business to attend universal spectators.

1- Customers of Facebook

- **Users**- Facebook customers mostly include its users, who communicate with different people and interact globally. It now has its concentrated area of shopping where people can buy or sell the property like clothes, jewellery, and even CSR activities also take place through Facebook because of its higher penetration among audience like fundraising for the respective cause.

Figure 1. Facebook business model

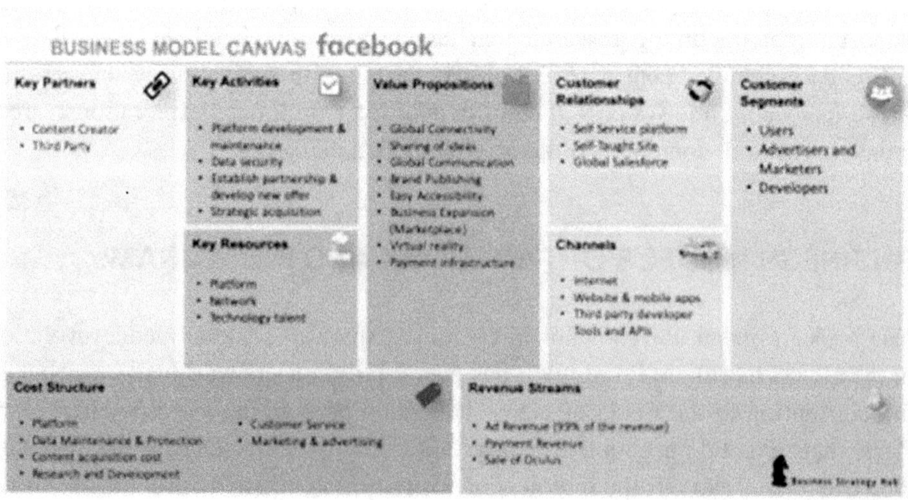

- **Advertisers and Marketers**- Brands and advertisers are a part of its computer-based that helps in earning revenue for the venture by placing offers and promotional ads.
- **Developers-** The platform also has its app and game development platform where the users can play and the game developers like Zyng and Facebook both benefits, respectively.

2. **The Value Proposition of Facebook**

- **Global Connectivity**- The main objective or goal of Facebook is to spread a free medium of communication and connectivity across the world despite their nationality, religion, culture, or background.
- **Sharing of Ideas**- It is the first social media digital platform where different people interact with others and share their ideas or commonalities and get the highest exposure for themselves to different culture, experiences, and ideas.
- **Business Expansion**- It has become a platform to utilize for the business purpose where you can be a sponsor, seller, or buyer from either your own company or any other company.
- **Virtual Reality** – With the acquisition of Oculus, Facebook is now its hand in virtual reality hardware which helps in the innovation in the presentation of products, photos, or videos in 360 views.

3- Channels of Facebook

- **Internet-** The first prerequisite is the internet for its services. Facebook operates through the internet via laptops, computers, tablets, or smartphones.
- **Website and Mobile apps**- It makes the usage of its website and mobile apps to reach more users.

4- Customer Relationship for Facebook It is user friendly and easily accessible for its users, it may assist new users by making their accounts and identities individually. It is a self-learning site, here one can expand its online visibility by finding more interactions through its new profile on Facebook community-building applications. Facebook has an extensive global sales organization that works directly with advertising and seller sales work to attract, retain, and support advertisers.

5- Key Partners of Facebook- The content creators like movies, TV shows, gaming, music, and news sharing articles, the third party also play a vital role on Facebook partners as e.g., mobile operating systems (IOS, Android), handset manufacturers (Apple, Samsung etc), and browse developers (Safari, Chrome, Firefox) all have collaborated with Facebook.

6- Key Activities of Facebook - Facebook are a platform that brings a myriad of activities, it also invests in the data maintenance and security of the data and take care of user's privacy, complying with laws in different countries is essential for Facebook operations. For e.g., North Korea residents have no access to Facebook, China and Iran are the only countries where access to Facebook is actively restricted in a wholesale manner.

7- **Revenue Stream of Facebook** Facebook's major money-making system is its advertising program. Most of its revenue generated from advertising only. The two categories in it (Self- Advertising and Engagement Ads). Facebook charge an amount for any business transaction on its platform whether it be- market featured deals, sales of digital products, sale of apps from developers, money transfer to friends, fundraisers transaction fees etc.

Facebook just keeps on giving, it keeps a safe place without any image harm in terms of revenue or public image. Although many social media platforms have risen after it but still Facebook is the most popular amongst others. Facebook also acquire WhatsApp, and Instagram too, all in all, Facebook is the one that will remain constant in the long run and help in driving innovations for new entrepreneurs by giving them a global market audience and digital platform.

INSTAGRAM

It is launched by Kevin Systrom and Mike Kriege in 2010, presently it is one of the most popular social networks worldwide. After its launch, it has developed very

Figure 2. Facebook money model

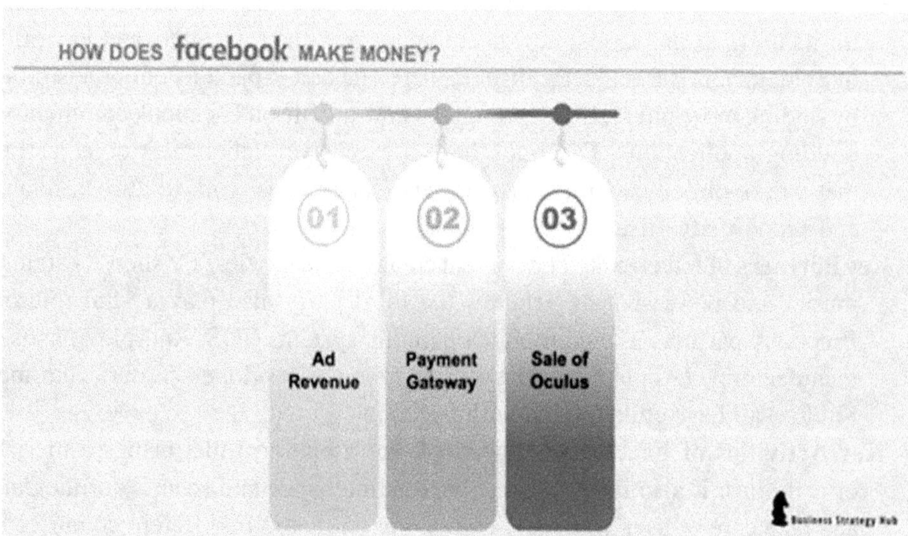

quickly. The application has seen tremendous growth from 1 million users amid the initial two months to 1 billion users by June 2018, with such a vast user base there is the question in people mind that how Instagram makes money?

When Facebook purchased this mobile photo-sharing application Instagram for around $1 billion in cash &stock in April 2013 it was two years old & had no revenue. At present, the organization is estimated to be worth more than $100 Billion according to the data compiled by Bloomberg.

Instagram is a Digital social networking platform that enables the user to share photos, videos, from their lives. It also gives a real time-sharing platform, helps in interaction with the masses. In this application, one can apply filters add captions, making reels and so many other interesting activities can be done on this site.

The Instagram business model is the same since its launch, a free picture sharing mobile application. It just requires a user profile to interface with others. This business model empowers individuals to share, explore, and chat with one another on mobile phone globally. It mainly targets the segment that has a smartphone. The

Figure 3. Timeline of Instagram

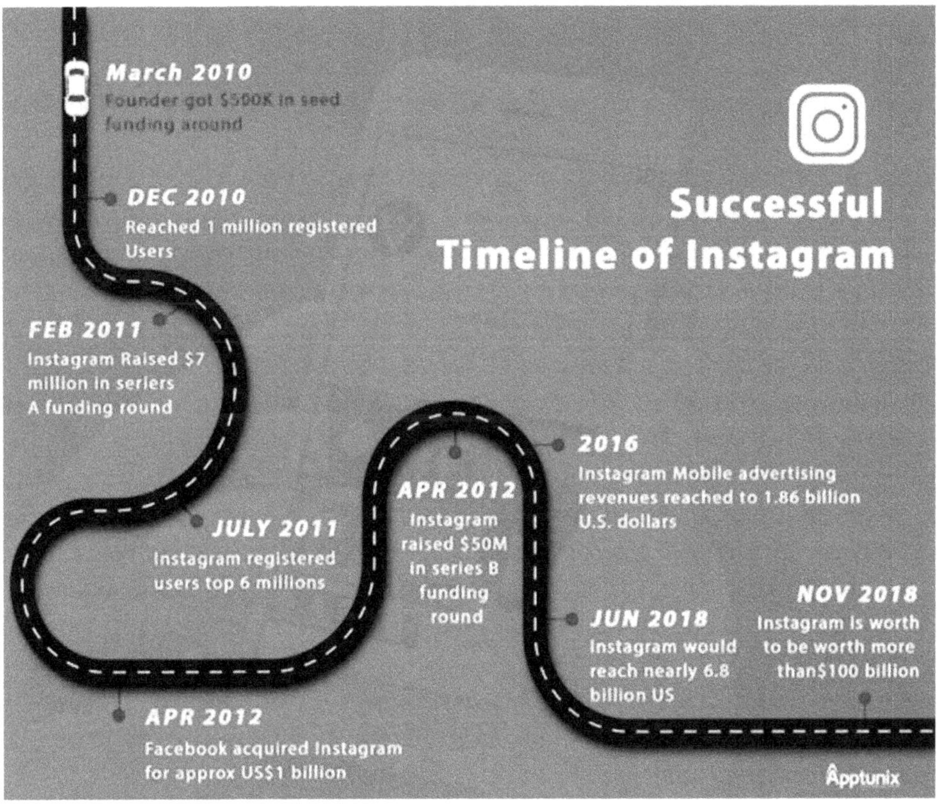

Figure 4. Instagram business canvas

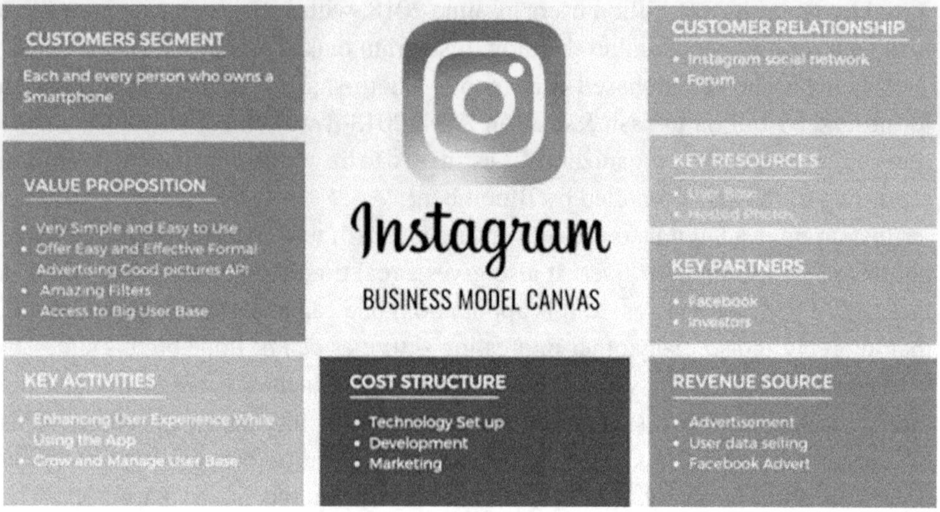

business model of Instagram adopts a customer-first approach by sponsoring easy to understand and engaging feature in the application. It was not the first nor the 10th photo sharing application, but it stands with full power because its user-friendly and provide real value to photo lovers and photographers.

This application does not have any clear revenue model. Pronounced share of their revenues is contributed through advertisement and E-commerce. The engagement of advertisement is the key to the revenue generation for Instagram. According to the business model of Instagram, one should always plan business with the most fundamental approach. Test the market to make implementations. Setting a USPs is very important for setting your product or service. As Instagram is a digital platform with a vast reach globally, the objective should be very clear figured out the desired audience and all should be done before the development procedure and seen very clear in your app development approach. The network strategy of Instagram is very different from others it just not simply uses the pre-existing social network for sharing but to make its network. (Brem, Judith Behrens, & Ronny Baierl, 2019)

Since it is a photo-sharing application it is a platform for branded promotions, a various famous organization whose brand visuals are promptly recognizable for e.g.- Nike, Puma, Adidas, Urbanic etc. Instagram business model brought a revolution not just a photo-sharing app but come with a business that reaches out to serve users by advertising their products in a benchmark way. Presently Instagram positioned to win mobile advertising which brings innovation in the business marketing strategy.

Most important in an Instagram business model that it enables an organization to market their product through means of videos, visual appealing quality help in enhancing, digital marketing with sound and motion.

DIGITAL BUSINESS MODEL

Figure 5. Digital business mode

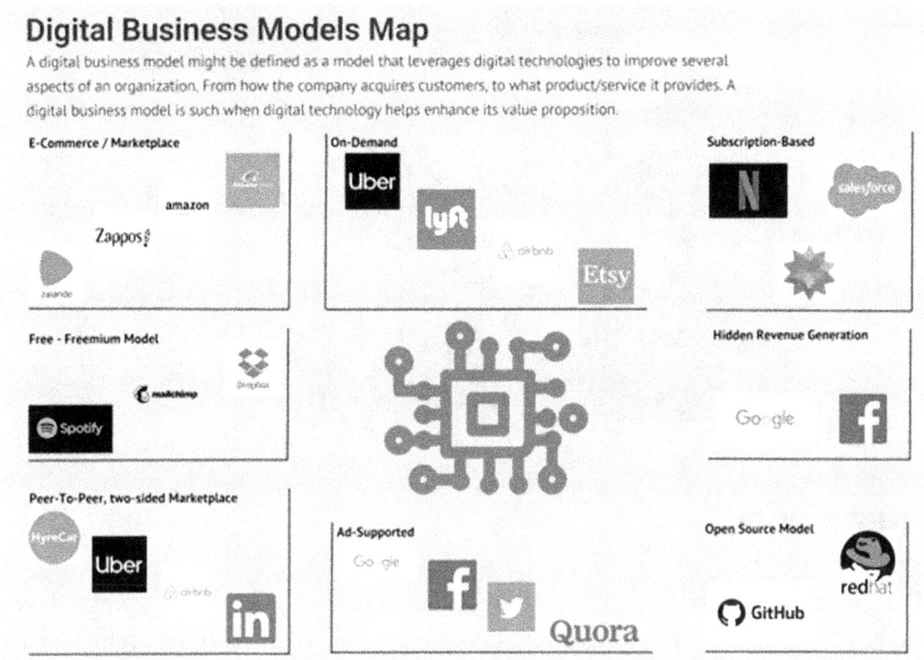

OPEN-SOURCE MODEL

This model makes free access which spread it very quickly. In 2018, Red Hat generated over $2.9 billion in revenues of which $2.57 from subscription and $346million from training and services. The Mozilla business model makes money through partnerships and distribution agreements with search engines.

Figure 6. Freemium business model

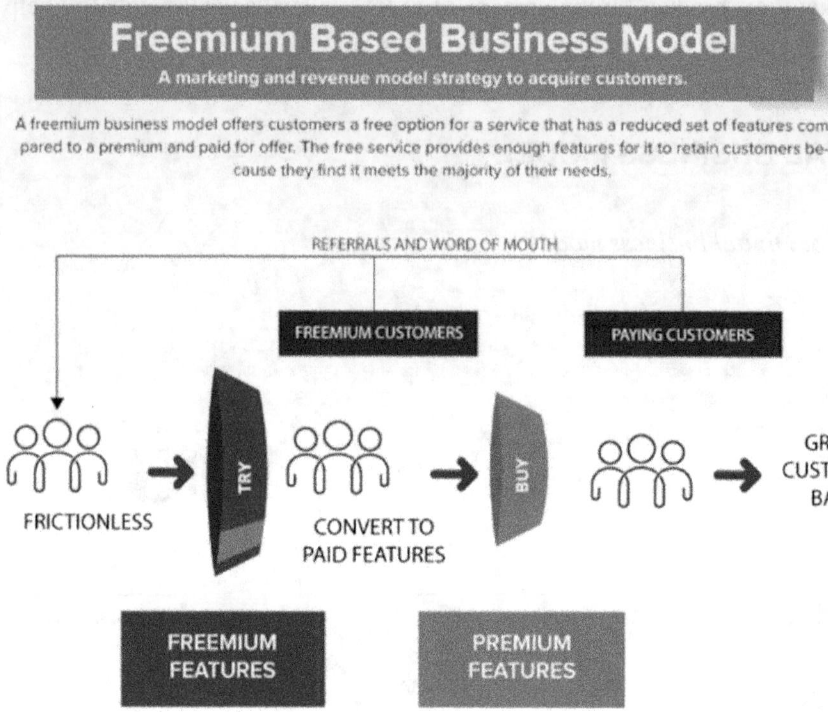

FREE MODEL

The free model has become quite inescapable on the web. This model worked well for products that scaled up quickly, companies like Google and Facebook have started this way. After attracting angel investor, venture, and capitalist but sooner they turn to the advertising model to monetization their users to avoid being left without cash and investors.

SUBSCRIPTION-BASED MODEL

Presently we are living in the subscription economy of the world, from Netflix to Spotify and Amazon prime follows a subscription model. It has its advantages like a loyal user base, continuous predictable revenue. Many companies are subscribing to this model as it allows them to provide sustainable revenue. Companies like Netflix, and Spotify spends billions of dollars in producing original content that can make subscriber renew their plans.

Peer to Peer, Two-Sided Market Place

It is usually two-sided who are participating in a transaction, which can be either product or service. (Uber, Ola, LinkedIn). In the case of Uber, enough drivers on the road to offer an on- demand and convenient service when riders need it.

E-Commerce Model

The first companies that proved the web was not only made just to communicate or connected computers but presently people ready to purchase physical stuff on it. Amazon started as a bookstore the company soon branched to sell music, clothes, grocery etc. Nowadays the e- commerce business model is taken for granted and is among the most used digital business model. (Morabito, 2022)

HIDDEN REVENUE GENERATION MODEL

This model explains the hidden revenue generation which states making money while people who use that most of the services barely realize that. (fourweekmba, 2015)

The models of digital entrepreneurship discussed shows social media has provided a digital platform of business. The different characteristics of digital platforms have proffered a plethora of opportunities to entrepreneurs. Facebook and Instagram have a well-structured framework that helps in connecting people. The models discussed shows; designed on the dimensions of global engagement, revenue generation, ubiquitous, open-source and one-to-many. The study analyses the entrepreneurship models of Facebook, Instagram propagated on online platforms. The analysis of the entrepreneur models of Facebook and Instagram maps how digital technology employed at various stages of entrepreneurship from acquiring customers to understanding what product/service is preferred. (Allen, 2019)

The models reflect the idea that the customers discover and engage with brands through sharing and reposting. The business models of Facebook and Instagram have brought upon revolutionary transformation in entrepreneurship.They have emerged as not just a photo-sharing app but a business app which reaches out to serve users by advertising their products. Instagram positioned to win mobile advertising which brings innovation in the business marketing strategy. This digital business model empowers individual to share, explore, and chat with one another on mobile phone globally. It mainly targets the segment who have a smartphone. The business model of Instagram and Facebook adopts a customer-first approach by sponsoring easy to understand and engaging feature in the application. It was not the first nor the 10th photo-sharing application, but it stands with full power because it is user-friendly and provides real value to photo lovers and photographers. The Facebook business model has extended its circle from the social networking site to Facebook pages. Facebook pages allow buying or selling clothes, jewelry, etc. It even shoulders corporate social responsibility through posts like fundraising for the respective cause. This application does not have an explicit revenue model, but it generates revenue through shares generated through advertisement and e-commerce. (Göcke, Mariusz Soltanifar, & Mathew Hughes, 13 November 2020) The engagement in advertising and promotion are the keys to the revenue generation for Instagram.

CONCLUSION

The framework of Digital entrepreneurship has a branding phenomenon; netizens are their target customers. The well-structured models have the power to involve people, expanding the scope of reaching people directly. The discussions on social media platforms about the brands reflect how it engages people and foster brand loyalties. In this age of digital society and social networks, the practice of digital entrepreneurship has extended to online platforms, beyond the geographical confinements, exhibiting the business goals to a large canvas of online platforms. Digital Entrepreneurship has witnessed a whirl of the transformation over the period; the dependency over social media to connect with people has expanded. The diversified nature of social media and its potential to shape public opinion have incorporated digital tools to develop a brand community. The framework of these digital entrepreneurship manifests the obscured aims of entrepreneurs. The framework of Facebook and Instagram entrepreneurship do not reflect direct revenue generation approach. Thus, there is no conspicuous impression of revenue generation in the minds of customers. The model enables an organization to market its product and amplify the brand an industry-leading product or service today is not enough. Customers search for products that comply with their values.

The way customers discover and engage with brands has changed. Today, an industry-leading product or service is not enough. Customers actively seek out brands that align with their values and live out those values with reliability. The model highlights the structure to connect with current and prospective customers as the model derives its shape from the sharing-resharing concept.

The model strategy attempts to strike the attention of customers. As can be observed, social media is all about real-time sharing; hence the brand ensures public participation with the posts. The framework unequivocally illustrates the business plans that target the customers by tickling their emotional instinct. As the youths of this generation are highly active on the social media platform, the idea is to webcast information on a worldwide stream and connect with people across the globe.

Table 2. Facebook and Instagram revenue generation framework

Model	Innovative Framework	Business Strategy	Revenue Generation	Product Branding
Facebook	In analysis, it shows Facebook has grown into the largest social networking service which encouraged entrepreneurs and welcome new ideas and fresh perspective. It gives a new gateway to small and local ventures to present their ideas, products, and services globally. Facebook approach to innovation involves implementing new changes without seeking the approval of its users. Facebook aggressive approach is the key to its innovative success.	After the in-depth study of the business model of Facebook it reflects that they went against conventional wisdom and focused more on acquiring users instead of jumping straight into revenue generation. This strategy has allowed them to conquer huge amounts of market share and become the de-facto social network. Facebook works targeted advertisement concept.	Facebook generates revenue through hidden charges. It generates revenue from selling advertising to the marketers. As, marketers pays for ads based on the number of impressions delivered or the number of actions like clicks. I also generate revenue from language translate apps like Jibbigo which allows Facebook post and chats to be translated in multiple languages which give opportunities to the companies to advertise their product in several languages. Facebook also generate huge revenue through its other apps e.g. – Instagram and WhatsApp.	Facebook is an interdependent platform that offer a plethora of opportunities to the advertisers to proliferate and promote their brands. The like, sharing and resharing feature of Facebook assists in product branding.
Instagram	The framework of Instagram shows that it has emerged as a commercial platform. It has delivered a unique social media experience for users via innovation. Instagram was first to introduce photo filters that enhance special moments of daily life. But now it expanded itself through the new innovation of multiple avenues for sharing moments, products and services. Instagram also open new digital space for advertisers and businesses.	Instagram business strategy is very exceptional and developing. The Instagram business model empowers the individual to share, explore with other globally. The business strategy of Instagram adopts a customer first approach by sponsoring easy to understand and engaging feature in the application. Most important in an Instagram business model that it enables an organization to market their product through means of videos, visual appealing quality help in enhancing, digital marketing with sound and motion. Presently, Instagram positioned to win mobile advertising which brings innovation in the business marketing strategy.	This application does not have any clear revenue model. Pronounced share of their revenues is contributed through advertisement and E-commerce. Since it is a photo-sharing application it's a platform for branded promotions, a various famous organization whose brand visuals are promptly recognizable for e.g.- Nike, Puma, Adidas, Urbanic etc. Instagram business model brought a revolution not just a photo-sharing app but come with a business that reaches out to serve users by advertising their products in a benchmark way.	Instagram is one of the aesthetically appealing online platforms. It assists in product branding through uploading about the products, connecting with engaged followers and boosting the brand with customer's comment, like and engagement.

REFERENCES

AdrieReinders, M. (2019). *The E factor, entrpreneurship in the social media age*. BenBella.

Allen, J. P. (2019). *Digital Entrepreneurship*. Taylor & Francis. doi:10.4324/9780429506567

Brem, Behrens, & Baierl. (2019). Digital Entrepreneurship (Interfaces Between Digital Technologies and Entrepreneurship). Springer International Publishing.

Carsrud, L. S. (2020). Exploring diversity in enterpreneurship (M. E. Carsrud, Ed.). Springer.

EE-HUB. (2017, APRIL). *Policy recommendation*. Retrieved from The Europeon entrpreneurship education network: http://ee-hub.eu/component/attachments/?task=download&id=492:EE-HUB-Policy-Recommendations-web

Göcke, Soltanifar, & Hughes. (2020). *Digital Entrepreneurship*. Springer International Publishing.

Horst, S.-O. (n.d.). *Digital Media Entrepreneurship: Implications for Strategic Identity Work and Knowledge Sharing of Beginning*. Academic Press.

Leick, Assadi, & Vinogradov. (2021). Digital Entrepreneurship and the Sharing Economy. Taylor & Francis.

Morabito, V. (2022). *Digital Entrepreneurship Management, Systems and Practice*. Cambridge University Press.

Rezvani, M. L. (2018). Organisational entrepreneurial alertness framework in opportunity discovery. *Academy of Entrepreneurship Journal*.

Satalkina, L. (2020). *Digital Entrepreneurship and its Role in Innovation Systems: A Systematic Literature Review as a Basis*. Academic Press.

Statistica. (2020). *Statistica*. Retrieved from https://www.statista.com/topics/1164/social-networks/

Turi, A. N. (2020). *Technologies for Modern Digital Entrepreneurship*. Apress Publisher. doi:10.1007/978-1-4842-6005-0

Vineela, G. S. (2018). *Digital Entrepreneurship*. Academic Press.

Chapter 3
Corporate Governance Attributes, Sustainable Innovations, and Financial Performance of Selected Manufacturing Firms:
A Case Study of a Developing Country

Emmanuel Uniamikogbo
Rhema University, Nigeria

Ikedinachi Ayodele Power Wogu
https://orcid.org/0000-0001-9050-8817
Rhema University, Nigera

Peter Ifeanyichukwu Ali
Imo State Polytechnic, Omuma, Nigeria

Sanjay Misra
https://orcid.org/0000-0002-3556-9331
Department of Applied Data Science, Institute for Energy Technology, Halden, Norway

Manju Khari
Jawaharlal Nehru University, New Delhi, India

ABSTRACT

This study considered how several aspects of corporate governance impact the financial performance of a few manufacturing companies in a developing country leading to sustainable innovations. Nigeria was considered for the study since it is a

DOI: 10.4018/978-1-6684-5871-6.ch003

fast-growing economy and the most populous country in Africa. Tobin's Q methods of analysis and purposive sampling techniques were utilized for analyzing the data gathered from annual reports of companies selected between 2011-2020. Both descriptive statistics and econometric analysis employing panel data techniques were used in the study. Results indicate that board independence and board size had substantial negative impact on Tobin's Q of manufacturing firms in Nigeria. The chapter reveales that audit committees should comprise people with the necessary accounting or finance knowledge and experience to embrace corporate governance procedures since they help interpret business performance in terms of Tobin's Q ratio.

1. INTRODUCTION

The global financial market has been significantly disrupted, and economic growth has been constrained due to the ongoing scandals, crises, and destruction of organizations. Arthur Anderson, Enron, Kmart, Adelphia Communications, and WorldCom were just a few of the several world wide organizations in the United States, South East Asia, and Europe that failed due to problems. Nigeria was not immune from the scandals that shook the global economy because many Nigerian businesses, including Intercontinental Bank, Oceanic Bank, Diamond Bank, Skye Bank, Cadbury Plc., etc., were negatively impacted. As a result, they played a significant role in the economic recession in Nigeria. Any organization's main goal is to increase shareholder value. The firm must be managed effectively, efficiently, ethically, and lawfully by the policies and practices of management, which must align with the interests of shareholders and other stakeholders if such an organization desire to be profitable and achieve long-term growth and continuation. In order to protect business interests and preserve conditions that are critical to the management and prevention of corporate failure and long-term economic depression, good corporate governance (CG) is required. All economic operations are critically dependent on effective corporate governance, particularly in developing and transitional economies like Nigeria.

According to the Organization for Economic Cooperation and Development (OECD) (2010), corporate governances are structure and system for managing and directing organizations. The Water Integrity Network (WIN, 2015) states that corporate governance structures outline the division of duties and authority among the board of directors, managers, shareholders, and other interested parties, as well as the policies and procedures for reaching agreements on business-related issues. Corporate governance offers the framework through which the company's goals, methods for accomplishing them, and measures of success are determined. According to Andrei and Robert (1997), good corporate governance lessens shareholders' and creditors' "control rights" over managers, which increases the possibility that managers will invest in initiatives with a positive net present value. Therefore, transparency with shareholders and fairness to other interested parties should be hallmarks of the board's and management's operations, as Jensen and Meckling (1976) predicted. Doing so would lower agency costs and enhance the organization's financial performance.

Corporate financial performance is a crucial idea that pertains to the extent to which the capital resources available to an organization are wisely employed to meet the overall business goals of an organization, which in itself, is the maximization of shareholders' wealth. A successful corporate performance keeps the company in business and increases the likelihood of future innovative and sustainable possibilities and outcomes. Corporate organizations must prepare for the challenges of globalization in light of the current dynamic economic environment, where businesses that can't adapt to modern business culture risk not surviving. Therefore, to improve their financial performance, businesses must identify and adopt the finest sustainable and innovative corporate practices used elsewhere in the globe. Based on the claim above, this study aims to determine whether a firm's corporate governance characteristics really affect its financial performance. As a result, this study investigates how corporate governance traits affect the financial success of selected manufacturing companies in Nigeria.

1.1 Statement of the Problem

One of the key elements in attaining business goals leading to sustainable innovations is corporate governance, which is concerned with the interactions between a company's management, board of directors, shareholders, and other stakeholders. Corporate governance is a non-financial factor that affects how well businesses operate and raises the amount of external financing available, contributing to sustainable economic growth. Reduced likelihood of organizational failure due to subpar financial performance is a byproduct of good corporate governance. On the other hand, the lack of distinction between ownership and control of an organization is cited as the primary cause of weak corporate governance, which leads to fraudulent practices like mismanagement and theft of company funds, corruption, a lack of transparency and accountability, infringement of the rights of minority shareholders, official rashness among managers and directors, a weak internal control structure, insider abuses, and subpar financial performance.

Corporate failure is undoubtedly linked to companies with ongoing concerns and issues brought on by agency conflict, where directors and managers act in their best interests (egotism) without considering the interests of the shareholders they are supposed to represent by generating returns on investment and maximizing shareholders' wealth. As a result, the corporate governance mechanism was introduced to ensure that boards of directors uphold transparency and fairness of firms' activities to shareholders and other stakeholders to end agency costs, which had a consequent adverse effect on corporate performance.

The impact of corporate governance on financial performance has been studied extensively in the financial sector, while the industrial sector in Nigeria has seen relatively less research. Furthermore, studies conducted by academics who used the manufacturing sector as the basis for their research used corporate governance indicators and mechanisms that were quite different from those used in this study, with mixed and inconclusive results ranging from positive to negative, no relationship, statistically significant to insignificant influence. These findings were unquestionably influenced by the various periods covered, the various research methodologies used, the types of data available and used, the types of variables taken into account, the various measures of corporate governance indicators used, and the various jurisdictions and study areas. This study was influenced by the diverse and contradictory viewpoints of earlier researchers. In light of this, the study uses data specific to Nigeria to investigate the impact of corporate governance traits on the financial performance of a sample of manufacturing enterprises. This study is motivated by the information gap mentioned above.

Examining how several aspects of corporate governance affect the financial performance of a few chosen industrial companies in Nigeria is the study's main goal. However, determining the impact of board gender diversity, board independence, board ownership structure, board size, and audit committee size, respectively, on Tobin's Q of chosen manufacturing enterprises in Nigeria are the particular objectives.

2. LITERATURE REVIEW AND HYPOTHESES DEVELOPMENT

2.1. Corporate Governance

Corporate governance, according to Gompers, Ishii, and Metric (2003), is the process by which the board of directors raises the value of the shareholders by policing the behavior of managers responsible for the day-to-day operations of the company. Corporate governance, according to Mayer (1997), is concerned with strategies to align the interests of shareholders and executives and make sure that businesses are operated for the advantage of shareholders. According to Alexander and Matts' definition of corporate governance from 2003, this term relates to the organization of the board and its operating procedures as well as corporate decision-making and control. According to Ahmed (2004), the word refers to the coordination between the firm's managers and owners, notably addressing the issue of how managers communicate the firm's financial health to the owners. Corporate governance is "the method by which firms are directed and governed," according to the Cadbury Committee (1992).

Corporate governance examines the relationship between internal corporate governance structures and societal perceptions of the extent of corporate accountability (Deakin & Hughes, 1997). Corporate governance, according to Strandberg (2001), is influenced by how much equity is held by internal and outside investors. According to Fama and Jensen (2012), corporate governance is a system that oversees and protects the interests of all an organization's stakeholders. Employees, clients, shareholders, management, suppliers, the government, investors, creditors, the board of directors, and others are examples of stakeholders. These stakeholders believe that protecting and preserving investments made by both shareholders and stakeholders is the core purpose of corporate governance.

2.1.1. Board Size

Board size is the total number of directors, including executive and non-executive members, whose numbers may vary from one country or culture to another (Zabri, Ahmad, & Wah, 2016). There is no generally recognized minimum requirement for the number of directors on a board. However, while some businesses opt for a small board size in the hope that monitoring will be effective, better, and faster for decision-making, others favor a larger board size in the hope that higher-quality decisions will result from larger boards. According to (Hermalin and Weisbach's 2003) argument, larger boards are likely to be less effective than smaller ones because agency issues may worsen when there are too many directors who are perceived as freeloaders on the board. This claim is consistent with research by (Effiok, Effiong, & Usoro, 2012), who claimed that the financial performance of companies would not be significantly impacted by increasing the number of board members to 12. In addition, Lipton and Lorch (1992) recommended that the number of directors on a board be limited to seven or eight members for the CEO's ease of control because a large board may result in less meaningful discussion because expressing one's views in a large group is typically challenging, time-consuming, and frequently results in a lack of board cohesion. However, research by Ahmed and Hamdan (2015), Shukla, Oduor, and Mbabazize (2015), as well as Odiwo, Chukwuma, and Kifordu (2013) found that a 12-member board would improve the efficiency, effectiveness, and financial performance of businesses. In light of this, the study aims to confirm if board size does, in fact, have any impact on the financial performance of a sample of Nigerian manufacturing enterprises. As a result, below is how the first hypothesis is expressed in the null:

$\mathbf{H_{01:}}$ Board size has no significant effect on the financial performance of selected manufacturing firms in Nigeria.

2.1.2. Board Gender Diversity

Board gender diversity refers to the split between male and female directors on a company's board of directors. While those who support board gender diversity feel that having more women on the board than their male counterparts will improve organizations' financial performance, others who are opposed to board gender diversity think that financial performance would be hindered with more women on the board. Gender diversity on boards is a useful governance tool for reducing managers' actual corporate manipulation actions. Female directors enhance boards' capacity for oversight and reduce the frequency of financial reporting errors and fraudulent activities in businesses, according to Wahid (2018).

Female directors are more socially conscious and ethical at work and are less likely to engage in dishonest practices like fraud and profit manipulation, claim Olugbode, Petracci (2015), and Wahid (2018). According to Garcia Lara, Garcia Osma, Mora, and Scapin (2017) and Gull, Nekhili, Nagati, and Chtioui (2018), female directors enhance the corporate board's ability to analyze the value of financial reporting techniques and, as a result, discourage aggressive accounting reporting. According to Gull, Srinidhi, and Tsui (2007), companies with more female directors tend to have lower earnings management and greater earnings quality. Similarly, Arun, Almahrog, and Ali-Aribi (2015) claim that companies with more female directors use more conservative methods of earnings management. This study aims to ascertain whether board gender diversity has any discernible impact on the financial performance of particular Nigerian manufacturing enterprises by doing so. Thus, the formulation below serves as our second hypothesis:

$\mathbf{H_{02:}}$ Board gender diversity has no significant effect on the financial performance of selected manufacturing firms in Nigeria.

2.1.3. Audit Committee Size

A board of directors committee, called the audit committee, is in charge of overseeing the financial reporting process, choosing the independent auditor, and receiving the audit results for both internal and external users of the organization. According to the Nigerian Companies and Allied Matters Act (CAMA), 1990, the audit committee should be composed of six members, three of whom should represent the shareholders and three of the management/directors.

The committee ensures that the financial statement conforms to all applicable laws, regulations, and accounting standards. They must deliver a trustworthy, reputable financial statement to the board with the best possible information. This committee evaluates the external auditors' report, keeps an eye on it, calls the accountant in to answer questions, and, where necessary, recommends to the shareholders that sanctions be taken. As a result, rather than the board of directors, the audit committee answers to the shareholders. There is a positive but minor correlation between the number of people that make up an audit committee and a company's financial performance, as indicated in the research works by (Osundina, Olayinka, & Chukwuma, 2016; and Kajola, 2008). Contrarily, the works (Narwal & Jindal, 2015) discovered a significant inverse relationship between audit committee size and firm financial performance. As a result, the size of the audit committee has a significant role in improving the financial performance of businesses. A larger audit committee benefits from a wider knowledge base and a wider range of experience, which allows it to carry out its duties more successfully. From those mentioned above, they authors hypothesized the statement in the null to represent the third hypothesis.

$H_{03:}$ Audit committee size has no significant effect on the financial performance of selected manufacturing firms in Nigeria.

2.1.4. Board Independence

A board of directors is said to be independent if all or most of its members are not connected to the business other than in their capacity as directors. For board members to be able to carry out their duties effectively and efficiently, they should not just be seen to be independent of thought. Through the monitoring and tactical functions of the directors, independence is a crucial component in ensuring board effectiveness. Having a sufficient number of independent directors on the board is a crucial component of board independence. Each director's ability, willingness, and board environment may contribute to their individual independence. When the study by (Kakabadse, Yang, & Sanders, 2010) looked at the effectiveness of non-executive directors in China, they discovered that the board members' qualifications, access to information, and incentives all play a role in determining the board's independence. However, the study also discovered that China's non-executive directors had a weak structure due to excessive meddling from controlling shareholders and a lack of understanding of their roles. Following the previous sentence, the authors present the fourth hypothesis in the null as follows.

$H_{04:}$ Board independence has no significant effect on the financial performance of selected manufacturing firms in Nigeria.

2.1.5. Board Ownership Structure

Board ownership is the situation in which a director assigned to manage the day-to-day operations of a company also owns a portion of the equity interest in that company. The board ownership structure describes the percentage of stock that investors own or hold. It establishes stockholders' ownership status and voting rights (Tariq & Naveed, 2016). Since management and other staff compensation is mostly a result or effect of the firm's owners' activities, and employee compensation significantly impacts the productivity and performance of a specific workforce, the role of the Board ownership structure is considered vital. Because it has both a positive and a negative impact on performance, studies on CG (Jensen & Meckling, 1976; AL-Najjar, 2015; Tariq & Naveed, 2016) have emphasized Board ownership structure as one key mechanism of CG (Irshad, Hashmi, Kausar, & Nazir, 2015). All shareholders, as well as the group interests of the owners, are intended to be represented by the board. Large, publicly traded firms, on the other hand, typically have extremely diverse ownership, including individuals, organizations, or owner groups with varying interests and time horizons for the company's expansion. Based on this, the fifth hypothesis was created to support the assumption:

$\mathbf{H}_{05:}$ Board ownership structure has no significant effect on the financial performance of selected manufacturing firms in Nigeria.

2.1.6. Average Tobin's Q

James Tobin, a Yale University graduate, and winner of the Nobel Prize in economics popularized Tobin's Q ratio in 1968. Nicholas Kaldor created the performance indicator in 1966. The market value of the representative firm divided by the capital stock's replacement cost serves as a proxy for the average Tobin's Q. According to Tobin, a firm's investment decisions are influenced by whether its q-ratio is more than or less than one. He asserted that a company's ability to increase investment depends on its q-ratio. Tobin said that if a company has a q-ratio larger than 1, its stock market value is higher than its replacement cost. When this ratio is greater than 1, investing in new capital goods is lucrative for the company because the projected return will outweigh the expense. A company cannot invest in new capital goods since doing so will result in a loss if its q-ratio is less than one, which means that the stock market values its capital assets at less than its replacement cost.

Given the aforementioned situation and the need for the banking industry to diversify and invest in various business portfolios in light of the current difficulties encountered in locating business funding, it would be necessary to increase the share price to ensure that its market value exceeds its book value for ease of investment and profitability.

2.2 Theoretical Framework: Stakeholders' Theory

Stakeholders' theory, developed by Edward R. Freeman in 1984, provides a more comprehensive view of corporate governance than agency theory, making it a better lens through which to view a company's performance in terms of corporate governance. The concept of the stakeholders' theory is frequently used in huge organizations, where the influence of businesses on society is so compelling that they must fulfill their obligations to numerous societal sectors rather than just to their owners. This theory has been widely applied in studies worldwide and is also regarded as the mainstay of governance theories in the discipline of accounting. Shareholders, employees, consumers, suppliers, lenders, creditors, managers, researchers, environmentalists, governments, etc., are some stakeholders interested in corporate organizations.

According to Freeman (1984), for an organization to succeed, it must simultaneously satisfy the owners, employees, unions, suppliers, customers, and other interested parties. Additionally, by advancing the idea of "internal stakeholders" as the channels to external groups, managers in various functional disciplines should be more sensitive to the external environment. To ensure that all parties have the same interests, executives should serve as the company's "corporate spokesperson" and human resource managers.

A change in the composition of boards by adding more outside directors to allay concerns about board members who are too subservient to management or employee representation at some level in corporate governance could address the diverse interests of stakeholders. Shareholder participation in important management decisions could also be increased. This theory is used to explain particular corporate governance traits and behaviors. Thus, it doesn't just focus on the interests of shareholders but also on those of other parties with a stake in the company. The stakeholders' theory strives to recognize the connections between management and achieving business goals by employing various instruments to reduce information asymmetry, enforce the law, and emphasize fairness to accommodate various stakeholder concentrations.

As businesses cannot operate in isolation without the support of other interests/stakeholders that ensure the sustenance and continued survival of these firms in terms of performance in their immediate operational context, the study on corporate governance and financial performance is grounded in the stakeholders' theory. Businesses are established not only to maximize wealth to the shareholders alone but also to protect the general interest of all stakeholders.

3. METHODOLOGY

The ex-post-facto research design (Marilyn, 2013; Wogu, Misra, Assibong, Adewumi Maskeliunas, and Damasevicius, 2018; Amu, Nwezeaku, Akujuobi, Ozurunba, Njie, Wogu, & Misra, 2019; Wogu, Njie, Katende, Ukagba, Edogiawerie, & Misra, 2020 and Wogu, Njie, Ezennwa, Chukwuedo, Ukagba, Misra, Uniamikogbo, & Olu-Owolabi, 2021) was used in this study. Twenty-six (26) manufacturing enterprises listed on the Nigerian Exchange Group (NGX) as of December 31, 2020, constitute the study's sample, which was chosen using the purposive sampling method. Following the global coronavirus (Covid 19) pandemic, which affected the majority of commercial activity, the 26 enterprises were chosen based on their capital base viability, solvency, profitability, stability, going concern characteristics, and data availability as of the 2020 financial year. From 2011 to 2020, secondary data from the audited annual reports of selected manufacturing enterprises listed on the Nigerian Exchange Group were used for ten years. Panel data analysis was used to analyze the data that was collected. The fact that the data is multidimensional and has both a time dimension and a cross-sectional dimension led to the selection of this regression method.

3.1 Model Specification

The study investigated the influence of corporate governance traits on the financial performance of particular Nigerian manufacturing enterprises. In keeping with the study's goals, the models under consideration are described in their functional and econometric specifications. The expression of a connection in a precise mathematical form is known as model specification. Indicators of corporate governance and financial performance, such as the size of the audit committee, the size of the board, the gender diversity of the board, the independence of the board, the ownership of the board, and Tobin's Q, are thus captured by this model.

Functionally, the model is presented as:

$$\text{CFP} = f(\text{CG}) \qquad (1)$$

Where;

CFP= Corporate financial performance
CG= Corporate Governance

When the variables are broken down into their measures, and the econometric form is specified, we have;

$$TQ_{it} = \beta_0 + \beta_1 ACS_{it} + \beta_2 BGD_{it} + \beta_3 BDI_{it} + \beta_4 BDO_{it} + \beta_5 BDS_{it} + u_{it} \quad (2)$$

Where;

TQ = Tobin's Q; ACS = Audit Committee Size; BGD = Board Gender Diversity; BDI = Board Independence; BDO = Board Ownership; and BDS = Board size.

4. DATA PRESENTATION AND ANALYSIS OF THE RESULT

This part of the paper presents and analyzes the estimates using various statistical methods. The descriptive statistics and the Pearson product-moment correlation findings were presented to analyze the preliminary studies. The findings of the panel regression were then given. Table 1 shows the findings of the descriptive Statistics.

According to the descriptive statistics data in Table 1, the banks' average Tobin's Q was 0.92, which indicates that they performed pretty poorly regarding their market significance. Compared to the mean, the standard deviation of 0.28 is quite small. This indicates that Tobin's Q-reported mean value is typically similar across the study's participating companies. Given that the standard deviation of 0.41 is also quite low, the average size of audit committee members, 6, supports an audit committee membership that is essentially ideal. This suggests that the audit committees of most companies in the study typically consist of six people and that these committees are common among the companies included in the sample.

The chosen companies' average level of board gender diversity was 15.08 percent, meaning that 15% of the board members are female.

Since male board members comprise 85% of the companies' boards, this generally does not suggest that they are especially diversified. The boards of the corporations appear to be more independent overall, as indicated by the average level

Table 1. Descriptive statistics

Variable	Mean	Max.	Min.	Std. Dev.	Skewness	Kurtosis	J-B	Prob.
TQ	0.92	2.55	0.08	0.28	2.47	13.03	750.97	0.00
ACS	6.06	9	4.00	0.41	2.94	29.41	4393.45	0.00
BGD	15.08	60	0.00	10.78	0.74	4.15	21.17	0.00
BDI	58.56	90	21.43	12.27	0.68	3.60	13.38	0.00
BDO	9.08	72	0.00	14.01	2.34	8.64	322.21	0.00
BDS	13.85	21	5.00	3.19	-0.33	3.03	2.65	0.27
FS	9.00	10.77	8.11	0.44	0.24	3.65	3.93	0.14

Source: Researchers' compilation (2021).

of board independence of 58.56 percent. The very low average board ownership of 9.08 percent shows that, on average, board members only own 9.08 percent of the companies. However, the maximum figure for board ownership is 72%. A moderate board membership across the firms is also shown by the average board size of 13.85 or roughly 14 members.

The correlation matrix for the datasets reported in Table 2 of the article shows the initial pattern of relationships between the study's variables. For the governance factors, the levels of the association are minor. Most correlation indicators suggest that there is often a negative relationship between the variables. For instance, since board independence has a strong negative correlation with board gender diversity, a more gender-varied board tends to be less independent. Similar to how board ownership and independence are negatively correlated with board size, larger boards exhibit lower levels of independence across organizations. The substantial negative link between board ownership and board size also demonstrates that companies with smaller boards usually have greater firm ownership structures. There is a poor correlation between board independence and audit committee size as well as between board ownership and size. The highest positive correlations between corporate governance variables for board ownership, board independence, board size, and audit committee size show that larger boards also typically have larger audit committees.

It is necessary to apply panel unit root tests to determine whether the data are stationary because the study's data show both common (homogeneous) and sector-specific (individual heterogeneity) characteristics. This is especially true for data that combine the two sectors. In this study, the homogeneous panel's stationarity properties were evaluated using the test created by Levin, Lin, and Chu (LLC). The

Table 2. Correlation matrix

Variable	TQ	ACS	BGD	BDI	BDO	BDS
ACS	0.00					
	(0.92)					
BGD	-0.08	-0.01				
	(0.10)	(0.78)				
BDI	0.04	-0.15	-0.14			
	(0.37)	(0.00)	(0.00)			
BDO	-0.04	-0.16	-0.07	0.15		
	(0.43)	(0.00)	(0.13)	(0.00)		
BDS	-0.09	0.13	-0.01	-0.19	-0.14	
	(0.08)	(0.01)	(0.85)	(0.00)	(0.00)	
FS	-0.14	0.27	0.11	-0.23	-0.32	0.64
	(0.01)	(0.00)	(0.02)	(0.00)	(0.00)	(0.00)

Source: Researchers' compilation (2021).

*Table 3. Panel Data Unit Root Tests Results *in levels*

Variable	Homogenous Unit Root Process		Heterogeneous Unit Root Process				Remarks
	Intercept and Trend						
	LLC		IPS		ADF-Fisher		
	I(0)	*I*(1)	*I*(0)	*I*(1)	*I*(0)	*I*(1)	
TQ	-34.6**	-28.16**	-19.16**	-14.76**	8.411	291.2**	I[0]
ACS	-2.374**	-3.72**	-1.293*	-4.03**	126.58*	155.2**	I[0]
BGD	-1.543*	1.66*	-1.170*	-1.93*	90.2	78.2*	I[0]
BDI	-4.41**	-15.12**	-2.84**	-7.53**	120.7**	205.3**	I[0]
BDO	-5.36**	-5.24**	-0.81	-2.87**	101.2**	121.1**	I[0]
BDS	-3.97**	-5.55**	-1.76*	-4.42**	94.8*	137.3**	I[0]
FS	-1.51*	-7.99**	1.06	-4.91**	94.1*	155.4**	I[0]

Source: Researchers' compilation (2021).

test assumes that each firm's cointegration vectors are the same. The common unit root assumption may not be sufficiently realistic because many enterprises are likely to display variances in their operational and overall performance characteristics. The Im, Pesaran, and Shin (IPS, 2003) and Augmented Dickey-Fuller tests permit heterogeneity in the panel's cross-section and assume a null hypothesis of no *cointegration* in the panel data, are employed to get around this special assumption for the companies in the sample. Table 3 displays the test outcomes. Table 3's unit root results show that all variables are stationary, according to the coefficient of the test for the variables in levels (given that the critical test values are higher than the test statistic). Given this circumstance, it is demonstrated that the variables are all integrated in the same order (i.e., I[1]), allowing for the co-integrated analysis of the variables to produce useful results.

The unit root results strongly suggest that the variables are all I[0] and that their stationarity status is equal. The results of the Pedroni and Kao panel cointegration tests on the panel and group assumptions are also included in Table 4, along with

Table 4. Panel Cointegration Test Result

Tobin's Q ratio equation	Panel Statistics	Group Statistics	Kao (ADF)
Variance ratio	1.285	--	-4.46**
Rho	1.685	3.932	
IPS	-10.96**	-6.73**	
ADF	1.018	0.926	

***Note:* **, * indicates the rejection of the null hypothesis of no cointegration at the 0.01 and 0.05 level of significance, respectively**

Source: Researchers' compilation (2021).

the corresponding variance ratios and rho statistics (non-parametric tests). For both the panel and group assumptions, the coefficients of the IPS and Augmented Dickey-Fuller test statistics are significant at the 5% level. In light of this, panel cointegration is well supported by both the ADF-t and non-parametric-t statistics. The Kao panel cointegration test, which is likewise significant at the 5 percent level, complements these findings. As a result, the cointegration test results indicate that the study variables have a significant long-term link.

4.1 Empirical Results on the Panel Analysis

This section's econometric research examines the specific contributions that corporate governance system indicators make to the prediction of performance among a sample of companies listed on the Nigerian Exchange Group using a panel data analytic approach. Tobin's Q ratio was used as the study's performance indicator. The approach demonstrates how the firm's performance correlates with operational depth and broad market performance. Table 5 presents the test's findings.

The main goals of the regression results analysis are finding the strength, significance, and direction of corporate governance's effects on the performance variable. The standard Hausman test for random effects is utilized when deciding whether the panel analysis method should be employed. The random sections argument's Chi-Square statistic is significant at the 5% level, indicating that the null hypothesis, according to which there is no random effect in the cross sections of the data, is true. As a result, the random effect result is successfully disproved as the most effective way to represent the relationships in the panel, and it is shown that the analysis would be better served by using the Fixed Effects (FE) estimates.

Tables 6 show the fixed effects estimates for how corporate governance affects the performance of the chosen organizations. Overall, the goodness of fit numbers is remarkable. The model accounts for approximately 98 percent of the systematic differences in TQ between the firms, as shown by the adjusted R-squared value of 0.988. At the 5% level, the model's F-value is also noteworthy. This shows that the dependent variable and all of the explanatory factors together have a substantial relationship. By taking into account each explanatory variable's individual coefficient, the major effect of corporate governance variables on company performance (TQ) can

Table 5. Hausman Test for Cross-Section Random Effects

Model	*Chi-Sq. Statistic*	*Chi-Sq. d.f.*	*Prob.*
Tobin's Q	12.41	6	0.019

Source: Researchers' compilation (2021).

Table 6. Static Results for Manufacturing Firms

Variable	Coefficient	t-ratio	prob.
Constant	3.498	94.649	0.00
ACS	0.076	28.007	0.00
BGD	0.013	11.616	0.00
BIND	-0.006	-4.299	0.00
BOWN	0.022	8.309	0.00
BSIZE	-0.022	-22.685	0.00
FS	-0.307	-71.973	0.00
Adj. R-sq	0.988		
F-stat	1986.0		

Source: Researchers' compilation (2021).

be seen. The outcome shows that all of the explanatory variable coefficients pass the significance test at the 1% level. This demonstrates unequivocally that all corporate governance factors significantly impact the firms' Tobin's Q ratio performance.

The coefficient of audit committee size is significant at a 5 percent level with a positive sign. This shows that bigger audit committees are important for enhancing companies' market success. This finding demonstrates that increasing the audit committee membership within a company can increase operational efficiency. The market performance of the corporations is demonstrated to improve by 0.076 percent for every one percent increase in the audit committee's membership.

The predicted outcome includes a positive and significant coefficient for board gender diversity. This implies that having a gender-diverse board tends to indisputably increase the performance of the nation's industrial enterprises. Additionally, it is implied that improving the representation of women on boards will improve business success. The board independence coefficient's results show that it is less than 1% and significant. The fact that more independent boards in the manufacturing sector appear to be linked to worse performance in the firms in the manufacturing sector in Nigeria makes this negative sign extremely unexpected. Board independence may tend to amplify agency issues in manufacturing companies, undermining their operational operations and market performance in Nigeria.

Tobin's Q ratio for the firms is significantly influenced favorably by the board ownership coefficient. This positive correlation shows that strong board ownership generally improves the companies' financial results. This conclusion serves as an indirect confirmation of the detrimental effects of board independence on bank performance. The findings show that to assure improved performance of the enterprises in Nigeria, limiting the independence and external impacts on board-management structures could be more advantageous. The negative and substantial coefficient of board size demonstrates that larger boards have a negative impact on the performance of the firms as a whole. Thus, it can be seen that large boards are ineffective for manufacturing companies in Nigeria as they lower their market performance.

4.2 Discussion of Result

This study looked at a few Nigerian industrial companies' financial health and corporate performance. The claim was that businesses function not only to serve the interests of their owners but also those of other stakeholders, who may or may not be sources of funding for the expansion and viability of the company. The study's findings show that board independence and board size substantially negatively impacted Tobin's Q of Nigerian manufacturing firms. In contrast, board gender diversity, audit committee size, and board ownership greatly impacted the firms. Large boards have been proven to be ineffective for Nigerian manufacturing companies since they lower their performance on the market.

The study's findings are consistent with those made by (Narwal & Jindal, 2015; Mora & Scapin, 2017; Gull, Nekhili, Nagati, & Chtioui, 2018; Ahmed & Hamdan, 2015; Shukla, Oduor, & Mbabazize. 2015; and Odiwo, Chukwuma & Kifordu, 2013), who looked at corporate governance traits and financial performance of firms in their various economic environments and discovered a significant relationship between these two factors. Their research showed that adding more members to the board would improve a company's efficiency, effectiveness, and financial performance. The results of this study contradict those of (Osundina, Olayinka, & Chukwuma, 2016; Effiok, Effiong, & Usoro, 2012; and Hermalin & Weisbach, 2003), who looked at the connection between corporate governance traits and the financial performance of firms and discovered that there was no discernible connection. As a result, there is little correlation between corporate governance traits and a firm's financial performance.

5. CONCLUSION AND RECOMMENDATIONS

In the financial literature, the function of boards in shaping organizations' growth patterns across all business sectors has gained significant attention. This study proved that to map the performance trajectory of Nigerian manufacturing enterprises with the capacity for sustainability and innovations, corporate governance structures that are sustainable and innovative are crucial. The outcome, in particular, demonstrates how substantial leverage can be created for the financial performance of manufacturing firms in Nigeria by expanding the size of audit committees, boosting the representation of women on boards, and strengthening the ownership drive of enterprises by the boards. Similarly, organizations' operational performances typically improve when there is more diversity of gender on the board. Surprisingly, the study revealed that more independent boards might hinder efficiency or worsen performance among financial firms in Nigeria. In order to achieve long-term efficiency that could bring about viable, sustainable, and innovative growth in the future of organizations, businesses must consequently have the best board structures possible.

The empirical research findings in this study offer a solid context and ramifications that allow for specific policy and practical advice for practitioners and policymakers.

The study demonstrated that larger boards are ineffective or inefficient in monitoring and controlling the firms in the market investment systems; therefore, it is important for Nigerian businesses to optimize board size to support companies' long-term, sustainable performance.

The board of directors must weigh in on the best course of action when deciding on overall investment policies, given the crucial responsibilities that board members play in choices that affect dividends for enterprises. This is especially true given that the firm's investment strategy is related to Tobin's Q. If the aim is to ensure efficiency in investment and market performance of the firms that would be sustainable and innovative, then fewer autonomous board members for the organizations should be encouraged.

Firms must strive for gender diversity, which is ideal given that having more women on boards tends to boost the market performance of the companies over time. The majority of studies in this field have demonstrated how variety improves performance.

To ensure more significant CSR engagements, it is also essential to consider the makeup of the standing committees on boards, particularly the audit committee. We advised that the audit committee should consist of people with the necessary knowledge and experience.

REFERENCES

Abdulazeez, D. A., Ndibe, L., & Mercy, A. M. (2016). Corporate governance and financial performance of listed deposit money banks in Nigeria. *Journal of Account Mark*, *5*(1), 1–6.

Abdullah, H., & Valentine, B. (2009). Fundamental and ethics theories of corporate governance. *Middle Eastern Finance, and Economics*, *4*, 89–96.

Ahmed, E., & Hamdan, A. (2015). The effect of corporate governance on firm performance: Evidence from Bahrain Exchange. *European Journal of Business and Innovation Research, 3*(5), 25–48.

Ahmed, S. (2004). Affective Economies. *Social Text, 22*(2), 117-139.

Ajala, O. A., Amuda, T., & Arulogun, L. (2012). Evaluating the effects of corporate governance on the performance of Nigerian banking sector. *Review of Contemporary Business Research, 1*(1), 32–42.

Akingunola, R. O., Olusegun, B., & Adedipe, E. (2013). Corporate governance and banks performance in Nigeria (post bank consolidation). *European Journal of Business and Social Sciences, 2*(8).

AL-Najjar, D. (2015). The effects of institutional ownership on firm performance: Evidence from Jordanian listed firms. *International Journal of Economics and Finance, 7*(12), 97–105. doi:10.5539/ijef.v7n12p97

AL-Najjar, D. (2015). The effects of institutional ownership on firm performance: Evidence from Jordanian listed firms. *International Journal of Economics and Finance, 7*(12), 97–105. doi:10.5539/ijef.v7n12p97

Alexander, V. N., & Matts, R. (2003). *Corporate governance mechanisms and firm performance: Evidence from Finland.* Working Papers 497, Hanken School of Economics.

Amu, C. U., Nwezeaku, N. C., Akujuobi, L. E., Ozurunba, B. A., Njie, S. N., Wogu, I. A., & Misra, S. (2019). The Politics of Public Debt Management Among Rising Hegemonies and the Role of ICT: Implications for Theory and Practice for 21st Century Polities. *International Journal of Electronic Government Research, 15*(3), 72–83. doi:10.4018/IJEGR.2019070105

Andrei, S., & Robert, W. V. (1997). A survey of corporate governance. *The Journal of Finance, 52*(2), 737–783. doi:10.1111/j.1540-6261.1997.tb04820.x

Arun, T. G., Almahrog, Y. E., & Ali-Aribi, Z. (2015). Female directors and earnings management: Evidence from UK companies. *International Review of Financial Analysis, 39*, 137–146. doi:10.1016/j.irfa.2015.03.002

Babatunde, M. A., & Olaniran, O. (2009). The effects of internal and external mechanisms on governance and performance of corporate firms in Nigeria. *Corporate Ownership and Control, 7*(3), 330–344. doi:10.22495/cocv7i2c3p1

Barney, J. B. (2002). Strategic management: From informed conversation to academic discipline. *The Academy of Management Perspectives, 16*(2), 53–57. doi:10.5465/ame.2002.7173521

Berghe, V. D., & Baelden, T. (2005). The complex relation between director independence and board effectiveness. *Corporate Governance, 5*(5), 61–83.

Bernard, A. B., & Jensen, J. B. (1999). Exceptional exporter performance: Cause, effect, or both? *Journal of International Economics, 47*(1), 1–25. doi:10.1016/S0022-1996(98)00027-0

Bhattacharyya, N., Mawani, A., & Morrill, C. (2008). Dividend payout and executive compensation: Theory and evidence. *Accounting and Finance, 48*(4), 521–541.

Cadbury, A. (1992). Report of the committee on the financial aspects of corporate governance. Gee Gee Ltd. (Professional Publishing Ltd.).

Chung, K. H., & Pruitt, S. W. (1994). A Simple Approximation of Tobin's q. *Financial Management, 23*(3), 70–74. doi:10.2307/3665623

Dar, L. A., Naseem, M. A., Rehman, R. U., & Niazi, G. S. K. (2011). Corporate governance and firm performance: A case study of Pakistan Oil and Gas Companies listed in Karachi Sick Exchange. *Global Journal of Management and Business Research, 11*(8).

Deakin, S. A., & Hughes, J. (1997). Board of directors and corporate financial performance: A review and integrative model. *Journal of Management, 76*(13), 291–334.

Effiok, S. O., Effiong, C., & Usoro, A. A. (2012). Corporate governance, corporate strategy, and corporate performance: Evidence from the financial institutions listed on the Nigerian Stock Exchange. *European Journal of Business and Management, 4*(18), 84–95.

Eyenubo, A. S. (2013). The impact of bigger board size on financial performance for firms: The Nigerian experience. *Journal of Research in International Business and Management, 3*(3), 85–90.

Fama, E., & Jensen, M. (2012). Separation of ownership and control. *The Journal of Law & Economics, 26*(12), 1–32.

Famogbiele, A. (2012). Failure of the universal banking system in Nigeria: The role of corporate governance. Paper Presented at the *1st Annual International Conference on Accounting, Finance and Management*, Obafemi Awolowo University, Ile Ife.

Fanta, A. B., Kemal, K. S., & Waka, Y. K. (2013). Corporate governance and impact on bank performance. *Journal of Finance and Accounting*, *1*(1), 19–26. doi:10.11648/j.jfa.20130101.12

Freeman, R. E., Wicks, A. C., & Parmar, B. (2004). Stakeholder theory and corporate objective revisited. *Organization Science*, *15*(3), 364–369. doi:10.1287/orsc.1040.0066

Ganguli, S. K., & Agrawal, S. (2009). Ownership structure and firm performance : An empirical study on listed mid-cap Indian companies. *The IUP Journal of Applied Finance*, *15*(12), 37–52.

García Lara, J. M., García Osma, B., Mora, A., & Scapin, M. (2017). The monitoring role of female directors over accounting quality. *Journal of Corporate Finance*, *45*, 651–668. doi:10.1016/j.jcorpfin.2017.05.016

George, T. P., & Karibo, B. B. (2014). Corporate governance mechanisms and financial performance of listed firms in Nigeria: A Content Analysis. *Global Journal of Contemporary Research in Accounting, Auditing and Business Ethics*, *1*(2).

Gompers, P., Ishii, J., & Metric, A. (2003). Corporate governance and prices. *The Quarterly Journal of Economics*, *118*(1), 107–155. doi:10.1162/00335530360535162

Gul, F. A., Srinidhi, B., & Tsui, J. (2007). *Do female directors enhance corporate board monitoring? Some evidence from earnings quality.* Working Paper, the Hong Kong Polytechnic University.

Gull, A. A., Nekhili, M., Nagati, H., & Chtioui, T. (2018). Beyond gender diversity: How specific attributes of female directors affect earnings management. *The British Accounting Review*, *50*(3), 255–274. doi:10.1016/j.bar.2017.09.001

Habbash, M. (2010). *The effectiveness of corporate governance and external audit on constraining earnings management practice in the UK* [Doctoral thesis]. Durham University.

Hermalin, B. E., & Weisback, M. S. (2003). *Board of Directors as an Endogenously Determined Institution: A Survey of the Economic Literature.* Center for Responsible Business. Working Paper Series; Paper 3.

Imam, M.O. (2006). *Firm Performance and Corporate Governance through Ownership Structure: Evidence from Bangladesh Stock Market.* Academic Press.

Irshad, R., Hashmi, S. H., Kausar, S., & Nazir, M. I. (2015). Board effectiveness, ownership structure, and corporate governance: Evidence from Pakistan. *Journal of Business Studies Quarterly*, *7*(2), 46–60.

Irshad, R., Hashmi, S. H., Kausar, S., & Nazir, M. I. (2015). Board effectiveness, ownership structure, and corporate governance: Evidence from Pakistan. *Journal of Business Studies Quarterly*, *7*(2), 46–60.

Iskander, M. O., & Chamlou, N. (2000). *Corporate governance: A framework for implementation*. The World Bank Group. doi:10.1596/0-8213-4741-1

Jensen, M. C. (1993). The modern industrial revolution, exit the failure of internal control systems. *The Journal of Finance*, *48*(3), 831–880. doi:10.1111/j.1540-6261.1993.tb04022.x

Jensen, M. C., & Meckling, W. H. (1976). Theory of the firm: Managerial behavior, agency costs, and ownership structure. *Journal of Financial Economics*, *3*(4), 305–360. doi:10.1016/0304-405X(76)90026-X

Johari, N. H., Saleh, N. M., Jaafar, R., & Hassan, M. S. (2008). The Influence of Board Independence, Competency and Ownership on Earnings Management in Malaysia. *International Journal of Economics and Management*, *2*(2), 281–306.

Jose, M. L., Nichols, L. M., & Stevens, J. L. (1986). Contributions of diversification, promotion, and research &development to the value of multiproduct firms: A Tobin's q Approach. *Financial Management*, *15*(4), 33–42. doi:10.2307/3665778

Kajola, S. O. (2008). Corporate governance and firm performance: The case of Nigerian listed firms. *European Journal of Economics, Finance, and Administrative Sciences, 14*.

Kakabadse, N. K., Yang, H., & Sanders, R. (2010). The effectiveness of non-executive directors in Chinese state-owned enterprises. *Management Decision*, *48*(7), 1063–1079. doi:10.1108/00251741011068770

Karamanou, I., & Vafeas, N. (2005). The association between corporate boards, audit committees, and management earnings forecasts: An empirical analysis. *Journal of Accounting Research*, *43*(3), 453–486. doi:10.1111/j.1475-679X.2005.00177.x

Kothari, S. P. (2001). *Capital market research in accounting*. Paper presented to JAR Rochester Conference. 10.1016/S0165-4101(01)00030-1

Krishnan, G. V., & Parsons, L. M. (2008). Getting to the bottom line: An exploration of gender and earnings quality. *Journal of Business Ethics*, *78*(1/2), 65–76. doi:10.100710551-006-9314-z

Kyaw, K., Olugbode, M., & Petracci, B. (2015). Does gender diverse board mean less earnings management? *Finance Research Letters*, *14*, 135–141. doi:10.1016/j.frl.2015.05.006

Lang, L., Stulz, R., & Walkling, R. (1989). Managerial performance, Tobin's q, and the gains from successful tender offers. *Journal of Financial Economics*, *1*(24), 137–154. doi:10.1016/0304-405X(89)90075-5

Liem, M. C. (2016). Corporate governance in Banking Industry: An explanatory study. *Research Journal of Finance and Accounting*, *7*(6), 30–48.

Lipton, M., & Lorsch, J. W. (1992). A modest proposal for improved corporate governance. *Business Lawyer*, *48*(1), 59–77.

Lubabah, M., & Bawa, A. (2013). Board composition, executive duality and performance of banks in the post consolidated era in Nigeria. *International Journal of Academic Research in Economics and Management Sciences*, *2*(1).

Luo, J. H., Xiang, Y., & Huang, Z. (2017). Female directors and real activities manipulation: Evidence from China. *China Journal of Accounting Research*, *10*(2), 141–166. doi:10.1016/j.cjar.2016.12.004

Maher, M., & Andersson, T. (1999). Corporate governance: Effects on firm performance and economic growth. OECD.

Mallin, C. A. (2007). Corporate governance (2nd Ed.). Oxford.

Marilyn, K. (2013). *Ex-post facto research: Dissertation and scholarly research, Recipes for success*. Dissertation Success LLC. http://www.dissertationrecipes.com/wpcontent/uploads/2011/04
/

Mayer, C. (1997). Corporate Governance, Competition, and Performance. *Journal of Law and Society*, *24*(1), 152–176. doi:10.1111/1467-6478.00041

McConnell, J. J., & Servaes, H. (1990). Additional evidence on equity ownership and corporate value. *Journal of Financial Economics*, *27*(2), 595–613. doi:10.1016/0304-405X(90)90069-C

Narwal, K. P., & Jindal, S. (2015). The impact of corporate governance on the profitability: An empirical study of the Indian Textile Industry. *International Journal of Research in Management, Sciences, and Technology*, *3*(2), 81–85.

Nelson, J. (1996). *Feminism, Objectivity and Economics*. Routledge.

Odiwo, W. O., Chukwuma, C. S., & Kifordu, A. A. (2013). The impact of corporate governance on the performance of manufacturing firms in Nigeria. *International Journal of Scientific Research (Ahmedabad, India)*, *5*(9), 924–933.

OECD. (2010). *Global corporate governance forum, background document*. https://www.oecd.org/dataoecd/63/60/46435512.pdf

Olayinka, M. U. (2010). The impact of board structure on corporate financial performance in Nigeria. *International Journal of Business and Management*, *5*(10), 45–827.

Olumuyiwa, Y., & Babalola, Y. A. (2012). Impact of corporate governance on capital structure decision of Nigerian Firms. *Research Journal in Organizational Psychology and Educational Studies*, *1*(2), 121–128.

Osisioma, C. B., Egbunike, A. P., & Adeaga, J. C. (2015). Investigating the impact of corporate governance on banks' performance in Nigeria: A field experiment. *International Journal of Economics and Business Administration*, *1*(2), 98–112.

Osundina, J. A., Olayinka, I. M. & Chukwuma, J. U. (2016). Corporate governance and financial performance of selected manufacturing companies in Nigeria. *International Journal of Advanced Academic Research/Social and Management Sciences*, *2*(10), 29 – 43.

Ping, Z., & Wing, C. W. (2011). Corporate governance: A summary review of different theoretical approaches. *International Research Journal of Finance and Economics*, 68.

Qureshi, M. A. (2007). System dynamics modeling of firm value. *Journal of Modelling in Management*, *2*(1), 24–39. doi:10.1108/17465660710733031

Rimon, E., Aiman, R., & Sandy, K. (2014). The effect of corporate governance on firm performance: Evidence from Egypt. *Asian Economic and Financial Review*, *4*(12), 1865–1877.

Sanda, A. U., Mukaila, A. S., & Garba, T. (2005). *Corporate governance mechanisms and firm financial performance in Nigeria*. Final Report Presented to the Biannual Research Workshop of the AERC, Nairobi, Kenya.

Sanda, A. U., Mukaila, A. S., & Garba, T. (2011). *Board independence and firm financial performance: Evidence from Nigeria*. African Economic Research Consortium (AERC) Research Paper 213.

Shleifer, A., & Vishny, R. W. (1997). A survey of corporate governance. *The Journal of Finance*, *52*(2), 737–783. doi:10.1111/j.1540-6261.1997.tb04820.x

Strandberg, R. (2001). Corporate governance and firm performance: Evidence from Pakistan. *Pakistan Development Review*, *45*(4), 231–244.

Tariq, I., & Naveed, M. (2016). Effects of board & ownership structure on firm financial performance: An economic value added perspective. *Developing Country Studies*, *6*(8), 1–9.

Tariq, I., & Naveed, M. (2016). Effects of board & ownership structure on firm financial performance: An economic value added perspective. *Developing Country Studies*, *6*(8), 1–9.

Thiruvadi, S., & Huang, H. (2011). Audit committee gender differences and earnings management. *Gender in Management*, *26*(7), 483–498. doi:10.1108/17542411111175469

Thuraisingam, R. (2013). The effects of corporate governance on company performance: Evidence from Sri Lankan Financial Services Industry. *Journal of Economics and Sustainable Development*, *4*(17), 103–109.

Tobin, J. (1969). A general equilibrium approach to monetary theory. *Journal of Money, Credit and Banking*, *1*(1), 15–29. doi:10.2307/1991374

Udeh, F. N., Abiahu, M. F. C., & Tambou, L. E. (2017). Impact of corporate governance on firm's financial performance: A Study of Quoted Banks in Nigeria. *The Nigerian Accountant*, *2*(50), 54–62.

Wahid, A. S. (2018). The effects and the mechanisms of board gender diversity: Evidence from financial manipulation. *Journal of Business Ethics*, *159*(3), 1–21.

Wahla, K. U. R., Shah, S. Z. A., & Hussain, Z. (2012). Impact of Ownership Structure on Firm Performance: Evidence from Non-Financial Listed Companies at Karachi Stock Exchange. *International Research Journal of Finance and Economics*, *84*(1), 613.

Wang, L. (2009). Corporate governance, industry clustering, and corporate performance. The Business Review, 12(1).

Wernerfelt, B., & Montgomery, C. A. (1988). Tobin's q and the importance of focus in firm performance. *The American Economic Review*, *78*(1), 246–250.

WIN. (2015). Semantics, Analytics, Visualization. Enhancing Scholarly Data.

Wogu, I. A., Njie, S. N., Ezennwa, E. O., Chukwuedo, C. N., Ukagba, G. U., Misra, S., Uniamikogbo, E., & Olu-Owolabi, E. F. (2021). The Politics of Climate Change and the Rising Demand for Global Energy in the 21st Century: Implications for Human and Economic Development. *International Journal of Energy Optimization and Engineering*, *10*(3), 1–23. doi:10.4018/IJEOE.2021070101

Wogu, I. A., Njie, S. N., Katende, J. O., Ukagba, G. U., Edogiawerie, M. O., & Misra, S. (2020). The Social Media, Politics of Disinformation in Established Hegemonies, and the Role of Technological Innovations in 21st Century Elections: The Road Map to US 2020 Presidential Elections. *International Journal of Electronic Government Research, 16*(3), 65–84. doi:10.4018/IJEGR.2020070104

Wogu, I. A. P., Sanjay Misra, J., Assibong, P. A., Adewumi, A., Maskeliunas, R., & Damasevicius, R. (2018). A Critical Review of the Politics of Artificial Intelligent Machines, Alienation and the Existential Risk Threat to America's Labour Force. In *Computational Science and Its Applications – ICCSA 2018. Lecture Notes in Computer Science* (vol. 10963). Springer. https://rdcu.be/5XTm https://link.springer.com/chapter/10.1007/978-3-319-95171-3_18

Wolfe, J., & Sauaia, A. C. A. (2003). The Tobin q as a Company Performance Indicator. *Developments in Business Simulation and Experiential Learning, 30.*

Wooi, H. C., & Ming, T. C. (2009). *Directors' Pay-Performance: A Study on Malaysian Government Linked Companies.* CenPRIS Working Paper No. 110/09, Universiti Sains Malaysia.

Xavier, M. S., Shukla, J., Oduor, J., & Mbabazize, M. (2015). Effect of corporate governance on the financial performance of the Banking Industry in Rwanda: A case study - Commercial Banks in Rwanda. *International Journal of Small Business and Entrepreneurship Research, 3*(6), 29–43.

Zabri, S. M., Ahmad, K., & Wah, K. K. (2016). Corporate governance practices and firm performance: Evidence from top 100 public listed companies in Malaysia. *Procedia Economics and Finance, 35*, 287–296. doi:10.1016/S2212-5671(16)00036-8

Chapter 4
Corporate Social Responsibility and the Financial Performance of Oil and Gas Entrepreneurial Marketing Firms:
An Appraisal of Firms in an Emerging Economy

Emmanuel Uniamikogbo
Rhema University, Nigeria

Ikedinachi Ayodele Power Wogu
https://orcid.org/0000-0001-9050-8817
Rhema University, Nigera

Osarenren Osasere Aigienohuwa
Nnamdi Azikiwe University, Nigeria

Sanjay Misra
https://orcid.org/0000-0002-3556-9331
Department of Applied Data Science, Institute for Energy Technology, Halden, Norway

Manju Kaushik
Amity University, Jaipur, India

ABSTRACT

Using an ex-post-facto research design, this study examined how listed Nigerian oil and gas entrepreneurial marketing companies' financial performance is impacted

DOI: 10.4018/978-1-6684-5871-6.ch004

by their commitment to CSR. A sample of 11 listed oil and gas entrepreneurial marketing companies in the Nigerian Exchange Group (NGX) for 2010–2019 was used. The sample companies' annual reports were used as data collection sources. The panel regression and Arrelano and Bond GMM estimation results were used for the study outcomes. The findings indicate that CSR significantly and positively affected the ROA, ROE, and share price of oil and gas entrepreneurial marketing firms in Nigeria. The study recommends that companies increase their CSR activity since it helps boost their financial performance. The state should develop a strong policy and develop an effective and enforceable modern CSR framework with effective state control in Nigeria.

1. INTRODUCTION

Financial and non-financial information that is pertinent, accurately portrayed, and helpful for vision-making is essential to aid all stakeholders in providing corporate reports (Umoren, Ogbari, & Atolagbe, 2016). Companies worldwide are currently concentrating on combining their financial and non-financial information as effectively as possible, especially when firms experience new environmental and societal changes. Therefore, every organization must disclose in its annual reports the many actions that impacted its stakeholders. The lack of this practice is turning into a major problem amongst these companies on a global scale.

Corporate social responsibility (CSR) is described by Umoren *et al.* (2016) as the internal monitoring and management as well as outward communication that enables organizations of all sizes to satisfy users' expanding information needs (internal and external). CSR communicates information about a company's economic, environmental, and social operations; the connected effects those operations have on the company and others as a result of its daily operations. Stakeholders (investors, the government, citizens, workers, clients, suppliers, trade associations, environmental organizations, etc.) count on businesses to generate reports that show their financial value, foster innovation, and advance learning. Long-term corporate success relies on strong social and environmental performance and a sound financial situation. One of the most important steps in creating a sustainable global economy is corporate social responsibility. CSR increases corporate responsibility, fosters confidence, promotes openness, spurs better creativity, boosts internal management and decision-making processes, lowers compliance costs, and provides a competitive edge (Umoren, et al., 2016).

Eccles and Krzuz (2010) contend that because even the most knowledgeable users need help understanding typical company reports, they are becoming less relevant and valuable for analysts and investors. Today's financial information users require data that will enable them to assess an entity's financial, social, and environmental responsibility. Businesses are expected to perform more than provide financial statements that comply with accounting rules. While companies are expected to conduct their operations in a way that minimizes their negative environmental effects, they should also make positive contributions to the communities in which they operate by considering the various requirements of their stakeholders.

Two schools of teaching emerged with different opinions regarding what CSR reporting and the financial performance of firms should be like. One of the schools of thought is that firms that embrace CSR activities are bound to improve their financial performance. Their argument is premised on the fact that a corporate and socially responsible firm to the host community would attract the attention of the people who patronize their products and provide an enabling environment for their business to strive. Thus, the mutual relationship between the firm and stakeholders would improve the firm's product sales and enhance its performance. On the other hand, those who opposed CSR activities lay credence to the fact that it is a waste of resources for a firm to embark on CSR activities, especially when the firm is not financially viable. That such funds made available to CRS would serve a better purpose when they are reinvested into the business for the expansion of the firm, as CSR activities have no link with a firm's financial performance. However, Ong'olo (2012) asserts that organizations that have maintained their competitiveness and experienced long-term steady growth have embraced CRS initiatives, allowing them to thrive in markets where sellers offer comparable products at comparable prices. This shows corporate social responsibility's importance to a firm's financial success. Similarly, Garriga (2004) discovered a substantial association between corporate social responsibility and the financial success of organizations. In the paper, he argued that numerous research studies had demonstrated this favorable relationship. However, according to (Sharma, Sharma, Ali, & Dadich, 2021 and Nripinder and Vikramjit, 2021), businesses that engage in CSR activities are unlikely to improve their financial performance because doing so would be an exercise in futility. Based on the claims mentioned above, this study aims to determine if entrepreneurial companies practicing corporate social responsibility may enhance their financial success.

1.1. Statement of the Problem

Corporate social responsibility is a concept in management that encourages businesses to incorporate social and environmental issues into their everyday operations and relationships with stakeholders. CSR has typically considered the means through which a business balances its responsibilities to economic, environmental, and social imperatives while meeting stakeholder expectations (also known as the

Triple-Bottom-Line Approach). Businesses must make profits for their investors while also fulfilling their cooperate responsibility, which has grown in importance for business researchers over the past ten years. Unfortunately, most businesses in emerging economies believe engaging in CSR is unimportant. In contrast, others who have done so do not feel that their CSR efforts must be adequately disclosed in their annual reports.

Similar issues with CSR practices and financial performance plague the majority of businesses in Nigeria. In addition to a need for more knowledge about what CSR entails, there is a need for the necessary details regarding how CSR activities must be reported in annual reports. These issues are part of corporate social responsibility initiatives, which also involve commitments to the community, the environment, human resources, and the satisfaction of customers. Firms experience these and many other related challenges. Hence, justifying one of the reasons for embarking on this study, with a view to ascertain CSR of firms has any influence on their financial performance in Nigeria.

In the past, many studies on corporate social responsibility and the financial performance of businesses in developed and developing economies around the world had been carried out with varying degrees of success; however, only a small number of these studies have been able to examine the environment in Nigeria with mixed and ambiguous outcomes. To our knowledge, no research in Nigeria recently considered CSR and the financial performance of oil and gas entrepreneurial marketing companies (2010 and 2019). According to the claims above, this study examines the impact of CRS on the financial performance of oil and gas entrepreneurial marketing enterprises in Nigeria using country-specific data to validate earlier research and resolve discrepancies in current literature. This study was influenced by the information gap mentioned above.

This study's primary goal is to investigate how Nigerian oil and gas entrepreneurial marketing companies' financial performance is impacted by their commitment to CSR. However, the precise goals are to examine how CSR affects the share price, return on equity, and return on assets of Nigerian oil and gas marketing companies.

2. LITERATURE REVIEW AND HYPOTHESES DEVELOPMENT

2.1 Corporate Social Responsibility

According to the World Business Council for Sustainable Development (WBCD, 1999), corporate social responsibility is the ongoing process of businesses acting in a way that contributes to a morally righteous society. It is management acting ethically in its interactions with the various stakeholders with a legitimate interest in the business and contributing to economic growth while enhancing the standard of living for the workforce, their families, and the local community. CSR is the beneficial result a business produces while managing its regular business operations. As a result, the company's obligation should be to treat all its stakeholders fairly, honestly, and respectfully.

CSR was viewed as a social obligation first (Carroll, 1979 and Maignan & Ferrell, 2000), who developed one of the best-known corporate social responsibility pyramids. This model views the various compositions encompassing the business's social responsibilities, including economic, legal, ethical, and philanthropic commitments. Businesses are creations driven by the profit motive, thus the main reason why firms constantly struggle to maintain customers and create new ones by engaging in various responsibilities. According to CSR, a long-term commitment to the growth of the community or the employees of a certain firm is made. By doing this, a corporation can structure its ethical spending practices in a way that directly benefits society as a whole. The standards, norms, and expectations that show consideration for what is just, fair, and respectful of the moral rights of stakeholders are what consumers, employees, shareholders, and the community view as ethical spending responsibilities.

2.2 Financial Performance

The financial health of an organization is gauged by financial performance. It is a subjective indicator of how well companies use the resources from their main revenue-generating business model. Financial performance is the main indicator of a company's overall financial health over time. Accounting key performance indicators are frequently used to gauge financial performance. Some of these measures include Return on Assets (ROA), Operating Profit Margin, Earnings Before Interest and Income Tax (EBIT), Return on Capital Employed (REC), and Return on Equity (ROE). These precautions have the benefit of being easily accessible.

2.2.1 Return on Asset (ROA)

A company's ability to create profit from its assets is gauged by the return on investment (ROA) profitability ratio. ROA measures how well a company's management uses its financial resources or helps to produce profits. The percentage of net income to total assets is used to calculate it. The ROA calculates the company's profit from each asset used in day-to-day operations. Return on assets is a measure of a company's capital intensity. In light of the foregoing, the study seeks to determine whether CSR impacts the financial performance of oil and gas marketing companies in Nigeria. As a result, the following is how the first hypothesis is expressed in the null:

H_{01}: CSR has no significant influence on the return on assets of oil and gas marketing firms in Nigeria.

2.2.2 Return on Equity (ROE)

The ratio of a company's profitability to its shareholders' equity is called return on equity (ROE). The company's net income is expressed as a percentage return to shareholders. The efficiency with which a company earns profit from each net asset (asset minus liability) utilizing invested capital from shareholders is measured by the firm's return on equity (ROE). It gauges the rate of return on the equity (shareholders' money) invested in common stock. ROE is calculated as the annual net income (before preferred stock dividends but before common stock payouts) divided by the total equity (excluding preferred shares). Following the above, the study seeks to know whether the presence of CSR activities of oil and gas entrepreneurial marketing firms has any relevance to financial performance in Nigeria. This research examines the effect of CSR on the ROE of oil and gas marketing firms in Nigeria. Hence, this paper formulates the second hypothesis in the null form:

H_{02}: CSR has no significant effect on the return on equity of oil and gas marketing firms in Nigeria.

2.2.3 Share Price (SP)

The cost at which one share of a company can be purchased is known as the share price (sometimes referred to as the stock price). It is the cost of a single equity share among several tradeable firm shares. The share price is the maximum price someone will pay for a claim or the lowest price at which a share may be purchased. A share's price is not fixed but changes with market conditions. Where the firm is considered to be performing well, the share price will possibly rise, whereas if the company fails to fulfill investors' expectations, the share price will likely fall. Accordingly, the third hypothesis is stated in the null:

H_{03}: CSR has no significant influence on oil and gas marketing firm share price in Nigeria.

2.3 Theoretical Framework

The stakeholders' idea, first formulated by Freeman in 1984, is the foundation of this study. According to the theory of stakeholders, a company's ability to develop and implement a corporate strategy that successfully manages its relationships with stakeholders is a prerequisite for its financial success. According to this theory, which was first proposed in "Freeman's Strategic Management: A Stakeholder Approach" in 1984, leaders should prioritize serving their stakeholders because they are crucial to the survival of their companies. As a result, companies are expected to engage in some stakeholder management. The stakeholders' theory is a system-oriented theory that presupposes that an organization is affected by the society in which it operates. This is because an organization must collaborate; it interacts with the people in the community where it conducts business. Similar to how the organization affects society, CSR includes economic, social, and environmental responsibilities. Financial and non-financial accomplishments are responsible for the survival and success of the company. Being socially conscious and maintaining positive relationships with stakeholders will provide them a competitive edge, enabling them to maximize profits and produce superior non-economic and economic results (corporate social performance).

2.4 Review of Empirical Studies

Muna, Kareema, and Wisam (2021) investigated the effect of social responsibility practices on the financial performance of banks in Iraq. The study illustrates the relationship between financial performance as measured by Return on Investment (ROI) and Return on Asset and social performance through the costs of social activities carried out by banks in three classified categories (the field of employees, community, consumers, etc.). A linear regression analysis was performed on the data gathered using a sample of 10 commercial banks that were listed on the Iraq Stock Exchange between 2012 and 2017 as part of the study. The findings indicated that social responsibility negatively impacts ROI when overall costs are included. However, ROI is positively impacted by individual responsibility (workers, community, and customers). Total social responsibility costs, as well as their corresponding areas, hurt ROA.

Sharma, Sharma, Ali, and Dadich (2021) examined how CSR affects the financial performance of a few Indian industrial and service organizations. The research establishes the connection between the CSR score and the ROE, ROA, and ROCE. The financial information for the Indian manufacturing and service industries from 2008 to 2017 was considered. The association between CSR score and the financial performance of the Indian manufacturing and service industries was investigated using the correlation technique. According to the study's findings, ROE, ROA, and ROCE have a positive correlation with the CSR Score of Service Sector Companies while having a negative correlation with the CSR Score of Manufacturing Sector Companies. The findings imply no meaningful relationship exists between CSR Score and the financial success of Indian manufacturing sector enterprises.

Nripinder and Vikramjit (2021) studied how corporate social responsibility (CSR) affects the Indian steel industry's financial performance (FP) in terms of value added (VAM), profitability measures (PM), market measures (MM), and growth measures (GM). For the study, secondary data from 40 organizations were gathered via CSR, annual reports, official websites, and the Prowess database across a 14-year period from 2004 to 2018. In the study, the panel regression analysis, MANOVA, and Univariate ANOVA were all used. The outcome showed that CSR has a favorable effect on financial performance in terms of VAM, PM, and GM, showing that increasing investments in CSR will increase profitability and sales as well as create wealth for shareholders. Additionally, this study finds no connection between MM and CSR.

Revlon (2020) studied the financial performance and corporate social responsibility of small and medium-sized manufacturing and service businesses in the United States. An ANCOVA,

statistic and multiple regression analysis were used to investigate the owner/managers' assessments of the level of social CSR, environmental CSR, and financial performance in a sample of 50 U.S.-based SME enterprises. The results revealed that when manufacturing and service SMEs participated in workplace and client CSR activities, the latter performed much better financially. Additionally, notwithstanding the business sector, a combination of social and environmental CSR initiatives revealed a negative but negligible impact on financial performance. According to the findings, U.S. SMEs should think about tracking their financial performance when making CSR investments and maximizing initiatives that are advantageous to them and society.

Xiaolin (2019) explored whether socially responsible corporate activity is rewarded with great financial success in China and the effect of corporate social responsibility on financial performance. For 2016 and 2017, information was gathered from CSR reports of 62 listed firms from the banking, real estate, and pharmaceutical industries. The values of corporate ESG data were gathered using the HKEX ESG Reporting Guide Content Index. Financial performance metrics were computed using the financial information in the annual business report. The association between CSR performance and financial performance was empirically investigated using the Least Square (OLS) regression approach. The findings demonstrated that, after adjusting for the fixed effect, every point raised in the CSR score significantly contributed to increases in ROA and ROE of 0.0608% and 0.172%, respectively. However, the impact of CSR performance on stock market returns is still being determined.

Abilasha (2019) analyzed the impact of CSR on the Indian financial performance of the new Companies Act 2013. The study's sample included 10 Indian businesses that were active between the years 2014 and 2017. The Annual Reports and the Moneycontrol.com website were used as the secondary source of data collecting.

Financial ratios, including profit before taxes, return on invested capital, return on equity, and return on asset, were used to gauge economic success. The impact of corporate social responsibility (the dependent variable) on financial performance (the independent variable), as proxied by PBT, ROCE, ROE, and ROA, was examined using the simple regression model. The study's findings indicate that while specific financial ratios like PBT, ROC, ROE, and ROA are minor, CSR has a considerable beneficial impact on the overall financial success of organizations.

Elizabeth (2018) examined business prosperity and social responsibility in the USA. The study specifically looks at the connection between monetary benefit and corporate social responsibility as defined by the sustainability standards established by the North American Dow Jones Sustainability Index. The performance of each index was compared to the others in the study, which looked at a ten-year data sample from the DJSI-NA, DJIA, S&P 500, and NASDAQ composite for the period between January 1, 2008, and December 31, 2017. The findings indicate that corporate social responsibility may have slightly improved stock performance and volatility. To ascertain the extent to which CSR impacts specific stock prices, a more thorough analysis of the effects of CSR will need to be done, given the numerous factors that affect the stock price.

Samira, Noor, and Muhammed (2018) analyzed the effects of CSR on the financial performance (FP) of Bangladeshi agribusiness sectors using a sample of four well-known agribusiness industries for three years between 2015 and 2017. The study employed a strategy known as purposive sampling. Data was gathered from the three years from 2015 to 2017 of the participating agribusiness industries' official financial statements. To analyze the data, regression, and correlation were applied. The results showed that while return on assets (ROA) and earnings per share (EPS) have no significant impact on financial performance in Bangladesh's agribusiness industries, return on equity (ROE) and net income have a significant impact on financial performance in favor of companies that practice corporate social responsibility.

Bushra and Rabia (2017) studied how corporate social responsibility affected the financial results of Islamic and conventional banks in different Asian nations. The impact of five independent corporate social responsibility variables—social welfare, health, education, public giving, and environmental protection—on the financial performance of Islamic and conventional banks was examined. The annual reports of the chosen Islamic and mainstream banks in Pakistan and Bangladesh from 2010 to 2015 were the source of the secondary data used for the study analysis. ROA and ROE were found to have a positive association, going by the results generated by the correlation matrix. According to the empirical investigation, a strong and positive correlation exists between corporate social responsibility and the financial success of a few Asian Islamic and conventional banks.

3. METHODOLOGY

The ex-post-facto research design (Marilyn, 2013; Amu, Nwezeaku, Akujuobi, Ozurunba, Njie, Wogu, & Misra, 2019; Wogu, Njie, Katende, Ukagba, Edogiawerie, & Misra, 2020 and Wogu, Njie, Ezennwa, Chukwuedo, Ukagba, Misra, Uniamikogbo, & Olu-Owolabi, 2021) was used in this study. This approach is suitable because it allowed the researchers to gather data from a pool of financial statements to assess the impact of corporate social responsibility on the financial performance of oil and gas marketing enterprises in Nigeria without manipulating the necessary data for the study. Eleven (11) Oil and Gas marketing companies operating in Nigeria as of December 31, 2019, and whose shares were listed on the Nigerian Stock Exchange constituted the study's population. Due to the availability and accessibility of data for the study period following the emergence of the Corona-Virus (Covid-19) pandemic in 2020, which entirely destroyed the global economy, this time frame has to be chosen. The complete study population makes up the study's sample size. A complete enumeration strategy was used to determine the study's sample size. The websites of the Nigerian Exchange Group and the annual reports and financial statements of the sampled oil and gas companies for the years 2010 through 2019 were used to gather the data for this study. The study's statistical methods included regression analysis, correlation matrix, and descriptive statistics.

The results of panel regression and Arrelano and Bond GMM estimate were used to analyze the study's data. The association between corporate social responsibility and the financial performance of oil and gas marketing enterprises in Nigeria was estimated using the panel data regression technique. To shed more light on the distributional dynamics of the model, the quartile regression estimates were also presented.

3.1. Model Specification

Corporate social responsibility (CSR), return on equity (ROE), return on asset (ROA), and share price (SP) were utilized to create a model that would sum up this study. As a result, the model is depicted below in a functional form:

$$CSR = f(ROE, ROA, SP) \ldots \ldots \ldots \ldots \ldots \text{ equ. } (1)$$

In a linear function, the above model is represented as follows:

$$CSR_t = \beta o + \beta_1 ROE_t + \mu_t \text{ ------ } Ho_1$$

$$CSR_t = \beta o + \beta_1 ROA_t + \mu_t \text{ - - - - - - } Ho_2$$

$$CSR_t = \beta o + \beta_1 SP_t + \mu_t \text{ - - - - - - } Ho_3$$

Where:

βo = Constant term; β_1= Regression coefficient of the independent variable; μ_t = Error Term for period t; CSR_t = Corporate social responsibility (Independent variable); ROE_t = Return on equity (Dependent variable); ROA_t = Return on asset (Dependent variable); and SP_t = Share price (Dependent variable).

4. DATA PRESENTATION AND ANALYSIS OF THE RESULT

The presentation, analysis, and interpretation of the data gathered for this study are all included in this section. Creating the foundation for the study hypothesis's testing necessitates the application of both mathematical and statistical methodologies. Therefore, it is an essential component of every investigation because it serves as the foundation for the conclusions and suggestions made at the end of the study. The models mentioned in section three were put to the test empirically. First, the data's preliminary analysis was carried out (descriptive and correlation analysis). The regression analysis was then performed. The outcomes of the descriptive statistics are shown in Table 1.

Table 1. Descriptive statistics

	Mean	Max	Min	Std. Dev.	Jarque-Bera	Prob
SP	34.48802	1555.99	0.5	115.0286	183895.3	0.000
CSR	0.911765	1	0	0.283869	1914.201	0.000
ROE	0.239651	2.5496	0.04	0.283278	2265.714	0.000
ROA	0.493801	2.966	0.006	0.302815	1856.99	0.000

Source: Researchers' compilation (2021) using Eviews 10.0.

The descriptive statistics for the variables are shown in Table 1. As can be seen, the mean share price is 34.488, with a standard deviation of 115.03, which is high and indicates that there is volatility in the share price behavior of the distribution of companies. The cost of the shares ranges from 0.5 at the lowest price to 1555.99 at the highest. The ROE ranged from 0 to 2.549 at its highest and lowest points. With a standard deviation of 0.2838 and a mean value of 0.911 for CSR, it is estimated that 91% of the enterprises in the distribution participate in charitable giving and community development activities. With a standard deviation of 0.283, ROE has a mean of 0.2396. With a standard deviation of 0.3028, ROA has a mean of 0.4938.

Table 2. Pearson correlation

	CSR-EP	ROE	ROA	SP
CSR-EP	1			
ROE	0.0418	1		
p-value	0.2979			
ROA	-0.04775	-0.0396	1	
p-value	0.2352	0.324		
SP	0.2761*	-0.1212*	-0.00536	1
p-value	0.000	0.0025	0.8941	

Source: Researcher's compilation (2021) using Eviews 10.0

This study investigated the association between CSR dimensions and business financial performance measurements using the Pearson correlation statistic. According to the findings, CSR has a positive correlation with ROE (r=0.0418) but is not statistically significant at 5% (p=0.2979), and a negative correlation with ROA (r=-0.04775) but is not statistically significant at 5% (p=0.2352). Additionally, CSR is significant at 5% (p=0.000) and strongly linked with SP (r=0.2761). The correlation analysis shows the direction and strength of the association between the variables. However, because it does not automatically imply functional dependence between the variables, it has a limited capability for inference. For this use, regression estimations work well.

4.1 Regression Analysis

The regression analysis aimed to determine the relationship between the dependent and independent variables and give the pertinent statistics for evaluating the effectiveness of the chosen model and verifying the study's hypotheses. The fixed and random effects estimates from the panel regression estimation were used in this investigation. The appropriate estimates were chosen and used in the inferential analysis based on the Hausman test. Panel effect models do not consider the endogeneity issue, even though they primarily compensate for unobserved heterogeneity (Cameron & Trivedi,

2005). Therefore, the Arellano and Bond (1991) GMM estimator, which manages potential endogeneity problems, was used to handle the endogeneity problem and provided a more reliable estimation parameter. Following are the findings, analyses, and interpretations:

Table 3. CSR and share price results

Variable	Aprori Sign	FE estimates	RE estimates	Arrelano and Bond GMM Estimates
C		-178.47* (9.699) {0.000)	-255.59* (46.590) {0.000}	-127.0343 (19.486) {0.000}
CSR-EWT	+	2.1896* (1.283) {0.088}	9.8775 (6.1364) {0.1080}	-25.8445* (4.41664) {0.000}
		Model Parameters		
R^2		0.6424	0.0739	0.2976
Adjusted R^2		0.6111	0.066	0.2896
F-statistic		26.862	9.929	
Prob(F-stat)		0.000	0.00	
Durbin-Watson		1.7	1.926	
		Model Diagnostics		
Hausman			0.042	
Ramsey Reset test		0.425		
Period Hetero.Test		0.209		
Cross-section Hetero.Test		0.120		
Pesaran CD for serial correlation		0.106		
Instrument Rank				10
j-statistics				5.8395
Prob-j-stat				0.21146
AR(1)				0.0491
AR(2)				0.8165

Source: Researcher's compilation (2021). * sig @ 5%, **sig@10%

The regression findings that looked at how CSR disclosures affected SP were displayed in Table 3. The FE estimate results are presented for the analysis in the study because the Hausman test statistic with a p-value of 0.042 suggests that the FE is the preferred model over the random effects model. The study also simulates the dynamic connection between share price and CSR declarations. The results are heteroskedasticity-free since the white-corrected standard errors were employed to account for any possible heteroskedasticity in the estimation. The estimations were tested for panel period heteroskedasticity (p=0.209) and cross-sectional heteroskedasticity (p=0.120); both were absent. The Peseran cross-dependency test [p=0.106] statistic shows no cross-sectional dependence in the residuals, which supports the likelihood that the errors will serially correlate. According to the FE calculations, R2 is 0.6424, with an adjusted R2 for the degree of freedom of 61.1%. The hypothesis of a significant linear relationship between the dependent and independent variables cannot be ruled out, according to the F-stat of 26.862 (p-value=0.00), which is significant at 5%. Additionally, it shows the combined statistical significance of the model.

According to the coefficient analysis, CSR has a favorable (2.1896) and statistically significant (p=0.088) impact on SP at a 10% level. According to the Arrelano and Bond estimation results, CSR has a significant (p=0.000) negative effect (-25.8445) on SP at 5%. The J-stat test for over-identifying limitations and the Arellano-Bond test for autocorrelation error are two things that should be emphasized regarding the GMM estimate results. All of the p-values produced by the J-stat tests are higher than 0.10, indicating that the null hypothesis could not be disproved. Therefore, prohibitions on over-identification are valid. While the AR(2) tests yield p-values over 0.10, indicating that a null hypothesis of no second-order serial correlation could not be rejected, the AR(1) tests show that the residuals in first differences are associated as expected. Thus, the GMM model's entire set of findings is reliable. The Ramsey Reset Test confirms the absence of misspecification errors for model specification [p=0.425].

Table 4. CSR and ROA Results

Variable	Aprori Sign	FE estimates	RE Estimates	GMM Estimates
C		0.41592* (0.07241) {0.000}	0.4566* (0.4536) {0.0023}	-0.80587* (0.09233) {0.000}
CSR	+	0.02516* (0.0112) {0.0251}	0.0030 (0.0107) {0.7772}	-0.2769* (0.0416) {0.000}
		Model Parameters		
R^2		0.6936	0.0734	0.358
Adjusted R^2		0.6901	0.066	0.112
F-statistic		195.12	9.895	
Prob(F-stat)		0.000	0.00	0.000
Durbin-Watson		2.1	1.97	2.071
		Model Diagnostics		
Hausman		0.006		
Ramsey Reset test		0.410		
Period Hetero.Test		0.81		
Cross-section Hetero.Test		0.431		
Pesaran CD for serial correlation		0.571		
Instrument Rank				8
j-statistics				3.0344
Prob-j-stat				0.2193
AR(1)				0.0023
AR(2)				0.274

Source: Researcher's compilation (2021) using Eviews 10.0. * sig @ 5%, **sig@10%

Table 4 displays the findings of the regression testing of how CSR affected Return on Assets (ROA). The FE is the preferred model estimate between the fixed and random effect estimates, according to the Hausman test statistic with p-value = 0.006. The white-adjusted standard error was used as a statistical safety measure to account for any potential heteroskedasticity in the estimation. As a result, the estimation findings are free of heteroskedasticity. Both panel period and cross-sectional heteroskedasticity were absent from the estimations (p=0.81 and p=0.431, respectively). The potential of serial correlation in the errors was confirmed using the Peseran cross-dependence test [p=0.571], and the statistic shows that the residuals are not cross-section dependent. The FE estimations reveal that the degree to which the explanatory variable can account for systematic fluctuations in the dependent variables is indicated by an R2 of 0.6936 with a degree of freedom adjusted R2 of 0.6901. The hypothesis of a significant linear relationship between the dependent and independent variables cannot be ruled out, according to the F-stat of 195.12 (p-value=0.00). Additionally, it shows the combined statistical significance of the model.

The study of the coefficients demonstrates that CSR has a positive (0.0251) and significant (p=0.0251) effect on ROA at 5%. The endogeneity issue is not considered by the FE models, even though they primarily control for unobserved heterogeneity (Cameron & Trivedi 2005). The Arellano and Bond (1991) GMM estimator adjusts for potential endogeneity problems to address this issue. Stronger betas in the Arrelano and Bond estimation findings demonstrate a significant departure from the FE estimates, supporting the assertion that the Arrelano and Bond estimation results are superior when endogeneity is taken into account. According to the examination of the coefficients, CSR has a negative beta (-0.2769) that is significant at 5% (p=0.000). We analyze the Arellano-Bond test for autocorrelation error and the J-stat test for over-identifying limitations. All of the p-values produced by the J-stat tests are higher than 0.10, indicating that the null hypothesis could not be disproved. Therefore, prohibitions on over-identification are valid. While the AR(2) tests yield p-values over 0.10, indicating that a null hypothesis of no second-order serial correlation could not be rejected, the AR(1) tests show that the residuals in first differences are associated as expected. Thus, the GMM model's entire set of findings is reliable.

Table 5. CSR and ROE results

Variable	Aprori Sign	FE estimates	RE Estimates	GMM Estimates
C		0.26889* (0.0173) {0.0000}	0.5455* (0.1134) {0.000}	0.33201* (0.1139) {0.0039}
CSR-EP	+	0.02226* (0.0097) {0.0221}	0.07414** (0.0408) {0.0696}	0.1061* (0.0326) {0.0013}
AR(1)	+	0.1273* (0.0467) {0.0066}	-0.0693 (0.0500) {0.1666}	0.22573* (0.0282) {0.0000}
		Model Parameters		
R^2		0.669	0.0238	0.537
Adjusted R^2		0.663	0.0159	0.5215
F-statistic		161.852	3.0318	
Prob(F-stat)		0.000	0.0103	
Durbin-Watson		1.9	1.46	
		Model Diagnostics		
Hausman			0.0119	
Ramsey Reset test		0.04		
Period Hetero. Test		0.738		
Cross-section Hetero. Test		0.265		
Pesaran CD for serial correlation		0.381		
Instrument Rank				8
j-statistics				4.4427
Prob-j-stat				0.731
AR(1)				0.392
AR(2)				0.681

Source: Researcher's compilation (2021) using Eviews 10.0 * sig @ 5%, **sig@10%

Table 5 displayed the findings of the regression testing how CSR affected Return on Equity (ROE). The FE is the preferable model estimate between fixed and random effect estimations according to the Hausman test statistic, which has a p-value of 0.0119. However, the generalized method of moments (GMM) estimator was also used to address the possibility of endogeneity bias. The estimation findings are free of heteroskedasticity since the white-adjusted standard error was utilized as a statistical precaution to account for any possible heteroskedasticity in the estimate. Both panel period heteroskedasticity and cross-sectional heteroskedasticity were demonstrated to be absent from the estimates (p=0.738 and p=0.265, respectively). The potential of serial correlation in the errors was confirmed using the Peseran cross-dependence test [p=0.381], and the statistic demonstrates that the residuals are not cross-section dependent. The FE estimations indicate that the degree to which the explanatory variable can account for systematic fluctuations in the dependent variables is indicated by an R2 of 0.669 with a degree of freedom adjusted R2 of 0.663. The F-stat is 161.852 (p-value=0.00), which is significant at 5% and indicates that it is impossible to rule out the possibility of a strong linear correlation between the dependent and independent variables. Additionally, it shows the combined statistical significance of the model.

According to the coefficient study, CSR has a favorable (0.0251) and significant (p=0.0221) impact on ROE at 5%. After accounting for endogeneity, the Arrelano and Bond estimation results significantly differed from the FE estimates, with greater betas demonstrating their superiority. According to the examination of the coefficients, CSR has a positive beta (0.1061) and is significant at 5% (p=0.000). We analyze the Arellano-Bond test for autocorrelation error and the J-stat test for over-identifying limitations. All of the p-values produced by the J-stat tests are higher than 0.10, indicating that the null hypothesis could not be disproved. Therefore, prohibitions on over-identification are valid. While the AR(2) tests yield p-values over 0.10, indicating that a null hypothesis of no second-order serial correlation could not be rejected, the AR(1) tests show that the residuals in first differences are associated as expected. Thus, the GMM model's entire set of findings is reliable.

4.2 Discussion of Results

The study used CSR as an independent variable and ROA, ROE, and share price as measurement indicators for financial performance, which is the dependent variable, to analyze the impact of CSR on the financial performance of Oil & Gas marketing enterprises in Nigeria. According to the study's findings, summarized in Table 3, an examination of the coefficients revealed that CSR has a favorable (2.1896) impact on SP and is statistically significant (p=0.088) at a 10% level. Arrelano and Bond's GMM estimation results showed that CSR had a negative influence on SP that was significant (p=0.000) at 5% and was -25.8445. Therefore, the null hypothesis that corporate social responsibility has no discernible impact on share price is rejected based on the Arrelano and Bond GMM calculation.

Additionally, Table 4 displayed the outcomes of the regression that looked at how CSR affected Return on Asset (ROA). According to the examination of Fixed effects coefficients, CSR had a favorable (0.0251) and significant (p=0.0251) impact on ROA at 5%. The Arrelano and Bond estimation findings after accounting for endogeneity are more striking, as evidenced by the Arrelano and Bond GMM estimation results, which significantly differed from the FE estimations and had greater betas. According to the examination of the coefficients, CSR has a negative beta (-0.2769) that is significant at 5% (p=0.000). The null hypothesis that corporate social responsibility has no discernible impact on Return on Assets (ROA) is disproved by Arrelano and Bond GMM estimation.

The regression results of the impact of CSR on ROE are finally displayed in Table 5. According to the examination of the fixed effects coefficients, CSR had a favorable (0.0251) and significant (p=0.0221) impact on ROE at 5%. The Arrelano and Bond GMM estimation findings showed a significant difference from the FE estimations with stronger betas, demonstrating that the Arrelano and Bond estimations results are more spectacular after adjusting for endogeneity. According to the study of the coefficients, CSR had a positive beta value of 0.1061, which was significant at 5% (p=0.000).

The null hypothesis that corporate social responsibility has no discernible impact on Return on Equity (ROE) is disproved by Arrelano and Bond's GMM calculation. The study's findings concur with those of Muna, Kareema, and Wisam (2021), Revlon (2020), Xiaolin (2019), Abilasha (2019), Elizabeth (2018), and Bushra and Rabia (2017), who, in separate studies examined the relationship between corporate social responsibility (CSR) and the financial performance of firms in Iraq, the United States, China, India, and Asian countries respectively and found a significant correlation. However, this study's findings contradict those of Sharma, Sharma, Ali, and Dadich (2021), Nripinder and Vikramjit (2021), and Samira, Noor, and Muhammed (2018), who looked into CSR and the financial performance of businesses in Bangladesh and India, respectively, and discovered no connection between the two.

5. CONCLUSION

CSR received little consideration and minimal importance in the goals of corporate corporations and amongst small and medium-scale entrepreneurial firms and industries (SMSI) businesses in the past. However, because the issue has garnered so much attention recently, it has emerged as an important issue. Examining whether a corporation or SMSI or entrepreneurial business engages in CSR reporting is one method of assessing its CSR behavior. A firm is seen to offer a fair account of its social impacts and business activities when it engages in CSR reporting, giving stakeholders a basis on which to assess the company's performance. The fact that CSR activity appears to have evolved more freely than compulsorily in recent years suggests that businesses can pick what information to report and may even choose not to disclose it.

Furthermore, there is huge room for improvement in the complicated relationship between CSR and business performance, whether at the corporate or entrepreneurial SMSE levels. This was supported by the field's empirical literature, which does not offer definitive conclusions. This study examined whether a company's socially responsible behavior could impact specific financial performance measures. To determine whether CSR activities could impact corporate performance metrics, the study examined some descriptive statistics and applied cross-section and panel data econometrical methodologies. The study's findings showed that CSR significantly impacted ROA, ROE, and share price of particular Nigerian oil and gas marketing enterprises. By implication, the same was found to be the case for SMSE and entrepreneurial businesses.

6. RECOMMENDATIONS

The study suggests that businesses may need to expand their CSR activity to improve their financial performance because corporate social responsibility substantially impacts corporate financial performance metrics for corporate multinational oil and gas marketing firms and entrepreneurial SMSE in Nigeria.

Similarly, the difficult circumstance of state policy weakness in developing an effective and enforceable CSR framework, particularly in most developing countries, supports the idea that modern CSR practices have dragged and evolved within a system skewed towards the spirit of free-market individualism without effective state direction. According to the survey, Nigerian businesses' CSR operations must be effectively regulated.

The credibility of CSR disclosures is the final concern. One issue with environmental disclosure is that the data supplied may tend to be selective, making it challenging to tell whether such disclosures go beyond corporate branding efforts driven by the desire to improve corporate image. As a result, CSR claims must be independently verified, and the accuracy and legitimacy of CSR disclosures recorded in accounting records must also be established.

REFERENCES

Abilasha, N. (2019). Impact of CSR on the financial performance of top 10 performing CSR companies in India. *Journal of Economics and Finance*, *10*(2), 49–55.

Amu, C. U., Nwezeaku, N. C., Akujuobi, L. E., Ozurunba, B. A., Njie, S. N., Wogu, I. A., & Misra, S. (2019). The Politics of Public Debt Management Among Rising Hegemonies and the Role of ICT: Implications for Theory and Practice for 21st Century Polities. *International Journal of Electronic Government Research*, *15*(3), 72–83. doi:10.4018/IJEGR.2019070105

Arellano, M., & Bond, S. (1991). Some test of specification for panel data: Monte Carlo evidence and an application to employment equations. *The Review of Economic Studies*, *58*(2), 277–297. doi:10.2307/2297968

Bushra, K., & Rabia, T. (2017). Corporate social responsibility impact on the financial performance of Islamic and conventional banks: Evidence from Asian countries. *Research Journal of Finance and Accounting, 8*(7), 20-28. www.iiste.org

Cameron, A. C., & Trivedi, P. K. (2005). *Microeconometrics: Methods and applications*. Cambridge University Press. doi:10.1017/CBO9780511811241

Carroll, A. B. (1979). A three-dimensional conceptual model of corporate social performance. *Academy of Management Review*, *4*(4), 491–509. doi:10.2307/257850

Eccles, R. G., & Krzus, M. P. (2010). Integrated reporting for a sustainable strategy: One Report has the potential to significantly change how companies operate and investors think, shifting the focus from meeting short-term financial goals to developing a long-term business strategy that not only commits to corporate social responsibility but also to a sustainable society. *Financial Executive*, *26*(2), 28-33.

Elizabeth, F. A., (2018). Corporate social responsibility and financial performance: An examination of the Dow Jones Sustainability North American Index. *Applied Economics Theses*, 33.

Garriga, E., & Melé, D. (2004). Corporate social responsibility theories: Mapping the territory. *Journal of Business Ethics*, *53*(1/2), 51–71. doi:10.1023/B:BUSI.0000039399.90587.34

Maignan, I., & Ferrell, O. (2000). Measuring corporate citizenship in two countries: The case of the United States and France. *Journal of Business Ethics*, *23*(3), 283–297. doi:10.1023/A:1006262325211

Marilyn, K. (2013). *Ex-post facto research: Dissertation and scholarly research, Recipes for success*. Dissertation Success LLC. http://www.dissertationrecipes.com/wpcontent/uploads/2011/04/

Muna, K. H., Kareema, A. J., & Wisam, H. A. (2021). Impact of corporate social responsibility on financial performance: Applied research in Iraqi commercial banks. *International Journal of Innovation, Creativity, and Change*, *12*(1). www.ijicc.net

Nripinder, K., & Vikramjit, S. (2021). Empirically examining the impact of corporate social responsibility on financial performance: Evidence from the Indian steel industry. *Asian Journal of Accounting Research*, *6*(2), 134–151. doi:10.1108/AJAR-07-2020-0061

Ong'olo, P. B. (2012). Relationship between corporate social responsibility practices and market share among supermarkets in Kisumu town [Unpublished MBA Research project]. University of Nairobi.

Revlon, W. (2020). *Corporate social responsibility and financial performance of U.S. manufacturing and service small- and medium-sized enterprises*. Walden University.

Samira, I. R., Noor, N. B., & Muhammed, H. (2018). 'Impact of CSR on firm's financial performance: A study on some selected agribusiness industries of Bangladesh. *American Journal of Economics, Finance, and Management*, *4*(3), 74–85.

Sharma, B. R., Sharma, A., Ali, S., & Dadhich, J. (2021). Corporate social responsibility and financial performance: Evidence from manufacturing and service industry. *Academic Journal of Interdisciplinary Studies*, *10*(3), 301–307. doi:10.36941/ajis-2021-0085

Umoren, A. O., Ogbari, M. E., & Atolagbe, T. M. (2016). Corporate social responsibility and firm performance: A study of listed firms in Nigeria. *ICAN 2nd Annual International Academic Conference on Accounting and Finance*.

Wogu, I. A., Njie, S. N., Ezennwa, E. O., Chukwuedo, C. N., Ukagba, G. U., Misra, S., Uniamikogbo, E., & Olu-Owolabi, E. F. (2021). The Politics of Climate Change and the Rising Demand for Global Energy in the 21st Century: Implications for Human and Economic Development. *International Journal of Energy Optimization and Engineering*, *10*(3), 1–23. doi:10.4018/IJEOE.2021070101

Wogu, I. A., Njie, S. N., Katende, J. O., Ukagba, G. U., Edogiawerie, M. O., & Misra, S. (2020). The Social Media, Politics of Disinformation in Established Hegemonies, and the Role of Technological Innovations in 21st Century Elections: The Road Map to US 2020 Presidential Elections. *International Journal of Electronic Government Research, 16*(3), 65–84. doi:10.4018/IJEGR.2020070104

Xiaolin, X. (2019). *The impact of corporate social responsibilities on financial performance in China. International master of environmental policy. Nicholas School of Environment & Sanford School of Policy*, Duke University.

Chapter 5
Awareness and Acceptability of Collaborative Consumption Platforms Amongst Youth

Abhishek Choudhary
https://orcid.org/0000-0001-7951-719X
Indian Institite of Crafts and Design, India

Amit Jain
Amity University, Jaipur, India

Toolika Gupta
Indian Institite of Crafts and Design, India

ABSTRACT

Collaborative consumption (CC) is an innovative model with the potential to transform how individuals produce and consume resources. CC is the concept of using technology to share resources for monetary or non-monetary gain. Although CC is common in many countries, the concept of sharing is relatively new to Indian customers. Increasing knowledge and acknowledgement of the benefits of CC, including efficient resource usage and sustainability, are leading to the emergence of numerous platforms in India. This study presents the outcomes of a three-month survey of 614 Indian customers between October and December 2022 to determine their awareness of CC categories and platforms. Using descriptive statistics, the information was evaluated. The study found that participants between the ages of 18 and 24 are highly motivated and aware of potential forms of CC and existing platforms. Some of the most well-known platforms are Ola, Airbnb, and Oyo. The study revealed the necessity to educate future CC users, particularly in the fashion and lifestyle market category.

DOI: 10.4018/978-1-6684-5871-6.ch005

INTRODUCTION

The "sharing economy" concept is associated with a wide range of actions beyond traditional consumerism. Due to generalized eco-empathy, anti-consumption behaviour such as redistribution, swapping, and sharing has gained popularity (Martin, 2016). To provide clients with temporary use of essential commodities, driven solely by hedonism and self-interest (Bardhi & Eckhardt, 2012; Lamberton & Rose, 2012), online companies (Airbnb and Uber) promote collaborative consumption by facilitating the exchange of privately-owned resources (Hamari et al., 2016). Business strategies that allow users to express their wants and preferences are gaining popularity. The "sharing economy," which includes these practices, has recently been a popular topic of discussion in many fields, including business and public policy. Many other types of tradable systems are possible thanks to the sharing economy concept, which allows for the distribution of both material and immaterial assets through online and offline mediums.

Collaborative Consumption (CC) is a rapidly evolving business concept based on communication and information technologies that are said to lay the groundwork for a "sharing economy." (Buczynski, 2013; Griffiths, 2013). However, given the rapid growth of the CC phenomenon, it is critical to gain a better understanding of this area through which people are more interested in having access to products rather than owning them. (Bardhi & Eckhardt, 2012;Chen, 2009). The CC model is well-established in both the US and European markets (Radwan et al., 2019). Since 2011, the topic has grown in popularity, with 559 papers in the Scopus database as of January 2022. Past studies have examined the context of CC and sustainability. Some concentrated primarily on the commercial models of CC and their implications. However, only a few studies have investigated customers' understanding of this notion and their use of cc services in depth.

Despite being young, the Indian sharing economy has flourished in transportation, hospitality, and co-working spaces. The introduction of Uber to the Indian market marked a turning point for the sharing economy. As the number of individuals with access to the internet and mobile devices grew, as did their willingness to experiment with new products and services, the company found success (McLean, 2015). From the perspective of a developing nation like India, the study on CC awareness and involvement in activities is valuable. Little research has been done on the CC from the consumer's perspective, its most crucial component, and driving force. Furthermore, previous studies have concentrated on the CC mostly from the views of developed countries and understanding perspective of respondents from developing world could lead to better insights regarding the phenomenon. countries with a developed emerging economy, which could be a good source of information. Due to the significant information gap between CC theory and practice in this domain, it is necessary to bridge the gap. This study addresses the question regarding India's depth of understanding and use of the CC service and platforms.

The study's goal is to assess the conventional and developing segments of CC and its platform and analyze and understand the degree of use in terms of customer perception in India. Data was obtained through a questionnaire from 630 respondents. The consumer's degree of awareness about CC services and platforms in India is evaluated and analyzed. Variations are investigated from the perspectives of age groups of respondents and the CC sector and their platforms.

LITERATURE REVIEW

The "sharing economy" refers to peer-to-peer access to underutilized resources (Lim, 2017). Although it was formerly limited to family and friends, sharing resources is not a new concept (Ter Huurne et al., 2017). Due to information and communication technology, new sharing possibilities are emerging. Strangers can exchange idle resources, including housing, tools, apparel, and rides(Lim, 2020; Belk, 2014). Sharing economy companies like Uber and Airbnb have revolutionized how people travel, work, and enjoy holidays.

"A sharing economy", according to Lessig (2008), is a cultural trend centered on social interactions to encourage a collaborative production system. As a result, the sharing economy exists to enable individuals and corporations to share everything. The concept highlights the relevance of products and experiences as critical components of the sharing economy. The sharing economy is one of the most important economic theories of modern times (Botsman & Rogers, 2010a). The sharing economy is often made easier by digital platforms that connect people who want to rent, swap, lend, or borrow things (peer providers or producers) with people who want to use them for a short time (peer consumers)(Cusumano, 2014). With this cultural phenomenon, a wide range of online activities relating to products like residences, automobiles, online content, information, etc., are developing (Ghasemkhani et al., 2018; Chen et al., 2015). The growth of the concept of "collaborative consumption" based on networks and structured systems to exchange services and goods is notable (Hamari et al., 2016; Möhlmann, 2015). The word has now become a benchmark for analyzing overall socioeconomic phenomena, attracting thousands of people to benefit and engage (Botsman & Rogers, 2010b). Collaborative consumption can connect unknown people and places (Belk, 2014b) due to economic and technological causes. There is a difference between sharing and exchanging in terms of collaborative consumption (Belk & Llamas, 2012). In a possession trade, ownership is transmitted from one person to another, and both products and ownership are shared. Thus, collaborative consumption is built on a transferable connection based on sharing, not on product ownership.

According to (Belk, 2014a), collaborative consumption occurs when a number of people work together to purchase and distribute a good or service in exchange for financial or other benefits. Collaborative consumption is studied by the business world as a kind of resources allocation that necessitates payment or other compensation (Belk, 2014; Bardhi & Eckhardt, 2012), while the sustainability field examines it as a form of involvement that must be environmentally responsible (Germann Molz, 2013; Heinrichs, 2013). These two viewpoints produce opposing perceptions of what characterizes a collaborative consumption platform. The essence of the CC, according to Frenken & Schor (2017) is consumers allowing one another temporary access to inadequately physical assets ("unused potential"), possibly in exchange for a fee. The European Commission offers a comprehensive definition of this phenomenon, referring to it as a "collaborative economy" (European Comission, 2016). "Collaborative economy refers to business models where activities are facilitated by collaborative platforms that create an open marketplace for the temporary usage of goods or services often provided by private individuals," managing transactions for financial gain or other purposes does not require a change in ownership.

Online platforms and resource sharing can facilitate CC. Access-based services provided to customers by businesses are an example of business-to-consumer (B2C) interactions, which are mostly conducted for commercial and charitable goals and are categorized by direct and negative mutuality (e.g., self-service technology, on-demand service delivery). While the internet platforms that enable CC, practices have their roots in the access framework (shifting away from ownership-based consumerism), the services supplied by peer groups utilizing their own assets put them apart from the access-based services provided by corporations. Social and business alignment collide in P2P markets. Peer service providers and customers need CC knowledge.

Numerous types of CC can be distinguished (Table 1). This phenomenon can be studied from several different perspectives, including peer-to-peer (P2P), customer-to-customer (C2C), (Guyader & Kienzler, 2019), and business-to-consumer (B2C). We can also distinguish CC based on the technology utilized, including online platforms (Ertz et al., 2019; Sutherland & Jarrahi, 2018) and offline platforms (Ertz et al., 2019). There are many other types of knowledge and information exchange that can take place in CC, including product, skill (Harvey et al., 2020),services (X. Cheng et al., 2019), monetary and exchanges (Barnes & Mattsson, 2016). Customers are the primary partners and suppliers in the supply chain of CC stores, unlike traditional stores. Three criteria distinguish CC from more traditional models of exchange: "(1) the quantity and type of participants, (2) the nature of the exchange, and (3) the directness of exchange"(Benoit et al., 2017). CC is a practical method of doing business that aids the environment by extending the usable life of products and reducing trash left behind after use (Gopalakrishnan & Matthews, 2018). Marketers and retailers can use the strategies to increase consumer acceptance of CC platform retail services. Adding a humane narrative that tells the story behind the product can be more effective than just providing basic product information like price and style. The psychological risks associated with the used product are distinct from those associated with new products, and strategies to alleviate these concerns should be implemented (Kim et al., 2021).

The above CC segments evolve at significantly various speeds. The accommodation and transportation sectors may be seen as the earliest examples of P2P commerce. (Schor & Cansoy, 2019; Zhang et al., 2019). The multiple studies by (Böcker & Meelen, 2017; Frenken & Schor, 2017; Godelnik, 2017; M. Cheng, 2016) also come to a conclusion about how people see the accommodation and transportation sectors as mainstream or conventional parts of the CC. These conventional CC businesses are predicted to grow far more in the future, as in technical services, collaborative finance, and domestic services (PwC, 2015)

OBJECTIVES

The study's objective is to analyze consumer understanding of the various segments of CC and its platform in India. The study will address the following aims in the current environment.

1. To check the awareness level for different formats of collaborative consumption amongst different demographic segments of consumers.
2. To what extent are consumers aware about collaborative consumption in different segments/domains?
3. To what extent are consumers aware of the existing platforms for CC?
4. To what extent do consumers use the services of selected CC platforms.

Table 1. Typology of collaborative consumption

Particular	Participation	Market	Mode	Key Segment
Form of CC	1. C2C 2. P2P 3. B2C	1. Offline 2. Online	1. Renting 2. Swapping 3. Sharing 4. Bartering 5. Lending	1. Collaborative Transportation 2. Collaborative Clothing & Lifestyle 3. Collaborative Accommodation 4. Collaborative Skill & Education

Based on the objectives mentioned earlier, the following hypotheses have been formulated for analyzing perception of Indian consumer.

a. Consumers are more acquainted with CC alternatives in Transportation and accommodation (traditional Segments) as compared to Clothing and education (emerging Segments).
b. Consumers prefer traditional segment platform services to emerging segment platform services.
c. The consumption pattern of CC varies across demographic segments.

METHODOLOGY

With an objective to analyze the given phenomenon from the perspective of Indian consumers the study examines the awareness and use of traditional and emerging CC services and their platforms. Based on the literature analysis, the transportation and accommodation segments are regarded as a conventional segment. The areas including apparel, education etc are regarded as emerging segments.

Data collection is an important phase in research planning, this includes the formulation of the questionnaire and finding an appropriate platform. Primary data were gathered using a self-designed questionnaire to elicit responses. The data gathering approach employed was quota sampling. With a structure consistent with quota features, the selection set matched the population structure. The data was collected online from 630 respondents. Only 614 responses were used for analysis out of a total of 630 completed online responses, as 16 were incomplete, this constituted a success rate of 97.45%.

The questionnaire has semi-closed questions that ascertain respondents' acquaintance with various forms of CC, their awareness of the presence of segment specific CC platforms, and their level of use of individual CC platforms. IBM-SPSS

Table 2. Demographic analysis (descriptive analysis)

Demographic	Frequency	Percentage	Female	Percentage	Male	Percentage
Age Group						
18-24	390	64%	198	50.76%	192	49.24%
25-30	224	36%	114	50.89%	110	49.11%
Profession						
Student	276	44.95%	159	57.60%	117	42.40%
Professional	338	55.05%	153	45.26%	185	54.74%

was used to analyze primary data received via questionnaire. The authors have used descriptive statistics tools. The relative frequencies were used to analyze respondents' awareness of CC types and platforms.

RESULTS

The authors determined the extent to which respondents are aware of the concept of CC using the study's framework. Majority of respondents were aware about the concept although only 80% have heard the term collaborative consumption.

The authors aimed to evaluate respondents' familiarity with various CC formats and their applicability to various types of businesses. According to the data in Table 3, the respondents' understanding of the various types of collaboration with respect to the sharing economy. Majority of the respondents are familiar with seven of the twelve forms reviewed. Car renting, two-wheeler renting, and room renting were most familiar with 90% or more respondents indicating awareness of these areas. Collaboration formats such as Sharing of room and car-pooling are also well-known. 80% or more of those responding to the survey said they were aware of these. Sharing of education and skill is ranked lower, with only 36% of respondents aware of its existence.

The authors subsequently ascertained the awareness of respondents regarding the existence of platforms/companies operating in the said domain (Table 4).

Table 3. Knowledge of forms of CC

Forms	N	%
Car Renting	591	96.25%
Two-wheeler renting	581	94.62%
Room Renting	576	93.81%
Sharing of Room	545	88.76%
Car-pooling	525	85.50%
Renting of apparel	344	56%
Renting of lifestyle products	300	48.85%
Sharing of apparel	291	47.40%
Sharing of lifestyle product	280	45.60%
Forms	N	%
Sharing of Education & Skill	222	36.15%
Swapping of apparel	214	34.85%

Table 4 demonstrates an understanding of the CC's unique platform. OLA (96 per cent) in the transportation segment, OYO (96 per cent) in the accommodation segment, and Uber (89 per cent) in the transportation segment may all be rated among the top three platforms in terms of familiarity. Other segment platforms are lesser known to the respondents. (e.g., Rapido, Flatmate, Trivago, Date the Ramp, and Kickstarter) were also mentioned by respondents but by few of them.

The authors determined how often respondents used specific CC platforms to get the services they offered (Table 5). Table 5 shows the degree of platform-specific CC user involvement among respondents.

As illustrated in Table 5, respondents make the most extensive use of the platform in the Transportation and accommodation area. According to respondents, car renting services and room rental platforms are the most frequently used CC platforms.

Table 4. Awareness of the platform of CC

Segment	Platform	N	%
Transportation	Ola	595	96.90%
	Uber	552	89.90%
	Zoom car	399	59.60%
	My Choice	319	51.95%
	Meru	245	40.71%
Accommodation	Oyo	590	96.10%
	Airbnb	505	82.25%
	Zolo	279	45.43%
	Couch Surfing	190	30.95%
Apparel	Flyrobe	305	49.67%
	Rent at Tali	291	47.39%
	The Clothing Rental	251	40.88%
	Rent It, Bae	225	36.65%
LifeStyle Product	Furlenco	258	46.41%
	Fab Rento	204	33.22%
	City Furnish	162	26.38%
Skill & Education	Coursera/EDX	208	33.87%
	Just Book	156	25.40%
	Padhega India	105	17.10%

Table 5. Use of the platform of Collaborative Consumption

Segment	Platform	N	%
Transportation	Ola	454	73.94%
	Uber	430	70%
	Zoom car	259	42.18%
	My Choize	182	29.64%
	Meru	125	20.35%
Accommodation	Oyo	475	77.36%
	Airbnb	354	57.65%
	Zolo	124	20.20%
	Couch Surfing	67	10.90%
Apparel	Flyrobe	193	31.92%
	Rent at Tali	168	27.36%
	The Clothing Rental	147	23.94%
	Rent It, Bae	115	18.72%
LifeStyle Product	Furlenco	121	19.70%
	Fab Rento	73	11.88%
	City Furnish	61	9.93%
Skill & Education	Coursera/EDX	148	24.10%
	Just Book	80	13.02%
	Padhega India	62	10.10%

Awareness of Collaborative Consumption Formats Amongst Respondents of Different Demographic Segments

The study also sought to determine the differences if any in the individual's awareness of the collaboration consumption formats across gender and age groups.

There was a statistically significant difference between the genders of the respondents in all eleven considered formats. In nine out of eleven cases, the group of male respondents is more aware of the opportunities for collaboration in comparison to the female respondents (Table 6).

An analysis was also carried out to see if there was a difference in familiarity with CC platforms across the genders. We employed 19 platforms for the analysis, with 5 each from the transportation segment, four each from the accommodation and Apparel sectors, and three each from the Lifestyle and education segments.

Table 7 reveals a statistically significant difference across genders in terms of awareness about the given CC platforms. Significantly, both genders demonstrated

Table 6. Differences in the perspectives of both genders on CC forms

Forms of Collaboration	Relative Frequency	
	Female (%)	Male (%)
Car Renting	74.73	89.08
Car-pooling	65.96	79.60
Two-wheeler renting	74.20	86.78
Sharing of Room	73.14	77.59
Room Renting	74.47	85.06
Sharing of Education & Skill	36.97	35.34
Sharing of apparel	62.50	75.00
Renting of apparel	51.60	43.10
Swapping of apparel	49.47	39.66
Renting of lifestyle products	42.82	60.34
Sharing of lifestyle product	41.76	43.39

equal understanding in the segment, and the data in table 8 confirms the existence of CC platforms. A statistically significant difference in general platform knowledge between males and females has been demonstrated in all sectors.

DISCUSSION

The study found that approximately half of the respondents believed they could use car renting, car-pooling, two-wheeler rentals, renting rooms, renting apparel, and lifestyle product renting. Less than half of those respondents understood that collaboration may be utilized in skill & education. The respondents are most aware of types of collaboration in conventional CC categories like transportation and accommodation (specifically car renting, carpooling, Two-wheeler renting, renting rooms, and sharing of rooms).

Using demographic data, we may conclude that the 18-25 age group is the more conscious of all analyzed forms of CC compared to the other age groups. The survey also shows that people are most aware of platforms in transportation (1st), accommodation (2nd), and clothing & lifestyle (3rd place). This is consistent with the finding of (Schor & Cansoy, 2019). In addition, there is a significant degree of awareness of the COURSERA/EDX platform as well as the Clothing rental platform from the apparel & lifestyle segment. This appears to be connected to the extensive media campaign that these platforms have been running in India for several years,

Table 7. Awareness about the Platforms in perspectives of the Gender

Segment	Platform	Relative Frequency	
		Female	Male
Transportation	Ola	79.79	89.37
	Uber	74.47	85.06
	Zoom car	47.34	66.38
	My Choize	36.70	48.28
	Meru	30.85	51.15
Accommodation	Airbnb	54.79	79.31
	Oyo	77.39	89.08
	Zolo	35.90	41.38
	Couch Surfing	26.60	25.86
Apparel	Flyrobe	47.34	25.00
	Rent It Bae	55.85	23.28
	Rent at Tali	54.79	26.15
	The Clothing Rental	61.70	24.14
Lifestyle Product	Fab Rento	20.74	29.89
	City Furnish	22.87	24.71
	Furlenco	33.51	37.93
Segment	Platform	Relative Frequency	
		Female	Male
Skill & Education	Padhega India	13.83	11.49
	Just Book	14.36	14.37
	Coursera/EDX	51.60	45.40

Table 8. General Awareness about the Segments of CC

Segments	Relative Frequency	
	Female	Male
Transportation	81.65	85.11
Accommodation	74.47	79.26
Clothing & Lifestyle	76.86	66.49
Skill & Education	62.77	53.19

particularly via television and digital. As a result, customers are more familiar with platforms in the transportation and lodging industries. The clothing and fashion industry come in third.

In terms of gender differences in acquaintance with CC platforms, we can say that the male has demonstrated a higher level of awareness than the female. Differential statistical significance was observed between transportation and accommodation platforms, along with across platforms in the other CC segments (Table 8).

The analysis also reveals that many respondents use two platforms that are part of the CC's largest categories. The transportation segment (89 percent) and the accommodation segment (89percent) are represented by the Ola and OYO platforms, respectively.

CONCLUSION AND LIMITATION

People in India, particularly those between 18 and 25 years old, may have a complete understanding of CC's potential applications. It illustrates that the degree of familiarity with a particular portal is primarily dependent on the mainstream popularity of a particular CC section or platform, regardless of whether it is positive or negative. Therefore, it would be essential to educate prospective users about CC's possible advantages and characteristics.

To increase CC acceptance, the public's trust in the usability and security of platforms must be reinforced. The CC platform must be designed in such a way that it not only provides value to customers but also influences their lifestyle, resulting in conversion (Kapoor & Vij, 2021). Both the government and the individual platforms have a role to play in clarifying the legal framework and promoting positive media coverage. As evident from the study increasing the base of CC amongst different demographic segment has tremendous potential. In this situation, the typical frugality, economy, and resource conservation associated with their age may be put to good use. The probability of growing participation in CC is increased by the fact that the barrier of low computer literacy within the age group is disappearing. This phenomenon will improve accessibility of scares resources for the population.

The research paper is useful for both academic and professional purposes. Theoretically, it contributes to our knowledge of CC variants other than the standard. The concept of "collaborative consumption" is cutting-edge, mostly unexplored, and in constant flux (Gerwe & Silva, 2020; Habibi et al., 2016). There isn't a simple typology that might be used to look into this phenomenon. It is impossible to create a universal topology for CC, however, due to the wide range of definitions and concepts that exist within the field. Based on the existing state of knowledge, the study suggests a classification system for CC file formats. As an added bonus on the cusp between theory and practice, the proposed research would increase our understanding of how widespread CC awareness is and how widely its platforms are used in developing countries like India. In this way, the study aids in filling a knowledge vacuum that is largely disregarded by academics outside of developed nations. The research has practical applications for both current platform operators and parties that could be interested in providing services within the context of a CC model, as well as for policymakers. For instance, the research's conclusions can be used to formulate a plan for persuading both current and future platform service users to change their behaviour.

Although the provided study is useful for generating new concepts, it has a number of methodological problems. The fact that this research was done in India — a developing country where these tendencies are just gaining traction — helps to explain them. The technique has also been a limitation, as it plays a role in choosing the appropriate CC formats and platforms. We understand that their definition was based on existing understanding, which will evolve. Finally, a limitation of the presented study is that it focuses on status rather than causal linkages, which was the authors' aim in this section of the research.

Future research directions can be identified from the perspective of the constraints. First and foremost, we might advocate doing comparative research on observed concerns on both developed and developing levels, within the framework of countries. It's also important to think about how demographic characteristics, such as income, education level, and geographic area, affect a person's level of comfort with and propensity to use certain CC strategies. Finally, we suggest research on how people feel about the CC and its many facets, including the positives and drawbacks; the degree to which it is regulated; and its economic, sociological, and ecological effects.

REFERENCES

Bardhi, F., & Eckhardt, G. M. (2012). Access-Based Consumption: The Case of Car Sharing. *The Journal of Consumer Research, 39*(4), 881–898. doi:10.1086/666376

Barnes, S. J., & Mattsson, J. (2016). Understanding current and future issues in collaborative consumption: A four-stage Delphi study. *Technological Forecasting and Social Change, 104*, 200–211. doi:10.1016/j.techfore.2016.01.006

Belk, R. (2014a). Sharing versus pseudo-sharing in web 2.0. *Anthropologist, 18*(1), 7–23. doi:10.1080/09720073.2014.11891518

Belk, R. (2014b). You are what you can access: Sharing and collaborative consumption online. *Journal of Business Research, 67*(8), 1595–1600. doi:10.1016/j.jbusres.2013.10.001

Belk, R., & Llamas, R. (2012). The nature and effects of sharing in consumer behavior. *Transformative Consumer Research for Personal and Collective Well-Being*, 625–646.

Benoit, S., Baker, T. L., Bolton, R. N., Gruber, T., & Kandampully, J. (2017). A triadic framework for collaborative consumption (CC): Motives, activities and resources & capabilities of actors. *Journal of Business Research*, *79*(May), 219–227. doi:10.1016/j.jbusres.2017.05.004

Böcker, L., & Meelen, T. (2017). Sharing for people, planet or profit? Analysing motivations for intended sharing economy participation. *Environmental Innovation and Societal Transitions*, *23*, 28–39. doi:10.1016/j.eist.2016.09.004

Botsman, R., & Rogers, R. (2010). *What's Mine Is Yours: The Rise of Collaborative Consumption*. Academic Press.

Buczynski, B. (n.d.). *Sharing is Good: How to Save Money*. Time and Resources Through Collaborative Consumption.

Chen, Y. (2009). Possession and access: Consumer desires and value perceptions regarding contemporary art collection and exhibit visits. *The Journal of Consumer Research*, *35*(6), 925–940. doi:10.1086/593699

Chen, Y.-J., Shanthikumar, J. G., & Shen, Z.-J. M. (2015). Incentive for Peer-to-Peer Knowledge Sharing among Farmers in Developing Economies. *Production and Operations Management*, *24*(9), 1430–1440. doi:10.1111/poms.12328

Cheng, M. (2016). Sharing economy: A review and agenda for future research. *International Journal of Hospitality Management*, *57*, 60–70. doi:10.1016/j.ijhm.2016.06.003

Cheng, X., Fu, S., Sun, J., Bilgihan, A., & Okumus, F. (2019). An investigation on online reviews in sharing economy driven hospitality platforms: A viewpoint of trust. *Tourism Management*, *71*, 366–377. doi:10.1016/j.tourman.2018.10.020

Cusumano, M. A. (2014). How traditional firms must compete in the sharing economy. *Communications of the ACM*, *58*(1), 32–34. doi:10.1145/2688487

Ertz, M., Durif, F., & Arcand, M. (2019). A conceptual perspective on collaborative consumption. *AMS Review*, *9*(1), 27–41. doi:10.100713162-018-0121-3

European Comission. (2016). Communication from the Commission to the European Parliament, the European Economic and Social Committee of the Regions: A European agenda for the collaborative economy. *Europe Commission*, 16. https://ec.europa.eu/germany/news/kollaborative-wirtschaft-eu-kommission-will-rechtliche-klarheit-für-neue-geschäftsmodelle_de?newsletter_id=188&utm_source=representations_newsletter&utm_medium=email&utm_campaign=EU-Aktuell&utm_content=Kollaborat

Frenken, K., & Schor, J. (2017). Putting the sharing economy into perspective. *Environmental Innovation and Societal Transitions*, *23*, 3–10. doi:10.1016/j.eist.2017.01.003

Germann Molz, J. (2013). Social networking technologies and the moral economy of alternative tourism: the case of couchsurfing.org. *Annals of Tourism Research*, *43*, 210–230. doi:10.1016/j.annals.2013.08.001

Gerwe, O., & Silva, R. (2020). Clarifying the sharing economy: Conceptualization, typology, antecedents, and effects. *The Academy of Management Perspectives*, *34*(1), 65–96. doi:10.5465/amp.2017.0010

Ghasemkhani, H., Li, Y.-M., Moinzadeh, K., & Tan, Y. (2018). Contracting Models for P2P Content Distribution. *Production and Operations Management*, *27*(11), 1940–1959. doi:10.1111/poms.12718

Godelnik, R. (2017). Millennials and the sharing economy: Lessons from a ‘buy nothing new, share everything month’ project. *Environmental Innovation and Societal Transitions*, *23*, 40–52. doi:10.1016/j.eist.2017.02.002

Gopalakrishnan, S., & Matthews, D. (2018). Collaborative consumption: A business model analysis of second-hand fashion. *Journal of Fashion Marketing and Management*, *22*(3), 354–368. doi:10.1108/JFMM-05-2017-0049

Goudin, P. (2016). The Cost of Non-Europe in the Sharing Economy: Economic, Social and Legal Challenges and Opportunities. European Parliamentary Research Service.

Griffiths, R. (2013). *The great sharing economy*. Co-Operatives UK.

Guyader, H., & Kienzler, M. (2019). “True Sharing” or “Sharing Economy” Fad? In A. G. B. Edvardsson Mary Jo Bitner & R. Verma (Eds.), *QUIS16 symposium: “Advancing Service Research and Practice”, 10-13 June 2019*. CTF Service Research Center, Karlstad University. http://urn.kb.se/resolve?urn=urn:nbn:se:liu:diva-160319

Habibi, M. R., Kim, A., & Laroche, M. (2016). From sharing to exchange: An extended framework of dual modes of collaborative nonownership consumption. *Journal of the Association for Consumer Research, 1*(2), 277–294. doi:10.1086/684685

Hamari, J., Sjöklint, M., & Ukkonen, A. (2016). The sharing economy: Why people participate in collaborative consumption. *Journal of the Association for Information Science and Technology, 67*(9), 2047–2059. doi:10.1002/asi.23552

Harvey, J., Smith, A., Goulding, J., & Illodo, I. B. (2020). Food sharing, redistribution, and waste reduction via mobile applications: A social network analysis. *Industrial Marketing Management, 88*, 437–448. doi:10.1016/j.indmarman.2019.02.019

Heinrichs, H. (2013). Sharing economy: A potential new pathway to sustainability. *GAIA - Ecological Perspectives for Science and Society, 22*(4), 228–231. doi:10.14512/gaia.22.4.5

Kapoor, A. P., & Vij, M. (2021). Want it, rent it: Exploring attributes leading to conversion for online furniture rental platforms. *Journal of Theoretical and Applied Electronic Commerce Research, 16*(2), 188–207. doi:10.4067/S0718-18762021000200114

Kim, N., Woo, H., & Ramkumar, B. (2020, July). The role of product history in consumer response to online second-hand clothing retail service based on circular fashion. *Journal of Retailing and Consumer Services, 60*, 102457. doi:10.1016/j.jretconser.2021.102457

Lamberton, C. P., & Rose, R. L. (2012). When is ours better than mine? A framework for understanding and altering participation in commercial sharing systems. *Journal of Marketing, 76*(4), 109–125. doi:10.1509/jm.10.0368

Lessig, L. (2008). *Remix: Making art and commerce thrive in the hybrid economy*. Penguin. doi:10.5040/9781849662505

Lim, W. M. (2017). Inside the sustainable consumption theoretical toolbox: Critical concepts for sustainability, consumption, and marketing. *Journal of Business Research, 78*, 69–80. doi:10.1016/j.jbusres.2017.05.001

Lim, W. M. (2020). The sharing economy: A marketing perspective. *Australasian Marketing Journal, 28*(3), 4–13. doi:10.1016/j.ausmj.2020.06.007

Martin, C. J. (2016). The sharing economy: A pathway to sustainability or a nightmarish form of neoliberal capitalism? *Ecological Economics, 121*, 149–159. doi:10.1016/j.ecolecon.2015.11.027

McLean, S. (2015). The rise of the sharing economy. *Computers & Law Magazine of SCL, 26*(1), 26–28.

Möhlmann, M. (2015). Collaborative consumption: Determinants of satisfaction and the likelihood of using a sharing economy option again. *Journal of Consumer Behaviour, 14*(3), 193–207. doi:10.1002/cb.1512

PwC. (2015). Consumer intelligence series 'The sharing economy.' PricewaterhouseCoopers.

Radwan, M. B., Patsiaouras, G., & Saren, M. (2019). To own or to access? An exploration of sharing and access practices by Arab millennials. In *Handbook of the Sharing Economy*. Edward Elgar Publishing. doi:10.4337/9781788110549.00012

Schor, J. B., & Cansoy, M. (2019). The sharing economy. The Oxford Handbook of Consumption, 51.

Sutherland, W., & Jarrahi, M. H. (2018). The sharing economy and digital platforms: A review and research agenda. *International Journal of Information Management, 43*, 328–341. doi:10.1016/j.ijinfomgt.2018.07.004

Ter Huurne, M., Ronteltap, A., Corten, R., & Buskens, V. (2017). Antecedents of trust in the sharing economy: A systematic review. *Journal of Consumer Behaviour, 16*(6), 485–498. doi:10.1002/cb.1667

Zhang, T. C., Gu, H., & Jahromi, M. F. (2019). What makes the sharing economy successful? An empirical examination of competitive customer value propositions. *Computers in Human Behavior, 95*, 275–283. doi:10.1016/j.chb.2018.03.019

Chapter 6
Green Entrepreneurship: A Way Ahead to Sustainable Development

Anadi Trikha
https://orcid.org/0000-0003-0792-0195
Rajasthan Technical University, India

Madhu Bala Kaushik
https://orcid.org/0000-0002-3336-6717
Manipal University Jaipur, India

ABSTRACT

As nobody opposes economic development, the words "entrepreneur" and "entrepreneurship" will continue to be a topic of conversation for generations to come. However, the concept of green entrepreneurship has added seasoning with the spices of sustainability, and its flavor is spreading globally. This chapter focuses on the fundamental notion of green entrepreneurship as well as a few Indian startups that have adopted the concept. In addition, the chapter describes the model used by NITI Aayog to accomplish the SDGs in India. In addition, the chapter discusses the prospects for green entrepreneurship in India.

INTRODUCTION

India is a very populous nation with a growing need for economic development to remain competitive in the international market. At the same time, this population requires employment opportunities and other material needs to maintain a high quality of life. Rapid population growth is not reciprocated by the required number

DOI: 10.4018/978-1-6684-5871-6.ch006

of jobs, and it is becoming an impossible task for the Indian government, and the youth are aware of this. This has paved the way for a range of start-ups and corporate houses to emerge in India, and the education sector has also caught wind of the shifting landscape. Now, higher education is likewise focused on cultivating entrepreneurs as opposed to creating job seekers. This sector receives a variety of grants and financial aid through business incubators, angel investors, and seed funding to foster innovation and creativity among students and encourage them to provide resources and funding for their enterprises, if necessary. If consulting services are also necessary, these are also offered. The government of India has established a separate department under the Ministry of Human Resource Development, which undertakes the training and development of competent faculty and teachers to facilitate innovation in classrooms.

The Ministry of Micro, Small, and Medium-Sized Enterprises is solely responsible for this sector and is monitoring the overall growth of this burgeoning entrepreneurial generation. In contrast, we have realised during the previous many years that destroying our ecology, civilization, forests, cultural heritage, environment, and, most importantly, mother earth, will not result in a new world. Future generations will not forgive us for our excessive use of resources, which has led to the depletion of the earth's natural resources and the contamination of its ecosystems with the waste of all types. If immediate corrective action is not taken, future generations will be deprived of fundamental requirements such as clean air and water to drink.

An emphasis was placed on green entrepreneurship as a response to this unavoidable and quickly deteriorating challenge. Although the term was coined by Berle, there are several examples of farmers and housewives employing eco-friendly practices in Indian traditional farming methods and Indian kitchens, as well as the process of recycling waste materials to create new and usable products. We are already familiar with the language of the tools and processes we will design for sustainability, and we have begun to incorporate the concept of creativity. To keep it alive, we must create, duplicate, recycle, and reinvent it, as is obvious from the preceding discussion. Green entrepreneurship seeks to purify the environment, conserve resources, and recycle waste that pollutes the air, water, and land. Further in the chapter aspiring green entrepreneurs of India is discussed.

BACKGROUND

The chapter sheds light on the origins of the various terms used in this chapter after examining many research papers, and it is reasonable to attempt from our side to offer the background information through a literature study.

Green Entrepreneurship

According to Berle (1991), he campaigns for waste reduction, material preservation, and energy saving as a green entrepreneur. Some startup ideas may be inspired by a combination of commonly accepted solutions to global problems, such as world hunger, world peace, and the requirement for resource reallocation (green businesses). Unfortunately, only a small fraction of people comprehend the need for green entrepreneurship, thus their contribution is negligible.

Isaak (2002) finished his paper on environmental entrepreneurship with several helpful pieces of advice. There were also other recommendations for expanding and boosting green industries.

According to Dixon and Clifford (2007), there is a significant relationship between entrepreneurship and the environment. The achievement of the organization's environmental, social, and economic objectives is solely facilitated by entrepreneurial instinct. The "Green-works business model" has been proposed and is effective due to its origins in the organic ties between enterprises and major corporate bodies that prioritise corporate social responsibility (CSR). They proposed an eco-entrepreneurial road to social and environmental sustainability.

According to Rao and Reddy (2012), who stated in their study on the rise of green consumerism that green products and services are now very popular due to the market's current degree of environmental awareness, the environmental goals of A better world are now met by the brand "green." Due to this foundation, entrepreneurs who recognise and adapt to social dynamics' trends and changes will be successful.

Sharma and Kushwaha (2015) developed a conceptual model of green entrepreneurship to analyse the opportunities for green entrepreneurs and sustainable development in India in light of market change and shifting circumstances.

According to Vaidya and Honagannavar (2017), green entrepreneurship is rapidly gaining acceptability and becoming a crucial engine of India's sustainable development.

Sustainable Development

Carley and Christie (2017) found that the earth's resource system must be governed since it is limited and interconnected with social systems, with economic, social, and political variables playing a significant influence. It is essential to regularly monitor the delicate environment and possess the requisite knowledge. It is vital to solve difficulties and eliminate obstacles to sustainable growth.

In addition to the essential components of sustainable development, namely economic, social, and environmental aspects, Pawowski (2008) emphasises the importance of other elements, such as political, legal, and technical factors. In addition to the fundamental aspects, he argues that political, legal, and technical

Table 1. 17 Sustainable Development Goals (SDGs) to transform our world

Goal 1	**No Poverty**	**Goal 10**	**Sustainable Cities and Communities**
Goal 2	Zero Hunger	**Goal 11**	Responsible Consumption and Production
Goal 3	Good Health and Well Being	**Goal 12**	Climate Action
Goal 4	Quality Education	**Goal 13**	Life Below Water
Goal 5	Gender Equality	**Goal 14**	Life on Land
Goal 6	Clean Water and Sanitation	**Goal 15**	Peace and Justice/Strong Institutions
Goal 7	Affordable and Clean Energy	**Goal 16**	Partnerships to achieve the Goal
Goal 8	Decent Work and Economic Growth	**Goal 17**	Reduced Inequality
Goal 9	Industry, Innovation, and Infrastructure		

Source: From wikipedia.org/wiki/Sustainable Development

considerations must be taken into account for humans to fulfil their environmental responsibilities efficiently.

Pearce and Warford examined sustainable economic growth in their book published in 1993. The significance of environmental protection and balanced economic growth was also heavily emphasised for emerging nations, as environmental degradation affects economic output and poses health hazards directly or indirectly.

The WECD Report defines sustainable development as meeting current demands without compromising future generations' ability to meet their own needs (1987). It was stated that the potential of the environment to meet current and future needs is bound by the current state of technology and societal structure.

Indicators of sustainable growth were developed by the Commission on Sustainable Development (CSD) to quantify and evaluate the sustainability of actions made during the economic development process.

MAIN FOCUS OF THE CHAPTER

Green entrepreneurship should not be discussed in terms of concepts and associated theories because they are ineffective at educating the masses and are more likely to remain in the dictionaries of the upper class, where they are employed for their benefit. Diverse authors hold divergent viewpoints, with the majority emphasising theoretical rather than practical ramifications. Through this chapter, we aim to engage the general public and disseminate information on green entrepreneurship from rural to urban areas so that anyone, regardless of age, will be able to define it and put it into practice for everything from small startups to established businesses.

Table 2. The CSD Indicators of Sustainable Development

• Poverty • Governance • Health • Education • Demographics • Natural Hazards • Atmosphere	• Land • Ocean, Seas, and Coasts • Freshwater • Biodiversity • Economic Development • Global Economic Partnership • Consumption and Production Patterns

Source: From Indicators of Sustainable Development: Guidelines and Methodologies (2007), UN

Roadmap of Government of India: The Indian Model of SGD Localization (NITI Aayog, 2022)

Given the variety of concerns at the local level and the size of the obstacles, attaining the SDGs in a country like India can only be done through localization. The SDGs have been endorsed by all twenty-eight states as well as eight union territories. Many states have made progress toward localising the SDGs. The different lessons that have come out of the localization process in the states and union territories can help other states and even other nations.

In a report titled "Localizing SDGs: Early Lessons from India," NITI Aayog and the UN in India have collaborated to chronicle learnings from the localization process in 2019. The study mentioned above is expanded upon and built upon in this publication, which offers a more nuanced view of the lessons learned during the process of achieving the SDGs. This report will serve as motivation for other states to participate in peer learning.

More importantly, this document shows an Indian model of localization that emphasises (a) institutional ownership, (b) the development of a strong review and monitoring system, (c) the growth of capacities for planning and monitoring SDGs, and (d) the promotion of a "whole of society" approach.

The NITI Aayog at the centre and the corresponding state and UT administrations at the sub-national level serve as the anchors of the Indian model of SDG localization, which is built around four interconnected pillars acting sequentially and concurrently at the national level.

The model's four main pillars are as follows:

Pillar 1: Creating institutional ownership
Pillar 2: Establishing a robust review and monitoring system
Pillar 3: Developing capacities for integrating SDGs in planning and monitoring.
Pillar 4: Promoting a "whole-of-society" approach

Figure 1. The localization imperative
Source NITI Aayog Report 2022

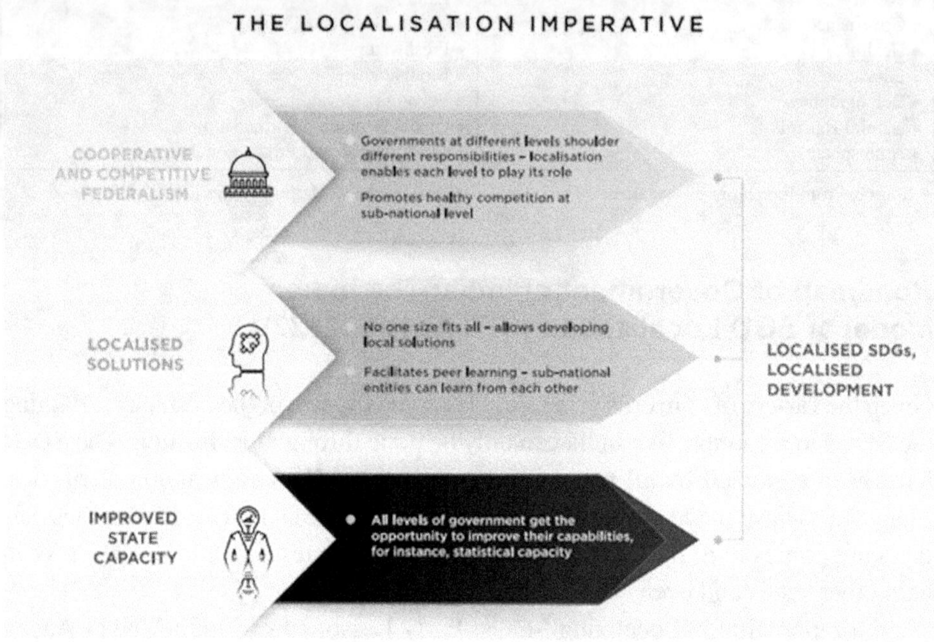

On January 1, 2016, Assam, a subnational government in the nation's northeast, formally embraced the SDGs. The SDGs were adopted and put into effect by the subnational government of Assam, which is recognised as the first. Other sub-national governments began a similar approach as a result of the Assam government's attempt to align its strategy with the SDGs. By encouraging and making it possible for local governments to link their vision, strategy, and action plan to the SDGs, NITI Aayog sped up this process by a large amount.

Over the past five years, sub-national governments have taken the lead in implementing SDG monitoring systems at various levels of governance, adapting SDGs at the local level, creating an institutional framework to support the 2030 Agenda, building capacity, and advancing the localization of SDGs at the district and local levels. High-level review procedures have been institutionalised by states and UTs for SDG monitoring. Indicator frameworks for the state, district, and even municipal levels have also been developed.

So far, three editions of the SDG Index by NITI Aayog have been published for the years 2018, 2019–20, and 2021–22. These reports rank states and UTs as well as highlight national performance on each objective. The Index Dashboard is a communication tool that offers representations and visualisations that help policymakers make data-based decisions more easily. The Index also acts as a vehicle

Figure 2. Indian model of SDG localization
Source NITI Aayog Report 2022

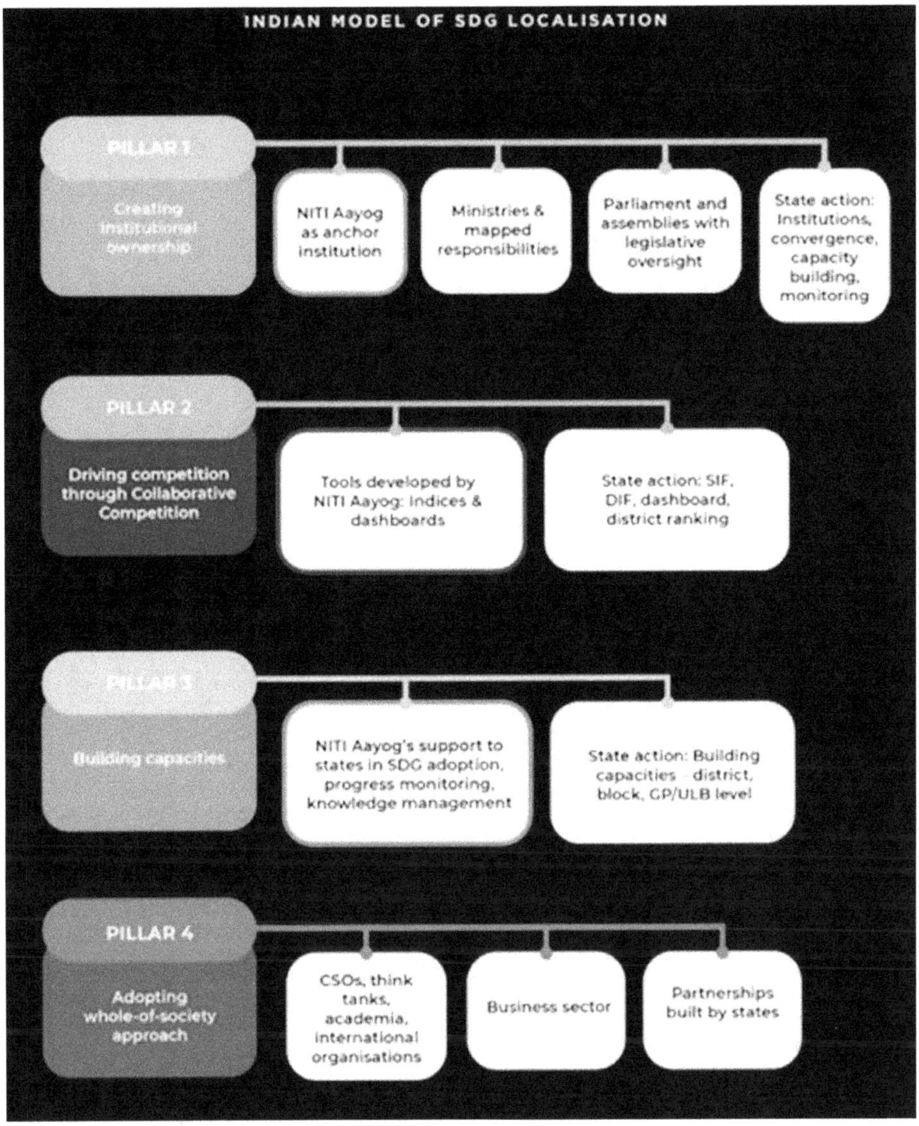

for advocacy, spreading the ideas of partnerships, resilience, and sustainability. The SDG objectives are covered in more detail, more often, and with higher quality and wider-coverage indicators in each edition of the Index than in the preceding one. The comprehensive index provides various insights, from the adoption and implementation of SDGs to the outcomes of SDGs.

Figure 3. Steps in SDG localization at the subnational level
Source NITI Aayog Report 2022

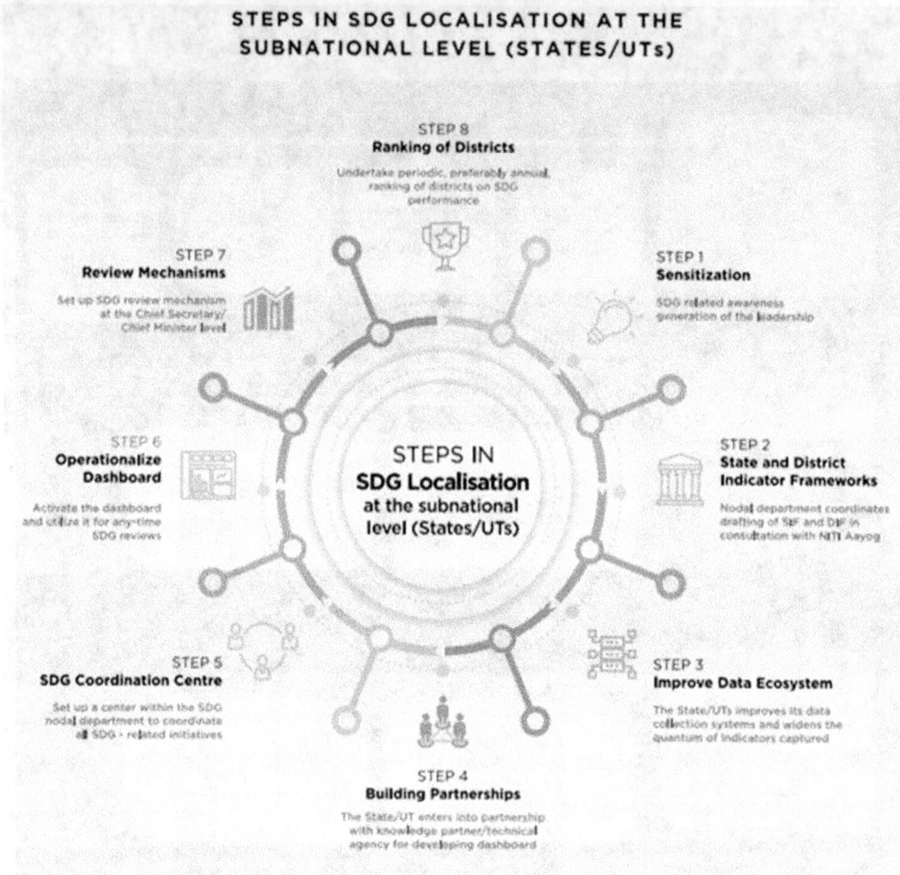

PROMISING GREEN ENTREPRENEURS OF INDIA

Ecoplore

In 2016, Prerna Prasad founded Ecoplore, combining her passion for travel with her desire to create an environmental effect. She is an advocate for sustainable tourism. Her websites feature hotels that are made of mud, wood, bamboo, stone, or any local architecture, maintain at least 33 per cent greenery on their campuses, and implement additional sustainable practices such as rainwater harvesting, solar panels, composting, no-plastic zones, organic farming, etc. Ecoplore has been recognised by the United Nations Environment Programme (UNEP) as meeting SDG 12.

Figure 4. Monitoring the progress of localization: SDG India index
Source NITI Aayog Report 2022

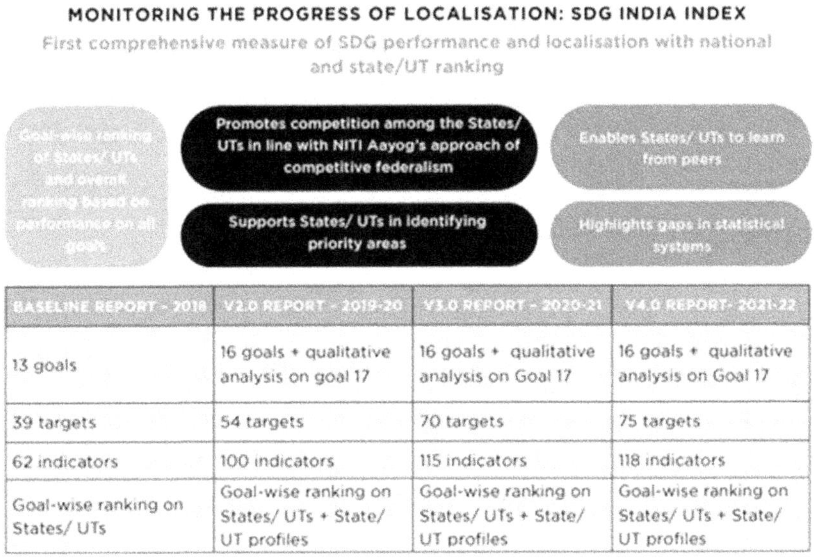

BASELINE REPORT - 2018	V2.0 REPORT - 2019-20	V3.0 REPORT - 2020-21	V4.0 REPORT- 2021-22
13 goals	16 goals + qualitative analysis on goal 17	16 goals + qualitative analysis on Goal 17	16 goals + qualitative analysis on Goal 17
39 targets	54 targets	70 targets	75 targets
62 indicators	100 indicators	115 indicators	118 indicators
Goal-wise ranking on States/ UTs	Goal-wise ranking on States/ UTs + State/ UT profiles	Goal-wise ranking on States/ UTs + State/ UT profiles	Goal-wise ranking on States/ UTs + State/ UT profiles

Ecoright

Nikita Barmecha and Udit Sood launched the online store Ecoright to market eco-friendly satchels and totes. Their corporate website states that "everything we do loops back to the world we love." The pair recently received a $30000 grant from Amazon as part of the latter's startup accelerator program, manufacturing with the $30,000 award and $10,000 in AWS Activate credits.

They provide consumers with ways to transition to conscientious consumption. They make products using recycled plastic and organic cotton as alternatives to new fashion trends and plastic pollution. Ecoright wants to expand globally sustainable processes and increase investment in ethical technologies.

Little Local

Through this platform, Antara Chatterjee aims to alter how Indians spend their vacations by introducing the idea of volunteering while on vacation. In the Himalayas, rural farmers, artisans, and micro businesses are connected directly to potential clients, who may shop locally and feel the farmers' blood, sweat, and tears. Little Local's products include information on the community that produced or grew them.

Sutrakaar

Neerja Palisetty comes from a family of weavers whose traditions date back 400 years. Sutrakaar was founded in 2017 to encourage experimental handloom weaving. They sell natural materials and paper-made products. Their goal is to transform paper trash into beautiful items by incorporating the four Rs (reduce, recycle, reuse, and respect) into their designs.

Bambrew

In Bengaluru, Vaibhav founded "Bambrew" in 2018 to produce alternatives to single-use plastic straws. But then he started producing regular packaging materials too. Bambrew is a manufacturer of bamboo, sugarcane, and seaweed-based goods. The website states that every item is 100% handcrafted and is a wonderful natural alternative to plastic, produced without the use of any chemicals or pesticides. They help communities while preserving the environment for future generations.

Chuk (Yash Pakka Pvt Ltd.)

Chuk is a product of Yash Pakka Pvt. Ltd., which creates compostable tableware (plates, trays, bowls, and delivery containers). The products are 100% biodegradable, microwaveable, and freezable. Launched in 2017, today with 150 plus elite customers Chuk is mobbing towards a cleaner planet, healthier family, and conscious business. It has also resulted in the company winning the India Design Mark, Red Dot, and CII design awards.

Ecokari

EcoKaari is a social company that was started by a group of people who wanted to build a community where sustainable growth from the bottom up is the key to making life better for all living things.

Eco implies environmentally friendly, while **Kaari** signifies Kaarigar (artist). As the name implies, local artisans and the environment are united. With the aid of Charkha and Handloom, they recycle plastic bags and cassettes to create handwoven carry bags in a variety of sizes and forms. They support recycling and reducing waste. The goal is to offer cutting-edge, environmentally friendly options.

Ecosys Cleaners

Ecosys are 100% soluble capsules that do not generate plastic waste and are firmly committed to the environment. Founders Prachi and Sumit worked on the idea of creating small capsules containing concentrations that can be added to water to make floor cleaners, handwash, etc. They want to eliminate unnecessary plastic waste in households and convert the approach to refilling and reusing. Make your cleaning solution using Ecosys refills; just find an existing plastic bottle.

Refillable

The founders Rahul, Lokesh, and Purav came up with the idea of a mobile convenience shop at your door that offers the full spectrum of home care items in the most sustainable and environmentally responsible manner during the struggling days of COVID-19 that usage of cleansers would become intense to fight it out. This was accomplished by modifying a pickup truck and fitting it with containers and dispersers, which the buyer could order through their website or WhatsApp and would be delivered in 48 hours. This start-up provides portable vending machines with a variety of liquid detergents, cleansers, disinfectants, etc. on demand in Bengaluru, Mumbai, and Surat. They are on a mission to eliminate 100,000 bottles from entering landfills in 2022.

CONCLUSION

Green entrepreneurship is the future of India, and the roadmap adopted by the Indian government will be instrumental in achieving it. The concept of "green entrepreneurship" is related to the creation of profitable businesses and start-ups that benefit the environment. Many companies in India, both start-ups and established ones, are pursuing green entrepreneurship programmes that will improve the country's overall environmental sustainability. Green entrepreneurship is now critical to combating climate change and the deteriorating environmental situation. To address environmental issues and help the environment, numerous innovative green technologies are being created by various industries, but there is still much to be explored in this field.

REFERENCES

About – Sutrakaar Creations. (n.d.). Retrieved December 13, 2022, from https://sutrakaar.in/about-sutrakaar/

Berle, G. (1991). *The Green Entrepreneur: Business Opportunities that Can Save the Earth and Make You Money* (1st ed.). Liberty Hall Press.

Commission on Sustainable Development, Department of Economic and Social Affairs. (2007). *Indicators of Sustainable Development: Guidelines and Methodologies* (3rd ed.). United Nations.

Dixon, S. E. A., & Clifford, A. (2007). Ecopreneurship- A new approach to managing the triple bottom line. *Journal of Organizational Change Management*, *20*(3), 326–345. doi:10.1108/09534810710740164

Ecoplore - Book your eco-hotel now! (n.d.). Ecoplore. Retrieved November 13, 2022, from https://ecoplore.com/

Humanising fashion. (n.d.). Retrieved August 12, 2022, from https://www.ecokaari.org/

Isaak, R. (2002). The Making of the Ecopreneur. In *Greener Management International* (pp. 81–91). Greenleaf Publishing Limited.

Kapoor, E. (2022, September 12). *This Amazon grant-winning startup is saving the environment, one tote bag at a time*. Business Insider. Retrieved September 15, 2022, from https://www.businessinsider.in/sustainability/news/this-amazon-grant-winning-startup-is-saving-the-environment-one-tote-bag-at-a-time/articleshow/94071570.cms

Krishnan, A. (2022, May 16). *Watch: Shocked by the viral video, he quit his job to make plastic-free bamboo packaging*. The Better India. Retrieved September 15, 2022, from https://www.thebetterindia.com/285540/plastic-free-packaging-bambrew-bengaluru-eco-friendly-startup/

Local, L. (n.d.). Retrieved November 13, 2022, from https://www.littlelocal.in/pages/about-us

Pawłowski, A. (2008). How many dimensions does sustainable development have? *Sustainable Development*, *16*(2), 81–90. doi:10.1002d.339

Pearce, D. W., & Warford, J. J. (1993). In *World without end: economics, environment, and sustainable development*. Oxford University Press.

Rao, K. N., & Reddy, G. V. K. (2012). Green Entrepreneurship- A Paradigm Shift towards Environment Consciousness. *Asia Pacific Journal of Management and Entrepreneurship Research*, *1*(3), 112–118.

Sharma, N. K., & Kushwaha, G. S. (2015). Emerging Green Market as an Opportunity for Green Entrepreneurs and Sustainable Development in India. *J Entrepren Organiz Manag*, *4*(2), 134.

Sustainable development and - India budget. (n.d.). Retrieved August 26, 2022, from https://www.indiabudget.gov.in/budget2019-20/economicsurvey/doc/vol2chapter/echap05_vol2.pdf

Sustainable Packaging Solutions: Bengaluru. (n.d.). Retrieved September 10, 2022, from https://www.bambrew.in/

Sustainable products for happy humans! (2022, August 23). Retrieved September 3, 2022, from https://www.ecoright.com/

This startup aims to eliminate 1 million plastic bottles in 2022 by refilling homecare liquids. (2022, July 19). Retrieved July 23, 2022, from https://www.indiatimes.com/news/india/refillable-mumbai-startup-offering-refilling-homecare-liquids-at-doorstep-575115.html#:~:text=Conceived%20in%202019%20during%20the,2020%20just%20by%20offering%20refills

Vaidya, P. N., & Honagannavar, D. V. (2017). Green Entrepreneurship towards Sustainable Environment. *International Journal of Commerce and Management Research*, *3*(1), 88–91.

Vig, A. (2020, September 6). *5 startups by 'green entrepreneurs' whose products are environmentally sustainable*. Retrieved September 2, 2022, from https://yourstory.com/socialstory/2020/09/startups-green-entrepreneurs-eco-friendly-products

WECD. (1987). *Our Common Future.* Report of the World Commission on Environment and Development. www.un-documents.net/our- common-future.pdf/

Chapter 7
Skill Building:
The Need for India

Damyanti Sodha
Manipal University Jaipur, India

Narender Singh Bhati
Manipal Univeristy Jaipur, India

ABSTRACT

India produces roughly a million graduates every year, yet only 3% are appropriately employable to skillfully accomplish productive jobs. About half of the country's people being young people, this presents a remarkable opportunity that can be tilized for the social, economic, and sustainable growth of the nation. Although India boasts of having approximately 3.4 million skilled workers, the country will need around 500 million skilled workers, according to a report by ILO (Indian Labour Organisation) by 2022. This proposition presents an imperative national priority to be addressed by addressing the issue of skill gap. Skill building is very important for making the aim of "Make in India," a campaign announced by the current prime minister, Mr. Narendra Modi. This chapter seeks to address the issue of skill gap and strives to present some key suggestions for skill building.

INTRODUCTION

Every year colleges and universities prepare millions of graduates in India, but it is surprising to see that lees than 3 per cent of workers possess the requisite skills to perform their jobs. According to the present status, half of the country's population is populated with people who are aged less than 25 years and this proposition offers a remarkable prospect to exploit nation's youth for long term economic growth and development.

DOI: 10.4018/978-1-6684-5871-6.ch007

Presently, the supply of skilled labour force in the country is roughly 34 lacs. As per the ILO, India needs 500 Mn skilled employees till 2022. Which means that we have just eight years to fill this huge gap of 496.6 million skilled labour force, which requires that skill enhancement must be made a critical national priority. The Companies Act of 2013 directive on CSR seeks renewed stimulus for companies to take heed to skill development in country.

We have around 62% people who are in the age bracket of 15 to 59 years and more than 50% people are less than 25 years of age. This young demographic dividend reinforces country's economic development is particularly noteworthy because elsewhere, the industrial world faces a sharp decline in labour force.

The country's labour force will rise by 32 percent in coming 20 years, however necessary workforce will go down by 4% hence it is imperative to provide skilled workers to fill skill gap across different industries.

Although this surplus young workforce boasts of giving the nation advantage, country confronts is challenge that majority of youth but unskilled work force seeking to get in the Indian Inc. The Economic Survey (2014-15) points to this trembling concern for the country that however, each year, nation is adding around 120 Lac to the labour market, but meagre 3 percent of these workers have gone through skill training of any sort.

Skill development is regarded as critical aspect for job conception. 60% young population brings with it unique demographic advantage. But to tap that dividend from this humongous work force, employability needs to be improved. Current statistics manifest that only 10% fresh graduates are employable by corporate. Although country's GDP is budding at rate 6-8%, job creation is not able to catch it up due to skill gap.

Gap highlights insistent requirement for considerable skill enhancement training which renders nation's labour force to not only get a rewarding livelihood but also generate noteworthy effect on country's economic & social growth and development. This proposition presents as an imperative national priority to be addressed by addressing the issue of skill gap. Skill building is very important for making the aim of "Make in India", a campaign announced by our current prime minister, Mr. Narendra Modi, a real success. This chapter seeks to address the issue of skill gap and strives to present some key suggestions for skill building.

REVIEW OF LITERATURE

We are living in dynamic, competitive and a globalised world. In contemporary knowledge economy, companies expect that academic institutions provide the required employability skills to the students (Bok, 2006). Cappelli (2008) points to the fact that the problems related to skills and talents are weaved together for both employers and job seekers. The responsibility lies on the educational institutions to prepare candidates which can be readily employed, whereas, employers need skilled workers to perform efficiently on their jobs resulting in cost leadership and profit maximisation.

Numbers of research studies have discovered that the institutes do not instil the adequate skills according to requirements of industry (Fugate and Jefferson, 2001). Cultural divergence, globalised market, skilled employees and collective & coordinated work patterns are some of the vital factors that impact triumph or demise of contemporary companies (Weisman, 2000).

Contemporary companies need employees that possess skills such as present ability, Communication, zeal for Learning, Team Building, Adaptability to work in different environments, Relationship management, pro-activeness, perseverance, creativity, innovation, problem solving, tech-savvy (D. Kumar & V. Jain (2010). Industries look for international outlook by job seekers (Barret and Beeson, 2002) and socially dependable perspective (Mumford et al, 2000).

However, companies have enormous anticipation gap in reference to employability skills. Profound skill gap is found between skills expected by companies and taught by institutes to students (Pfeffer and Fong, 2002).

Rajkumar Paulrajan (2011) asserts that vocational and selling skills are required at the entry level, whereas leadership, team building and decision making are required at managerial levels in the retail industry. Masura Rahmat et al (2012) assessed the requirement of information technology graduates in terms of software development, soft skills and entrepreneurial skills.

Padmini.I (2012) in her study, discusses actions taken by government for skill building of students and how can soft skills be aligned with curriculum to prepare students for rewarding employment. Nidhi Pandey.A (2012) identified important factors required by management students that make them employable. She found that life skills help in coping with loss and stress and also help in developing critical thinking.

Divya Shukla (2012) identified crucial employability skills among engineering graduates and concluded that curriculum should include apprenticeship programs and live projects with the industry and this will certainly improve the employability of students. Varwandkar Ajit (2013) in his study, suggested characteristics such as domain specific knowledge, responsiveness, communication and managerial abilities have momentous effect on employability.

Poornima Jain (2013) studied the skill development in the country, and sought to find the challenges in execution of government's action plan for skill development and suggested crucial measures to enhance the employability skills of job seekers.

There was imminent need of coordination between Government and departments accomplish aims of skill development.

Chithra. R (2013) compared the perception of skills required by employers and job seeking engineering graduates. She concluded augmenting skills and employment of specific education will allow workers to perform effectively. Rajanibala J. Shah et al (2014) suggested that academic institutes should provide continuous training and organise workshops to familiarize students about current market expectations of different sectors.

Hari Prasad.N et al (2014) studied skill deficiency in engineering graduates. Peer group & personal experiences play crucial role in development of skills. Networking and Focus group deliberations are essential to attain jobs. Rubvita Chadha et al (2014) stressed the need of appropriate teacher orientation, personality development workshops and continued industry-institute interaction in preparing the management students for the industry.

OBJECTIVES

The main objectives of the chapter are as given under:-

1. To understand the skill gap and its extent in India and implications in certain sectors/industries.
2. To present possible strategies for skill building.

MAIN TEXT AND FINDING

Skill Gap and Its Extent and Implications

Study piloted by the NSDC in 2014 reveals that India will need 109.73 mn skilled labourforce till 2022 for important sectors. It is projected 4.69% of workers in country have been through any training program for skills.

Several surveys organised assessment of employability, unveil an enormous gap between skills and requirement of market. Report prepared by Ernst and Young 75 percent (IT), 55 percent (manufacturing), 55 percent (healthcare) and 50 percent (Banking and Insurance) graduates are non-employable. Adding to that, NASSCOM upholds less than one third of graduates and 10% regular graduates are considered fit for employment. Hence, it becomes imperative to contemplate over probable reasons that result into low employability of regular graduates in general and engineering graduates specifically.

With a total population of approximately 130 crores people, and the largest youth population (57.2 crores population under the age of 24), labour is considered as a crucial factor of production in India. As per the economic survey 2014, working population in the country is anticipated to surge from about 58% (2001) to 64% (2021). Demographics stipulate that India will exceed China, with India's dependency ratio dipping from 61% (2002) to 36% (2020) and China ongoing constant at 44% (UN Department of Economic and Social Affairs).

Let us now look at some sectors/ Industries to look at the position of skill gaps and requirements.

Electronics and IT Hardware Industry

Consumer demand was anticipated INR 24 lakh crore by 2020. Government is making strenuous attempts to boost manufacturing.

IT and ITeS Sector

The sector's GDP contribution has immensely enhanced driven by noteworthy exports to western countries. It provides new job opportunities and at present employs around 3 mn directly and 9.5 mn indirectly.

Table 1. Breakup of Indian electronics and IT hardware sector

Subsector	Breakup
Consumer Electronics	26%
Computer and Peripherals	15%
Communication and Broadcasting equipment	34%
Semiconductor	6%
Others	19%

(Source: NSDC India)

Table 2. Incremental human resource requirement

Segment	Employment (In Million)		
Design & Manufacturing	1.45	1.75	2.06
Sales & Marketing	1.58	2.33	3.34
Repair, installation and Maintenance	1.30	2.16	3.54
Total	4.33	6.24	8.94

(Source: NSDC India)

Table 3. Demographical characteristics of workforce, emerging technologies and focus on skills requirement

	Demographical Characteristics of Workforce, Emerging Technologies and Focus on Skills Requirement
Demand for Specialist Roles & Niche Segments	· Requirement for roles like system integrator · Automotive & medical electronics would need enhanced specialist roles · Smart phones, tablets and DTH segments witness significant growth in human resource requirement
Migration	· Migration major challenge. · High cost of living in Electronics hubs dispirit migration from rural & semi urban areas
Modes of recruitment	· Recruitment through industry personnel visiting Institutions & ITIs · Government schemes like Apprenticeship play crucial role
Skill Premium	· No premium attached to trained people · Skill premium absent · Trained manpower barely recognized
Changing skill Requirements	· Emergence of new technologies viz. cloud computing, mobile applications · Shift from software to mobile applications. · Demand for hardware technicians replaced by networking engineers
Recruitment Preferences	· Focus on basic knowledge of technical operations for recruitment · Soft skills and product knowledge are key · Prior experience (unorganized) is important in repair and maintenance
Attrition	· Attrition low in manufacturing · High attrition levels across sales & marketing, for front-end workers. Attrition amongst entry and mid-level more than 30 percent annually.

(Source: NSDC India)

Incremental Human Resource Requirement

- Majority of employment generated by exports business
- Exports contribute 78 percent of employment
- Employment growth was high during FY02–09 period, however, started settling down with evolution of non-linear business models
- It anticipates to employ 5.1 mn professionals directly in FY22

- Southern states saw growth in intake capacity from 2005-06 and 2009-10.
- West, south west & eastern regions saw low growth.
- North eastern states & Bihar have lowest engineering seat density per million population showing potential for private players.
- Great demand of quality Institutes in Central India.

Table 4. Engineering education in India

Institutes, Colleges, Universities	No. of Institutes, Colleges, Universities	
Institutes of National Importance (IITs-15,NITs-20,IIITs-5)	40	Offer the best quality education
Deemed/Private Universities (Deemed-75,Private-66)	141	university status
AICTE Approved Engineering Colleges	3241	Quality varies across colleges

(Source: NSDC India)

Retail Sector

Sector has grown at steady pace by factors like changing lifestyles, rising incomes, demographics, and availability of easy credit. The retail sector contributes to 23% of the GDP. As far as FDI is concerned cumulative value of sector has doubled motivated by liberalization in single brand retail norms. Organized Retail no more an urban phenomenon. Tier 2 and smaller cities evolve fast to constitute majority share of organized retail in next few years.

STRATEGIES FOR SKILLS BUILDING

In order to make up for gap between demographic surplus and lack of skilled youth, both central and state governments should consider skill building as national priority.

National Skill Development Corporation (NSDC) to work closely with state governments and strive to align skilling & educational aims at competency levels. Ministry of Skill Development and Entrepreneurship needs to frame empowering ecosystem to instil employable skills to increasing workforce.

Industry can also play prominent role in skill development. Companies can provide pertinent operational expertise necessary to prepare capacity. It needs to provide handy atmosphere for skill training to workers. Companies need to play key role in assisting expansion of skill development.

ITIs were conceptualised for instilling vocational training to prepare trained workers that the nation needed desperately. But, these institutions have not been able to fulfil their aims due to various reasons like non-flexible training structure, unfitting vocational instructors, lacking state of art equipment and frail alignment with the industry. So a comprehensive plan should be carved which could involve government, ITIs and the industry to streamline the functioning of ITIs. Industry can assist in framing the course curriculum and design customised training programs

Table 5. Incremental human resource requirement

Sub Sector	Employment (In Million)		
	2013	2017	2022
Food & Grocery	19.6	21.36	24.44
Health & Personal Care	1.7	1.86	2.28
Home Improvements	4.4	5.11	6.63
Leisure	0.8	0.84	0.92
Lifestyle	4.5	5.17	6.10
Auto Sales	1.5	1.68	1.95
Jewellery Retail	1.5	2.04	3.14
Food Services	4.6	7.05	10.49
Total	38.6	45.11	55.95

(Source: NSDC India)

Table 6. Changing skills set requirements

Job Roles	Representative Skills Gaps
Customer Service Associate	· Inadequate product knowledge · Poor customer service orientation, Poor numeracy skills · Inadequate grooming and hygiene
After-sales Service Associate	· Inadequate communication skills · Poor customer empathy · Poor adaptation to changing technologies
Cashier	· Inadequate operational knowledge of POS terminal and payment processing · Inadequate book-keeping/ accounting skills, · Inadequate product knowledge
Supervisor, Assistant Departmental Manager, Departmental Manager	· Inadequate communication, people management and leadership skills · Inadequate coordination skills · Poor grievance handling skills

(Source: NSDC India)

as needed by the industry. ITIs can hire experts working in Industry to take some lectures and can be very handy in training. Industry associations can be made in areas of providing their premises for on-the-job trainings and for apprenticeship. For instance, Samsung technical schools through Advanced Repair and Industrial Skills Enhancement programme. More than 3,000 young people have graduated from these Schools since 2014. These have been working in close association with Ministry of MSME and Departments of Technical Education.

The other area which should be focussed upon is the vocational training and apprenticeship. Vocational training systems should be supplemented with on-the-job training frameworks. Government should work in close collaboration with industry which can also include MSME sector, to prepare a positive atmosphere to enhance the opportunities of apprenticeship in the nation. The Government also opines to bring services under the realm of apprenticeship. For example, Tata Motors is already running an Apprenticeship Training Program in Pune, Maharashtra. Each year over 3000 young people undertake apprenticeship training in their training program.

Skilling should also be integrated with the mainstream education. Skilling can be aligned with the mainstream formal education by carrying out vocational training classes having close linkage with the local economy. This can be done from class nine onwards. This integration ensures students have range of needed skills which shall help them when they join industry and they have already received long term training on the same. For instance, Hindustan Unilever (HUL) came out with a popular "Project Shakti" which aims to improve the source of revenue of rural women. The company trains rural females as entrepreneurs. Also named as "Shakti Amma", rural female entrepreneurs are trained about products and relevance in upholding health & hygiene.

Another significant measure for skill building is counselling. It creates ambition and lessens the attrition rates at the time of training and employment by assisting job seekers to take well informed decisions. With the plethora of training & new job roles, counselling is very pertinent for youngsters to take well informed career decisions. So, a well-crafted counselling framework needs to be devised which assesses the capabilities and behavioural assessments and guide them to take appropriate career paths.

During the contemporary rapidly changing and dynamic country, entrepreneurship certainly emerged as key source of meeting objectives of young. But, local entrepreneurs evolving each year in country is substantially less. The existing approach to entrepreneurship is disjointed and fragmented. India needs holistic all encompassing approach to support entrepreneurship development.

FLAGSHIP PROGRAMS/ INITIATIVES FOR SKILL DEVELOPMENT

Establishment of Training Institutes: It includes 15,154 ITIs (together with 11,892 private institutions); 36 Sector Skills Councils & 33 National Skills Training Institutes, and 2,188 training partners registered with NSDC.

Pradhan Mantri Kaushal Vikas Yojana: Flagship Pradhan Mantri Kaushal Vikas Yojana (PMKVY) scheme launched in 2015 covers short-term training, skilling through ITIs and apprenticeship scheme. It boasts of having trained 10 million youth since its launching.

SANKALP and STRIVE: SANKALP program focuses on district-level skilling ecosystem and STRIVE project aims at augmenting performance of ITIs.

Initiatives from Several Ministries: Around 40 skill development programs implemented by 20 central ministries/departments have resulted in training four crore people.

Mandatory CSR Expenditure in Skilling: Mandatory CSR spending under Companies Act, 2013 has resulted in investment of over 100, 000 crore in different social projects by Indian corporations.

TEJAS Initiative for Skilling: TEJAS (Training for Emirates Jobs And Skills), launched at the Dubai Expo, 2020 to train overseas Indians.

National Apprenticeship Promotion Scheme (NAPS): National Apprenticeship Promotion Scheme (NAPS) offers marches in offering prospects for young people.

Reduce Migration: Skill building programs reduce migration and enhance independence by way of creating self employment opportunities. Ministry of Skill Development & Entrepreneurship signed an MOU with Indira Gandhi Open University (IGNOU) in January 2022 to enable ways for opportunities for youth and strengthen vocational & technical training.

CONCLUSION

India can boast of a young demographic dividend and dream of getting a lucrative advantage out to a surplus young force but we face an imminent challenge of skill shortage and only 3% of our workers have undergone any kind of skill training. The gap reflects need of substantial skill enhancement campaigns that result in rewarding career and generate notable effect on country's economic & social landscape. Skill development improves scenarios of employability and creates productive employees for corporate and widens career opportunities. Skill development is crucial for personal development viz. professional network, and nurture innate talent required in desired fields. It also prevents dropout rates. Government needs to target skilling 70% people to fulfil the goal of $8 trillion by 2030. This proposition manifests as an imperative national priority to address the issue of skill gap. Skill building is thus the key to make the "Make in India", a real success. India has all the potential to achieve the precious dream of becoming "Developed India".

REFERENCES

Ahmad. (2012). Relationship between employability and graduates' skill. *International Business Management, 6*(4), 440-445.

Ajit, V. (2013). Factors Impacting Employability Skills of Engineers. *International Journal of Science and Research.*

Barrett, A., & Beeson, J. (2002). *Developing leaders for 2010.* The Conference Board.

Bok, D. (2006). Our Underachieving Colleges. Princeton University Press.

Cappelli, P. (2008). Talent management for the twenty-first century. *Harvard Business Review*, (March), 74–81. PMID:18411966

Chadha. (2014). Industry's Requirement for Employability of Management Student in Present Scenario. *International Journal of Business Quantitative Economics and Applied Management Research, 1*(3).

Chithra, R. (2013). Employability Skills-A Study on the Perception of the Engineering Students and their Prospective Employers. *Global Journal of Management and Business Studies, 3*(5).

Fugate, D. L., & Jefferson, R. W. (2001). Preparing for globalization: Do we need structural change for our academic programs? *Journal of Education for Business, 76*(3), 160–166. doi:10.1080/08832320109601304

Jain. (2013). Globalization and Developing Employability Skills: Challenges and their Solutions with Reference to NPSD & Government's Action Plan and role of Life Long Learning and Extension Departments. *Journal of Business Management & Social Sciences Research, 2*(5).

Kumar & Jain. (2010). Survival Skills of Business Management Graduates: A Study With Reference to Retail and Banking. *Far East Journal of Psychology and Business, 1*(1).

Mumford, M. D., Zaccaro, S. J., Harding, F. D., Jacobs, T. O., & Fleishman, E. A. (2000). Leadership skills for a changing world: Solving complex social problems. *The Leadership Quarterly, 11*(1), 11–36. doi:10.1016/S1048-9843(99)00041-7

NSDC. (n.d.). *Schemes and Initiatives*. Retrieved December 14, 2022 from https://nsdcindia.org

Padmini. (2012). Education Vs Employability-The Need to Bridge the Skills Gap among the Engineering and Management Graduates in Andhra Pradesh. *International Journal of Management & Business Studies, 2*(3).

Pandey. (2012). Awareness of Life Skills for Job Sustainability amongst Management Students. *Tripude's National Journal of Business Research, 4*(1).

Pant, N., & Mishra, M. (2015). *Bridging the Gap: Driving Scale and Impact in Skill Development and Employability through Corporate Social Responsibility*. IICA and Sattva.

Paulrajan, R. (2011). Employability Skills in Chennai Retail Market, India. Acta Universitatis Danubius, 7(5).

Pfeffer, J., & Fong, C. T. (2002). The end of business schools? Less success than meets the eye. *Academy of Management Learning & Education*, *1*(1), 78–95. doi:10.5465/amle.2002.7373679

Hari Prasad, N. (2014). Alarming Employability Skills Deficiency among Budding Engineering Graduates – A study on engineering graduates in Chittoor district. *SAMZODHANA – Journal of Management Research, 3*(1).

Shukla, D. (2012). Employability Skill among Professionals – Chagrin of HR Executives in Indian Labor Market: A Study on Engineering Graduates of Bhopal City. *VSRD International Journal of Business & Mngt. Research*, *2*(8).

Srivastava & Shah. (2014). A Study on Factors Affecting Employability Skills of Management Students. *International Journal of Management and Development Studies, 3*(2).

Weisman, V. L. (2000). The impact of facilitative leadership: Multi-rater measurement of behavioral outcomes of managerial leaders. *Proceedings of the Academy of Human Resource Development*, 20-28.

Chapter 8
Signal-Based and Model-Based Pipeline Leakage Detection and Localization Techniques:
A Comparative Study

C. Banerjee
Amity University, Jaipur, India

Arpita Banerjee
St. Xavier's College, India

ABSTRACT

In India, agriculture is the backbone of the economy, and its practices depend upon water usage. As per the statistics available, the source of fresh water in India is scare. Smart drip irrigation in agricultural process may prove to be a boon for the farmers aiding water conservation. Certain issues like leakage in the pipeline structure need attention to conserve water and reduce environmental and economic loss. There are various types of leakage detection techniques; however, optimization is needed to make it more convenient and economic to use. Also, the automation in leakage localization in pipeline structure is a matter of concern, and more accuracy is needed to pinpoint the location of leakage. The research study discusses the existing leakage detection techniques with their limitations and proposes a hybrid cellular automata-based leakage detection and localisation model through which the limitations may be addressed in a unique and comprehensive manner.

DOI: 10.4018/978-1-6684-5871-6.ch008

1. INTRODUCTION

Rapid growth of population worldwide is a serious threat to the continuous availability of water resources (Boretti, A., & Rosa, L., 2019). Around 84% of the total available water is being consumed for irrigation purpose (Dhawan, V., 2017). India constitutes approx. one sixth of the world's population, one fifthly of land and one twenty fifth of the water resources (Mol, A. A., et al., 2018). In water quality index, globally, India ranks 120th of 122 countries reporting that 70% of water is contaminated. Also, India contains around 4% of global freshwater with 16% of its population (Tripathi, B., 2018).

Due to its high share of jobs and the development of livelihoods, agriculture is the backbone of the Indian economy. In rural India, most of the population is dependent on agriculture. Agriculture makes a significant contribution to the country's GDP growth, but has remained the slowest moving sector of the Indian economy (Rathi, D., 2018). Water is important for agriculture and based on the statistics of the fresh water resources availability; there is a need to optimize the use of water in agricultural practice. Smart drip irrigation is a possibility to conserve water and optimize its use (Chaudhry, S., & Garg, S., 2019).

It is important to note that large amount around 25% (Krupakar, H., & Jayakumar, A., 2016) available water is being wasted due to leakage in water pipeline in irrigation system used in agriculture (Vardhini, H., & Janardhana Raju, G., 2020). Leakage in pipeline can be cause by change in pressure (Abdulshaheed, A., et al;, 2017), corrosion (Al Qahtani, T., et al, 2020), condition of pipe or any other external factor (Chan, T. K., et al., 2018). Through extensive research in leak detection technology, leakage in the water pipeline leads to the need to avoid the threat of leaks and mitigate their impact. It is possible to mount a leak detection device to identify leaks that can develop in these channels and minimize excessive water waste (El-Zahab, S., & Zayed, T., 2019).

Detection and localization of leak is a very important area in agriculture. With the use of available leakage detection and localisation techniques and new technologies like Internet of Things (IOT) and sensors the detection, localization, and prediction of leak in real time is a possibility. Many researchers, academicians, and industry personnel have contributed in this area but still scope exists for its optimization in terms of detection and localization. Through this research paper, we discuss the existing leakage detection techniques with their limitations and propose a hybrid cellular automata based leakage detection and localisation model through which the limitations may be addressed in a unique and comprehensive manner.

Apart from the introduction which is provided in section 1, the rest of the paper is arranges as follows: section 2 highlights some of the evident contribution of the researches as literature review and their limitations, section 3 discuss the various pipeline leakage detection and localization techniques and segregates them into Model based and Signal based techniques, section 4 presents a tabular form of the important parameters churned out as a comparative study of signal based and model based leakage detection and localization techniques, section 5 briefly suggests a proposed a hybrid cellular automata based leakage detection and localisation model for addressing the existing limitations and conclusion and future work is mentioned in section 6.

2. LITERATURE REVIEW

(Soldevila, A., et al., 2017) introduces a method based on Bayesian classifiers for leak localization in Water Distribution Networks (WDNs). For all possible leak scenarios, probability density functions for pressure residuals are calibrated off-line. To evaluate the position of leaks in the WDN, a Bayesian classifier is applied on-line to the computed residuals. In order to improve the precision of localization, a time horizon based logic combined with the Bayesian classifier is also proposed.

(Moser, G., Paal, S. G., & Smith, I. F., 2018) proposes a device identification technique known as falsification of the error-domain model is adapted for the performance evaluation of water delivery networks and, more precisely, for the detection of leaks in those networks. The use of falsification of the error-domain model for practical use in water delivery networks shows great potential.

(Rajeswaran, A., et al., 2018) presents a leak detection technique in WDNs, which includes making on-demand additional flow measurements and regular use of water balance. Graph partitioning is used to calculate the position of flow parameters, with the goal of minimizing the cost of measurement. Until the desired resolution is obtained, this method is recursively repeated.

(Cody, R., et al., 2018) presents an investigation of singular spectrum analysis (SSA) in removing leak components from noisy measurements. SSA is a non-parametric and adaptive approach that can decompose a signal without making assumptions of linearity or stationarity into interpretable components. As applied to noisy hydro-acoustic signals, the leak signatures are shown to be efficiently extracted.

(Blesa, J., & Pérez, R., 2018) proposes an original method of modeling the impact of uncertainties on WDN networks. In the absence of leakage, it is focused on the processing of real data in the water network. In order to extrapolate the potential residuals in the various leak scenarios, the difference (residual) between the calculated data and the one given by a network simulator in normal operation is used. The error is analyzed in terms of correlation intervals and leak localization evaluation between the approximation proposed and the actual one.

(Huynh, H. X., et al., 2018) suggest a new simulation method to predict the closing or opening of irrigation culverts based on a cellular automaton. Water quality parameters such as salinity, temperature, pH, dissolved oxygen, etc. have been calculated at culverts to solve this problem. Then, the opening or closure of the culverts is considered based on the water quality there. In order to reduce the amount of effort and time spent by farmers, it is necessary to have a measure to help predict the water quality in culverts, thus making farmers feel healthy to grow.

(Raei, E., Shafiee, et al., 2019) presents a new approach by building a list of candidate locations based on sensitivity to leaks that are simulated at all possible nodes in a network. The study introduces a new technique for placing a series of pressure sensors which intends to meet two goals i.e., the minimization of the number of sensors and the detection time, the selection of a set of sensors is explored. To examine trade-offs between these goals, the non-dominated sorting genetic algorithm (NSGA-II) is used. (Javadiha, M., et al., 2019) investigates the use of deep learning using pressure measurements for leak localization in Water Distribution Networks (WDNs). A Convolutional Neural Network (CNN) can be used to learn the different pressure maps that characterize each leak location by using a training data set containing appropriate samples of all possible leak locations. In addition to the purpose of filtering the effects of uncertainty and noise, a time horizon approach to Bayesian reasoning is used over each CNN instant classification output.

(Soldevila, A., et al., 2019) introduces a new data-driven approach for leak localization in water delivery networks. The proposed approach relies on the use of available pressure measurements in some of the selected internal network nodes and the use of Kriging spatial interpolation to estimate the pressure in the remaining nodes. By comparing current pressure values with their reference values, online leak localization is achieved. Thereafter, to consider the residual time evolution, a time horizon computation based on Bayesian reasoning is applied, resulting in an improved precision of leak localization.

(Sun, C., et al., 2020) introduces a novel leak localization method that uses a data-driven approach based on limit pressure measurements in two-stage WDNs, i.e. (1) two distinct linear discriminant analysis (LDA) machine learning classifiers and neural networks (NNET) are built to evaluate the probabilities of each node having a leak within a WDN and (2) Afterwards, Bayesian temporal reasoning is applied to rescale the probability of each potential leak position at each phase after a leak is detected, in order to improve the accuracy of the localization.

Limitations of the Existing Study

After reviewing of the existing work, following limitations were identified. They can prove to be potential research area to be carried out in future.

- Low leakage localization accuracy.
- Time-consuming and labour intensive.
- Less cost effectiveness.
- Focus on a single leak.
- Optimal sensor placement.
- Real-time data collection and result calculation.
- False alarm during processing the non-leakage data.
- Focused on predefined areas where a leak might occur.

3. PIPELINE LEAKAGE DETECTION AND LOCALISATION TECHNIQUES

Following section provides a brief study of the pipeline leakage detection and localisation techniques segregated into signal based and model based technique:

3.1 Signal Based Pipeline Leakage Detection and Localization Techniques

Basically there six types of signal based leakage detection and localizing techniques that has been identified and a brief overview of each technique is provided here.

1. Observation

The farmers faced a lot of difficulty in identifying leak through just observing it. The reason it is sometimes become difficult because of spreading of water. This spreadness is generally based on soil types. Much of the water gets wasted till they are identifying that a leak exist at a particular point (Rojek, I., & Studzinski, J., 2019).

2. Acoustic

This is the most common and traditional method of leak identification in water pipeline. It contains acoustic sensors and is powered by the water flow in the pipeline; as it shifts with the flow in the pipeline, the system records all noise activities. Any new signal different from the ones that are produced may give the intuition of leak possibility. The detection of leakage is efficiently dependent on the placement of sensor. The deployment cost of these fixed sensors are more and they required continuous monitoring which may sometimes not possible hence not suitable for small leak (Kumar, D., et al., 2017).

3. Infrared

Video cameras make it possible to detect gas leakage using infrared which is a special type of filter insensitive to a selected spectrum of infrared wavelengths is being used to absorb hydrocarbons from the spectrum. This creates a smoky image of leak on video cameras. This type of leak detection techniques can be used only for shorter distances where continuous monitoring is possible (Bach, P. M., & Kodikara, J. K., 2017).

4. Fibre Optic

Fibre optic cable pipeline tracking is a good choice for precisely detecting leaks. But it is only suitable for a limited distance. The location of using fibre optic cable and medium for which it is being used is very important. If it is a gas to be monitored then the cable should be installed above the pipeline as gas normally rises. When it comes to liquids, the cable should be installed below pipeline (Wong, L., et al., 2018).

5. Tracer Gas

There are certain combination of insoluble gases like ammonia, halogens and helium which are being used to identify leak and its location in an underground pipeline using physical detections. The lighter gas among the three flows out from the cracks, holes. It becomes easy for the gas to flow out as these gases are not pipe material dependent. They are not cost effective and hence not suitable for large pipelines. They are even not suitable for old networks of pipelines as gas may evade through the joints and hence not so efficiently technique (El-Zahab, S., & Zayed, T., 2019).

6. Ground Penetrating Radar

Electromagnetic waves are being used to identify and localize leak in underground pipeline. This technique is suitable for all types of pipe and does not require any expertise for use. Only disadvantage with this method is the efficiency of leak detection which lies with the position of leak and surrounding environment of pipeline. A lot of disturbance around the pipeline make leak identification impossible and is an expensive technique (Senin, S. F., et al., 2019).

Figure 1. Leakage detection techniques

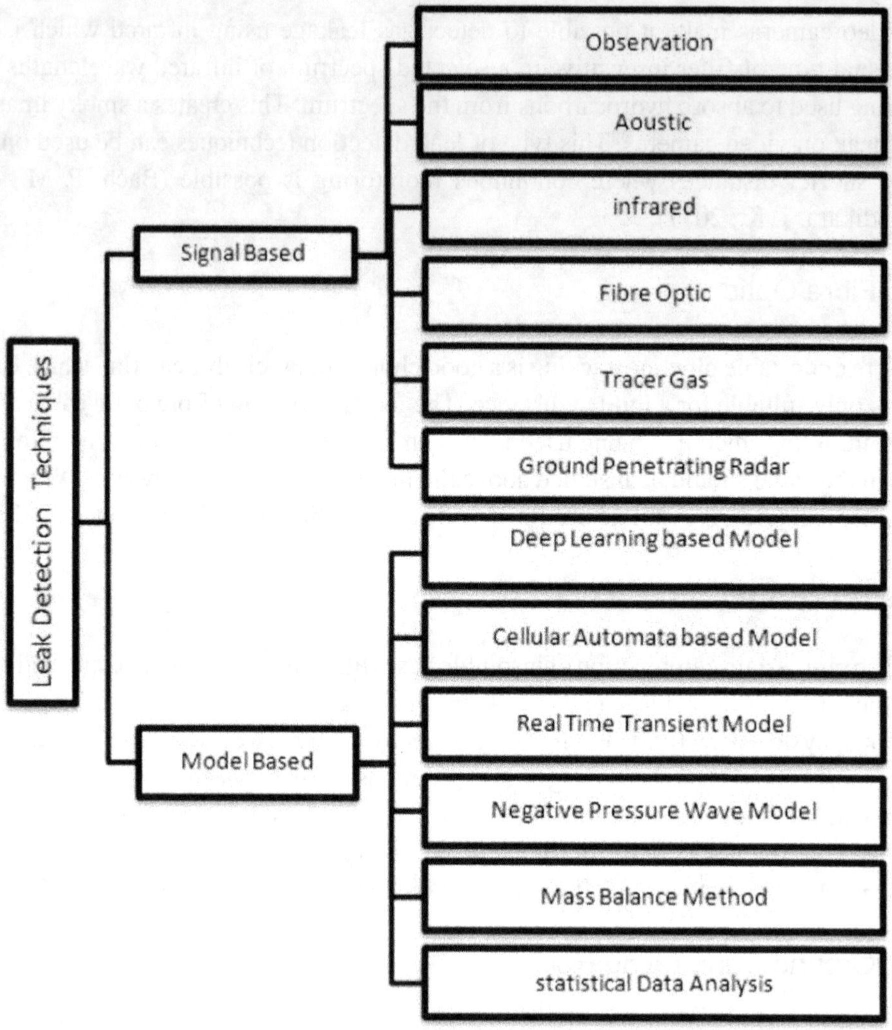

3.2 Model Based Pipeline Leakage Detection and Localization Techniques

1. Deep Learning Based

Automated continuous agricultural field monitoring by the farmer can be done with integration of deep earning algorithm which uses of logic based learning models like ANN and CNN. The study found that the higher the number of hidden layers in the ANN model, the more correct the analysis may be (Zhou, X., et al., 2019).

2. Negative Pressure Wave Model

This model is based on the availability of pressure signals. When a leak is being detected it transfers negative pressure waves in both directions of the leak. This method is affected by many parameters like speed of the wave, noise generating from device, variations in the pressure etc. Due to the variation of pressure while opening and closing of valve, chances of false alarm are high (Abdulshaheed, A., et al., 2017).

3. Mass Balance Method

This method is most suitable for small leaks. It is based on the difference in the flow rate at a particular location. Since it has a low detection rate this model is not suitable for leak localization (Yang, S., et al., 2018).

4. Real Time Transient Model

Real Time Transient Model (RTTM) is best as it is based on mathematical model for detection and localizing of leak in long pipelines. Transient model can easily differentiate between the noise of leak and normal flow in pipe line hence accuracy level is more that acoustic based leak detection model. Though this is an expensive technology, the leak detection speed is very fast and it requires an extensive instrumentation to guarantee a real time monitoring (Smith, J., et al., 2018).

5. Statistical Data Analysis

It is also one of the efficient methods to detect and locate pipeline leak. This model is very easy to learn and use and can be implemented to any pipe type. Since lot of data variation are being included in it so this makes the model costlier. It is not suitable for small leaks (Liu, J., et al., 2019).

6. Cellular Automata Based

Cellular automata are being used to detect, localize, and predict leak in oil and gas pipelines. The concept of changing the state of a cell according to its neighbouring cell with time is being used and it gives a prediction of leak in future on the basis of current state (Huynh, H. X., et al., 2018).

4. COMPARATIVE STUDY

The following section provides a comparative study of the signal based versus model based leakage detection and localisation techniques considering the parameters like initial setup cost, detection rate, accuracy, localisation, feasibility, and false alarm.

5. CELLULAR AUTOMATA BASED LEAKAGE DETECTION AND LOCALISATION MODEL

Considering the results of the comparative study, we propose cellular automata based leakage detection and localisation model. As is evident from the comparative study the cellular automata is best as it has a low initial setup code, can detect leak, it is highly accurate, can localise leakage with accuracy, and the false alarm is also low. Figure x provides a pictorial representation of the proposed model for leakage detection and localisation. We will discuss its implementation in our next paper.

Table 1. Comparative study of various signal based and model-based leakage detection and localization techniques

Techniques		Parameters					
		Initial set up cost	**Detection**	**Accuracy**	**Localization**	**Feasibility**	**False Alarm**
Signal based	**Observation**	Low	✓	Low	✓	Low	Low
	Acoustic	Low	✓	High	✓	Low	Low
	Fibre Optic	High	✓	Moderate	✓	Moderate	Low
	Tracer Gas	Low	✓	Low	✓	Low	Low
	GPR	Moderate	✓	Low	✓	Low	Low
Model based	**CA**	Low	✓	High	✓	High	low
	Deep Learning	High	✓	High	✓	High	Low
	NPV	Moderate	✓	Moderate	✓	Low	low
	Mass Balance Method	Low	✓	Low	X	Low	Low
	RTTM	High	✓	High	✓	High	Medium
	Statical Data Analysis	high	✓	High	✓	High	Medium

Figure 2. Cellular automata based leakage detection and localization in drip irrigation setup

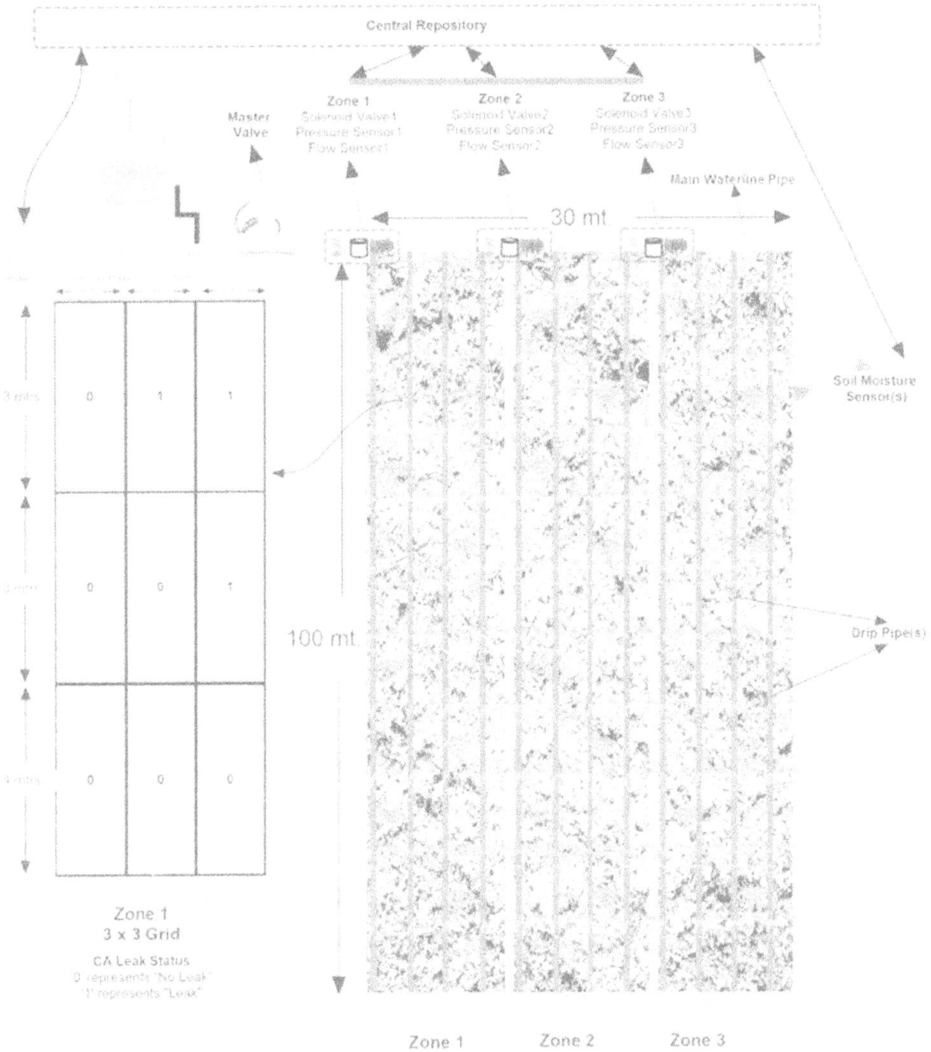

6. CONCLUSION AND FUTURE WORK

Water is scare due to over population and its improper use may have an adverse impact on the economy of a country. India is an agricultural driven economic country and water is an essential part of agricultural process. Water leakage is a serious issue which needs to be tackled in an intelligent manner. It is true that we may not eliminate the water leakage problem completely; however, we may adopt certain automated and innovative techniques for addressing the mentioned problem.

After the study of the various signal based and model based leakage detection and localisation techniques and after a thorough comparative analysis, it is evident that there are better prospects if the concept of cellular automata is employed for the leakage detection and localisation in a water pipeline structure which is non linear and considering the fact that small leaks may also develop. The proposed cellular automata based model is a first step towards realising the goal of leakage detection with less false alarm and accurate leakage location. The future work may involve implementation of the conceptual model in a practical way with some experimental results for its validation.

REFERENCES

Abdulshaheed, A., Mustapha, F., & Ghavamian, A. (2017). A pressure-based method for monitoring leaks in a pipe distribution system: A Review. *Renewable & Sustainable Energy Reviews*, *69*, 902–911. doi:10.1016/j.rser.2016.08.024

Abdulshaheed, A., Mustapha, F., & Ghavamian, A. (2017). A pressure-based method for monitoring leaks in a pipe distribution system: A Review. *Renewable & Sustainable Energy Reviews*, *69*, 902–911. doi:10.1016/j.rser.2016.08.024

Al Qahtani, T., Yaakob, M. S., Yidris, N., Sulaiman, S., & Ahmad, K. A. (2020). A Review on Water Leakage Detection Method in the Water Distribution Network. *J. Adv. Res. Fluid Mech. Therm. Sci*, *68*(2), 152–163. doi:10.37934/arfmts.68.2.152163

Bach, P. M., & Kodikara, J. K. (2017). Reliability of infrared thermography in detecting leaks in buried water reticulation pipes. *IEEE Journal of Selected Topics in Applied Earth Observations and Remote Sensing*, *10*(9), 4210–4224. doi:10.1109/JSTARS.2017.2708817

Blesa, J., & Pérez, R. (2018). Modelling uncertainty for leak localization in water networks. *IFAC-PapersOnLine*, *51*(24), 730–735. doi:10.1016/j.ifacol.2018.09.656

Boretti, A., & Rosa, L. (2019). Reassessing the projections of the world water development report. *NPJ Clean Water*, *2*(1), 1–6. doi:10.103841545-019-0039-9

Chan, T. K., Chin, C. S., & Zhong, X. (2018). Review of current technologies and proposed intelligent methodologies for water distributed network leakage detection. *IEEE Access: Practical Innovations, Open Solutions*, *6*, 78846–78867. doi:10.1109/ACCESS.2018.2885444

Chaudhry, S., & Garg, S. (2019). Smart irrigation techniques for water resource management. In *Smart Farming Technologies for Sustainable Agricultural Development* (pp. 196–219). IGI Global. doi:10.4018/978-1-5225-5909-2.ch009

Cody, R., Harmouche, J., & Narasimhan, S. (2018). Leak detection in water distribution pipes using singular spectrum analysis. *Urban Water Journal, 15*(7), 636–644. do i:10.1080/1573062X.2018.1532016

Dhawan, V. (2017, January). Water and agriculture in India. In *Background paper for the South Asia expert panel during the Global Forum for Food and Agriculture (GFFA)* (p. 15). Academic Press.

El-Zahab, S., & Zayed, T. (2019). Leak detection in water distribution networks: An introductory overview. *Smart Water, 4*(1), 5. doi:10.118640713-019-0017-x

Huynh, H. X., Huynh, N. T., Huynh, T. P., Van Tran, S., & Nguyen, L. T. T. (2018). Simulating the Irrigation Operations with Cellular Automata. In *Context-Aware Systems and Applications, and Nature of Computation and Communication* (pp. 195–210). Springer.

Javadiha, M., Blesa, J., Soldevila, A., & Puig, V. (2019, April). Leak localization in water distribution networks using deep learning. In *2019 6th International Conference on Control, Decision and Information Technologies (CoDIT)* (pp. 1426-1431). IEEE. 10.1109/CoDIT.2019.8820627

Krupakar, H., & Jayakumar, A. (2016). *A Review of Intelligent Practices for Irrigation Prediction.* arXiv preprint arXiv:1612.02893.

Kumar, D., Tu, D., Zhu, N., Hou, D., & Zhang, H. (2017). In-line acoustic device inspection of leakage in water distribution pipes based on wavelet and neural network. *Journal of Sensors, 2017*, 2017. doi:10.1155/2017/5789510

Liu, J., Zang, D., Liu, C., Ma, Y., & Fu, M. (2019). A leak detection method for oil pipeline based on markov feature and two-stage decision scheme. *Measurement, 138*, 433–445. doi:10.1016/j.measurement.2019.01.029

Moser, G., Paal, S. G., & Smith, I. F. (2018). Leak detection of water supply networks using error-domain model falsification. *Journal of Computing in Civil Engineering, 32*(2), 04017077. doi:10.1061/(ASCE)CP.1943-5487.0000729

Raei, E., Shafiee, M. E., Nikoo, M. R., & Berglund, E. (2019). Placing an ensemble of pressure sensors for leak detection in water distribution networks under measurement uncertainty. *Journal of Hydroinformatics, 21*(2), 223–239. doi:10.2166/hydro.2018.032

Rajeswaran, A., Narasimhan, S., & Narasimhan, S. (2018). A graph partitioning algorithm for leak detection in water distribution networks. *Computers & Chemical Engineering*, *108*, 11–23. doi:10.1016/j.compchemeng.2017.08.007

Rathi, D. (2018). India's backbone is break bone. *International Journal of Basic and Applied Research*, *8*(6), 622–627.

Rojek, I., & Studzinski, J. (2019). Detection and localization of water leaks in water nets supported by an ICT system with artificial intelligence methods as a way forward for smart cities. *Sustainability*, *11*(2), 518. doi:10.3390u11020518

Senin, S. F., Jaafar, M. S., & Hamid, R. (2019). Locating Underground Water Pipe Leakages Via Interpretation of Ground Penetrating Radar Signals. *IACSIT International Journal of Engineering and Technology*, *8*(2), 72–77.

Smith, J., Chae, J., Learn, S., Hugo, R., & Park, S. (2018, September). Pipeline rupture detection using real-time transient modelling and convolutional neural networks. In *International Pipeline Conference* (*Vol. 51883*, p. V003T04A016). American Society of Mechanical Engineers. 10.1115/IPC2018-78426

Soldevila, A., Blesa, J., Fernandez-Canti, R. M., Tornil-Sin, S., & Puig, V. (2019). Data-driven approach for leak localization in water distribution networks using pressure sensors and spatial interpolation. *Water (Basel)*, *11*(7), 1500. doi:10.3390/w11071500

Soldevila, A., Fernandez-Canti, R. M., Blesa, J., Tornil-Sin, S., & Puig, V. (2017). Leak localization in water distribution networks using Bayesian classifiers. *Journal of Process Control*, *55*, 1–9. doi:10.1016/j.jprocont.2017.03.015

Sun, C., Parellada, B., Puig, V., & Cembrano, G. (2020). Leak localization in water distribution networks using pressure and data-driven classifier approach. *Water (Basel)*, *12*(1), 54. doi:10.3390/w12010054

Tripathi, B. (2018, June). 40% of Indians will have no access to drinking water by 2030: NITI Aayog. *Business Standard*. Retrieved 24th Nov., 2020 from https://www.business-standard.com/article/current-affairs/40-of-indians-will-have-no-access-to-drinking-water-by-2030-niti-aayog-118062500074_1.html

Vardhini, H., & Janardhana Raju, G. (2020). Design of Internet of Things Based Smart and Efficient Water Distribution System for Urban and Agriculture Areas. *Journal of Computational and Theoretical Nanoscience*, *17*(9-10), 4688–4691. doi:10.1166/jctn.2020.9301

Wong, L., Deo, R., Rathnayaka, S., Shannon, B., Zhang, C., Chiu, W. K., & Widyastuti, H. (2018). Leak detection in water pipes using submersible optical optic-based pressure sensor. *Sensors (Basel), 18*(12), 4192. doi:10.339018124192 PMID:30513585

Yang, S., Talbot, R. W., Frish, M. B., Golston, L. M., Aubut, N. F., Zondlo, M. A., & McSpiritt, J. (2018). Natural gas fugitive leak detection using an unmanned aerial vehicle: Measurement system description and mass balance approach. *Atmosphere, 9*(10), 383. doi:10.3390/atmos9100383

Zhou, X., Tang, Z., Xu, W., Meng, F., Chu, X., Xin, K., & Fu, G. (2019). Deep learning identifies accurate burst locations in water distribution networks. *Water Research, 166*, 115058. doi:10.1016/j.watres.2019.115058 PMID:31536886

Chapter 9
Loss Minimization Strategy for Induction Motor-Driven Electric Vehicles

Manish Kumar
Netaji Subhas Institute of Technology, University of Delhi, India

Bhavnesh Kumar
Netaji Subhas Institute of Technology, University of Delhi, India

Asha Rani
Netaji Subhas Institute of Technology, University of Delhi, India

ABSTRACT

This chapter presents a loss model control (LMC) strategy for electric vehicles driven by poly-phase induction motors. The LMC is a widely used strategy for loss minimization of induction motor drives. The conventional LMC approach of reducing losses by minimizing the rotor flux/magnetizing current leads to surplus power loss caused by sudden increase in stator current during transient states. Therefore, to overcome the challenges, a new approach of LMC is presented for efficiency enhancement by equalizing the motor core losses and the copper losses. Furthermore, grasshopper optimization algorithm (GOA) is used to tune the PI controller that determines the optimal flux level for good efficiency. Compared with nominal flux operation, the proposed LMC is efficient, fast, and has smooth flux adaptation with high accuracy, versatile implementation, and can withstand transient mode. Simulation studies are performed on 5Hp IM using the proposed LMC method. The test results are provided and compared with the nominal flux method to validate the effectiveness of the proposed LMC.

DOI: 10.4018/978-1-6684-5871-6.ch009

I. INTRODUCTION

Transportation Systems are indispensable part of human life. These systems not only provide comfort in commuting people but also are of great help in case of emergency. Transportation systems driven by gasoline engines are in use from many decades. However, depleting oil reservoirs, inflated oil costs and degradation of the environment from the smoke produced by these systems is posing a challenge to their sustainability. Now a days, almost every country is putting efforts to develop electric motor driven transportation sustainability to handle the issues with traditional transportation systems (Kumar & Revankar, 2017).

Usually, Batteries feed the energy in electric motor to propel the transportation system (Bilgin & Emadi, 2014). Among all the electric motors available in the market, Induction motor (IM) is the most suitable-one in terms of cost, maintenance, mechanical sturdiness and performance. IMs are designed to operate at rated flux to ensure fast transient response as well as high torque per ampere at rated load. However, practically many times these motors operate with partial load leading to lower efficiency due to the excessive core losses. Flux weakening during partial loading can increase the electric vehicle efficiency (Sridharan & Krein, 2016). Indirect field-oriented control (IFOC) strategy is advantageous for flux control as it independently controls the flux and the torque; also, it improves dynamics of IM drive at minimum flux operation (Farhani et al., 2017).

Many flux optimization techniques have been suggested in the literature to balance the magnetic and electric loading of the machine with optimal condition of flux (Lim & Nam, 2004). Two broad categories of loss minimization are *i) Search Control & ii) Loss Model Control (LMC).* The first method is a feedback procedure that finds the maximum efficiency by continuously comparing the exact minimum input power without depending on the machine parameter. It suffers from high convergence time, objectionable torque pulsation and sluggish response (Yin et al., 2019). On the other hand, the second approach is based on the mathematical modelling of the motor drive to derive an expression for optimal flux level. It is a feedforward approach and completely depends on how accurately the model is derived. The main advantage of LMC is that it is fast and simple (Abootorabi Zarchi et al., 2019; Ali et al., 2016).

In (Lim & Nam, 2004), LMC strategy with rotor flux as a controlled variable has been used for loss minimization in the drive. The complete system-based loss is minimized with different approaches. In (Farhani et al., 2017), LMC strategy for direct field-oriented control drive is proposed. The loss model is derived in terms of rotor flux which is optimized as per the load torque. The rotor flux is calculated in two steps, one is suboptimal and the other being global minima. In (Shukla & Singh, 2018) a solar power-driven field-oriented control (FOC) drive is used for water pumping application with LMC approach in which the efficiency is improved by minimizing the magnetization current of IM. In (Borisevich & Schullerus, 2016) LMC approach is used for steady state operation and also for transient performance with suboptimal condition. This model is adjustable to transient as well as steady state mode.

In (Kioskeridis & Margaris, 1996) and (Kumar & Rani, 2018) LMC approach was used and the loss model was optimized with respect to rotor flux and its dependent current. But actually, minimizing the flux or current in the drive doesn't support full loss minimization, as the drive can operate at maximum efficiency only when its copper loss equals to the core loss which cannot be met with only flux minimization. Flux minimization decreases the corresponding current i_{ds} subsequently the torque dependent current I_{qs} increases. Perturbation in both current leads to increase in the stator current and ripples in torque profile, hence the losses actually increase at the minimum level of flux. This indicates that the value of flux at which losses are minimum is the local minima rather than the global minima.

In this paper, LMC approach is used in the IFOC drive to minimize the losses with flux reduction by actually finding the global minima of the flux which gives the maximum efficiency condition with reduction in torque ripple. Further Paper is organised in following sections. Section II represents a detailed IFOC drive with proposed control method, section III discusses proposed efficiency enhancement strategy, section IV discusses grasshopper optimization algorithm, section V discuss detailed analysis and results of drive followed by conclusion.

II. IFOC DRIVE WITH PROPOSED CONTROL METHOD

Control of IM becomes as simple as of DC motor when it is controlled with IFOC scheme (Bose, 2002). It works by decoupling the torque generating current i_{qs} and the flux generating current i_{ds} (Farhani et al., 2017; Lim & Nam, 2004). For decoupling the current vectors, a vector rotator θr is selected as per equation 1.

$$\theta_r = \int \omega_r + \omega_m \tag{1}$$

Where, ωr represents rotor frequency in rad/ sec and ωm $_r$epresents rotor mechanical speed in rad/sec (Bose, 2002). In this paper, a flux estimator is applied to regulate the value of rotor flux under different loading conditions. The proposed IFOC drive is shown in figure 1. The torque and speed of the motor are used as a variable in the proposed mathematical model to calculate the value of rotor.

Figure 1. IFOC drive model with proposed control

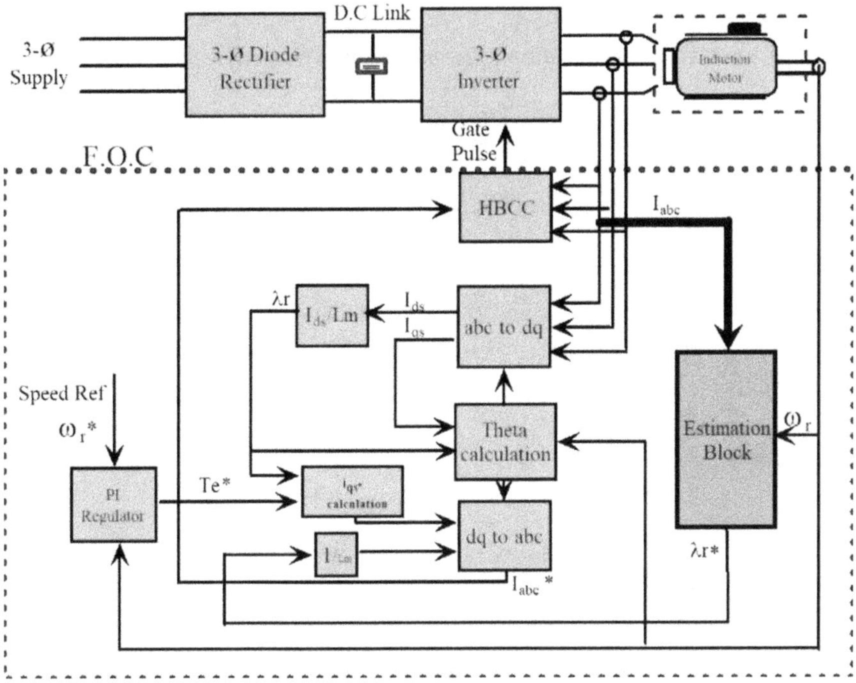

The d-q axis stator current component can be calculated as:

$$i_{qs} = \frac{2}{3}i_a - \frac{1}{3}i_b - \frac{1}{3}i_c \tag{2}$$

$$i_{ds} = -\frac{1}{\sqrt{3}}(i_a + 2i_b) \tag{3}$$

Rotor flux value can be computed as:

$$\psi_{dr} = \frac{L_r}{L_m}(\psi_{ds} - \sigma L_s i_{ds}) \tag{4}$$

Where; $\sigma = \left(1 - \frac{L_m^{\ 2}}{L_s L_r}\right)$ is the machine leakage factor and $(\psi_{ds} = \int (v_{ds} - R_s i_{ds}) dt)$ is the d-axis stator flux. Electromagnetic torque T_e developed by the motor is expressed as:

$$T_e = \left(\frac{3}{2}\right)\left(\frac{P}{2}\right)\left(\frac{L_m}{L_r}\right)\left(i_{qs}\psi_{dr} - i_{ds}\psi_{qr}\right) \tag{5}$$

Where; P is number of poles, L_m and L_r are mutual and rotor inductances. The d-axis stator current (i_{ds}) rotates in the direction of ψr and iq_s is along qe axis which forces $\psi qr_{=0}$ and $\psi dr=_{\psi r}$. T$_h$us, expression for the torque can be written as:

$$Te = kt\psi r_i qs \tag{6}$$

where $k_t = \left(\frac{3}{2}\right)\left(\frac{P}{2}\right)\left(\frac{L_m}{L_r}\right)$ and $\psi r = L_m id_s$

I$_I$I. PROPOSED EFFICIENCY ENHANCEMENT STRATEGY

Motors are used to drive the mechanical loads by converting electrical energy into mechanical energy. Various losses occur during this energy conversion in these machines. In IM, magnetic and electric loading affects core and copper losses. The stray load losses depend mainly on type of stator and rotor slots, length of overhang, and also on the harmonics in the supply voltage. Mechanical losses depend on application type. The sum of stary losses and mechanical losses does not exceed 30% of the total losses for a given load and speed and hence can be assumed constant (Abootorabi Zarchi et al., 2019; Ali et al., 2016; Lim & Nam, 2004; Sridharan & Krein, 2016). In IFOC induction motor drive, core losses ($Pc_{ore)}$ and copper losses (Pcu) can be expressed as:

$$P_{cu} = \left(\frac{R_s}{L_m^2}\right)\psi_r^2 + \left(R_s\frac{L_r^2}{L_m^2} + R_r\right)\left(\frac{T_e^2}{9\psi_r^2}\right)$$

$$P_{\substack{stator,rotor\\windings}} = R_s i_{ds}^2 + \left(R_r\frac{L_m^2}{L_r^2} + R_s\right)i_{qs}^2 \tag{7}$$

$$P_{core} = \left(K_h\omega_e + K_e\omega_e^2\right)\left(\left(\frac{L_sL_r - L_m^2}{3L_m}\right)^2 \frac{T_e^2}{\psi_r^{\,2}} + \left(\frac{L_m}{L_r} + \frac{L_sL_r - L_m^2}{L_rL_m}\right)^2 \psi_r^2\right)$$

$$P_{core} = \left(K_h\omega_e + K_e\omega_e^2\right)\left((\sigma L_s)^2 i_{qs}^2 + \left(\sigma L_s + \frac{L_m^2}{L_r}\right)^2 i_{ds}^2\right) \tag{8}$$

In IFOC drive these losses can easily be reduced by controlling the magnetic loading through the flux control (Hesari & Hoseini, 2017).

The efficiency is expressed as:

$$\eta = \frac{\omega_r T_e}{(\omega_r T_l) + R_s i_{ds}^{\;2} + \left(R_r \frac{L_m^2}{L_r^2} + R_s\right) i_{ds}^2 + (K_h\omega_e + K_e\omega_e^2)\left((\sigma L_s)^2 i_{qs}^2 + \left(\sigma L_s + \frac{L_m^2}{L_r}\right)^2 i_{ds}^2\right)} \tag{9}$$

For the strategies to maximize the efficiency, it is convenient to select T_e and ωr as independent variables (Bose, 2002). All other variables are derived in terms of the selected independent variable. The torque and speed are taken from the IM drive and the rotor flux needed is optimized so that the machine runs at maximum efficiency as per equation below.

$$maximize\ \eta(\mathrm{Te}_{,}\ \omega \mathrm{r}) \tag{10}$$

As per the basic theory, the maximum efficiency of IM occurs when the copper loss equals to the core losses at a given torque and speed, provided the amplitude of the stator current and flux does not exceed their specified maximum limits. Flux weakening without any constraint can cause burden on the machine by sudden increase in the stator current and thereby increasing the input power too. On the other hand, drive must be able to withstand the applied torque and also the transient condition must be handled well with the weakened flux (Sreejeth et al., 2019). In order to satisfy all these conditions, following a strategy of flux minimization is proposed:

Since EV operates at light load most of the time, maximum efficiency can be obtained by programming the rotor flux in accordance with the difference of copper loss and core loss. To control the amplitude of stator current and flux, constraints are implemented in the machine which can be specified as (Sridharan & Krein, 2016).

$$\psi_{r,\min} = \frac{T_e}{k_t i_{qs,\max}} \tag{11}$$

$$\psi r_{,\max} = \psi r_{,sat} \tag{12}$$

Where, $iq_{s,\max}$ is the maximum allowable q-axis current for given operating condition, $\psi r_{,\min}$ is the minimum value of flux that ensures the operation of the machine is in thermal limit and $\psi r_{,\max}$ is the maximum value of flux beyond which flux does not saturate. The losses can be computed in real time and correspondingly the flux can also be assigned to the system to operate with minimum losses as shown in figure 2. Equation 7 and equation 8 has been used in the IFOC model where the value of rotor flux is obtained by passing the difference of core loss and copper loss through a PI controller. This rotor flux value is worked as objective function for IAE (Integral Absolute Error).

Figure 2. Block diagram of loss minimization strategy

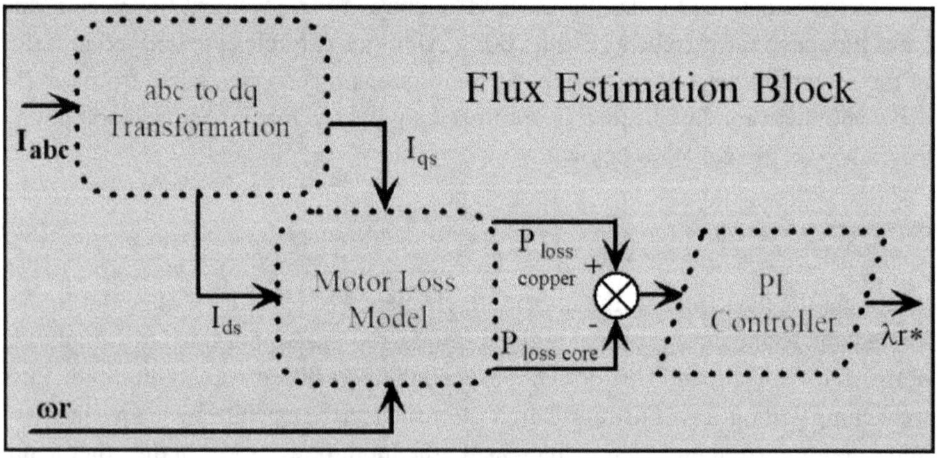

Variation of losses with respect to the variations in the stator current components (id_s and iq_s) on different speed profiles were examined to study the behaviour. Figure 3 shows the variation of losses with current id_s and iq_s with different speed profile.

Figure 3. Variation of Losses with variable stator current component

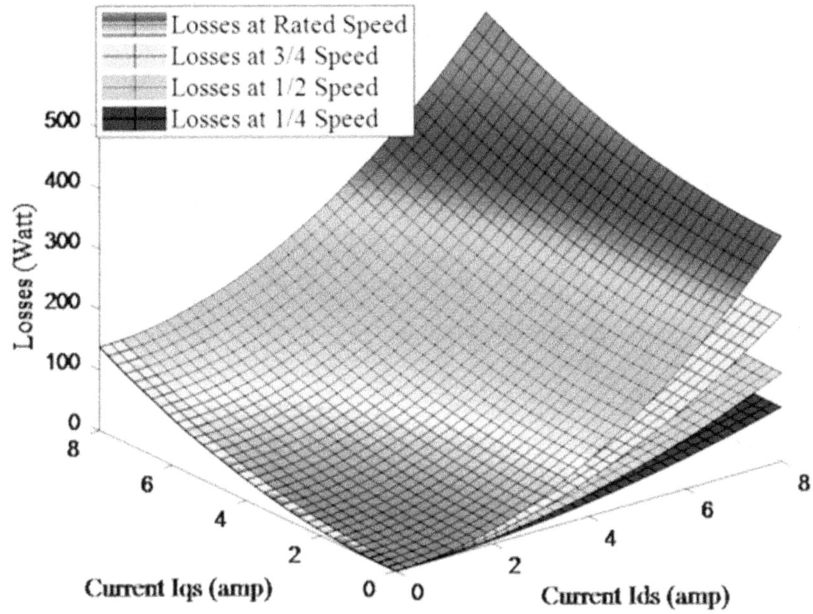

IV. GRASSHOPPER OPTIMIZATION ALGORITHM

Grasshopper optimization algorithm (GOA) is one of the finest swarm algorithm (Saremi et al., 2017). In this paper, GOA is applied for optimizing the gains (K_p and K_i) of the PI controller with an objective to reduce the integral absolute error (IAE) to a finite limit. Objective function for minimizing the IAE of the controller is:

$$Best\_Cost = a\int \left|0-(Copper\ loss - core\ loss)\right| dt \tag{13}$$

GOA takes the following necessary steps during optimization:

Step1. Generate and initialize the population and K_p and K_i

Step2. Based on the initialization step, the random behaviour of the gain parameters are generated with the help of equation 14.

$$X_i = S_i + G_i + A_i \tag{14}$$

Where X_i is position of the i_{th} grasshopper, S_i is the social interaction of the grasshopper, G_i is the gravity force on the i_{th} grasshopper and A_i shows the wind advection.

Step3. The fitness of the population is evaluated by the position of the grasshoppers. The required objective function is given in the following equation

$$K = \min(Best\_\cos t)$$

Where Best_cost is the absolute error.

Step4. After calculating the fitness of each individual, the best optimal solution based on value of K is updated and the target solution TA is updated if there is any better solution as $i=i+1$.

Step5. Finally, the termination step, check the stopping criteria if it is not met move to stem 3 again otherwise update the optimal solution.

The GOA was run up to 100 iteration with 50 population. Best cost value converges to 12.7561 at 61st iteration as shown in figure. 4. Optimal gain obtained by GOA are 9.9822 and 0.5528 for Kp and Ki respectively.

Figure 4. Convergence plot of GOA for 100 Iterations

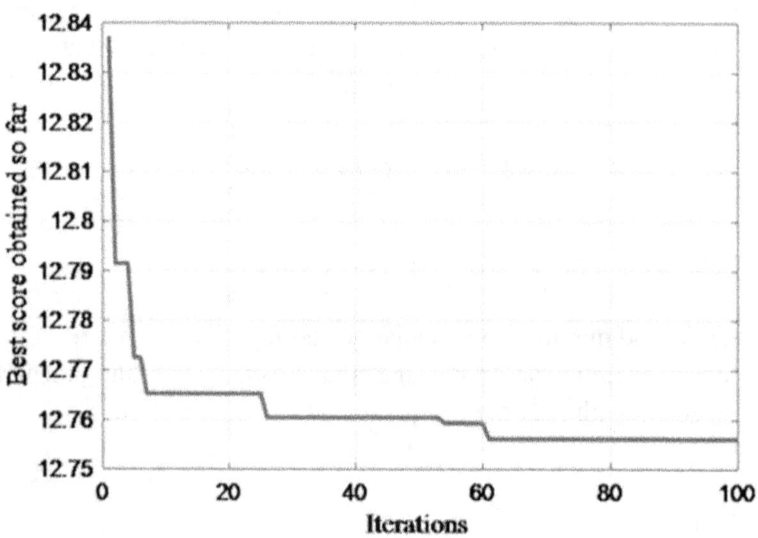

V. RESULTS AND DISCUSSION

A 3-phase, 5hp, 460V and 183rad/sec IM drive for a wide range of load torque and rotor speed operation is operated with constant (nominal) rotor flux and calculated optimal rotor flux. Parameters of the IM under consideration are given in appendix A. Drive performance was examined on the following test conditions:

(i) Under Varying Load

Loss curves for copper loss, core loss and total loss are plotted at half load and quarter load of the drive. It is clear from figure 5(a) that the nominal rotor flux of the drive is always greater than the proposed rotor flux but this value of rotor flux is actually a local minimum. On the other hand, the plotted core loss and copper loss curve always intersect with each other in the left side of the nominal rotor flux. This proposed value of rotor flux corresponds to global minima as both the losses equates at this value of flux. Table 1 gives the comparison between nominal rotor flux operation and proposed rotor flux operation. At 4.25 Nm load torque the losses in the drive with nominal flux operation and proposed rotor flux strategy are 174.6624 and 57.4040.

Figure 5a. Power losses with variable torque and rotor flux at 157rad/sec

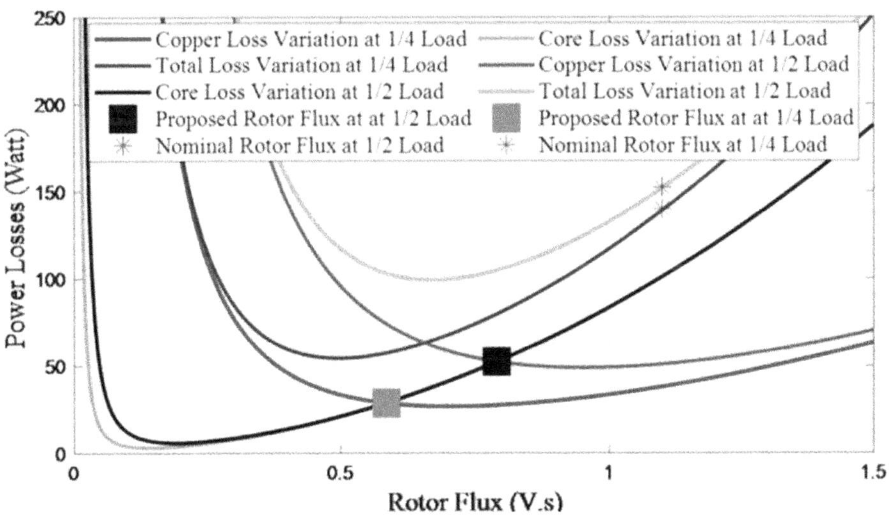

Figure 5b. Surface of power losses with variable torque and rotor flux at 157rad/sec

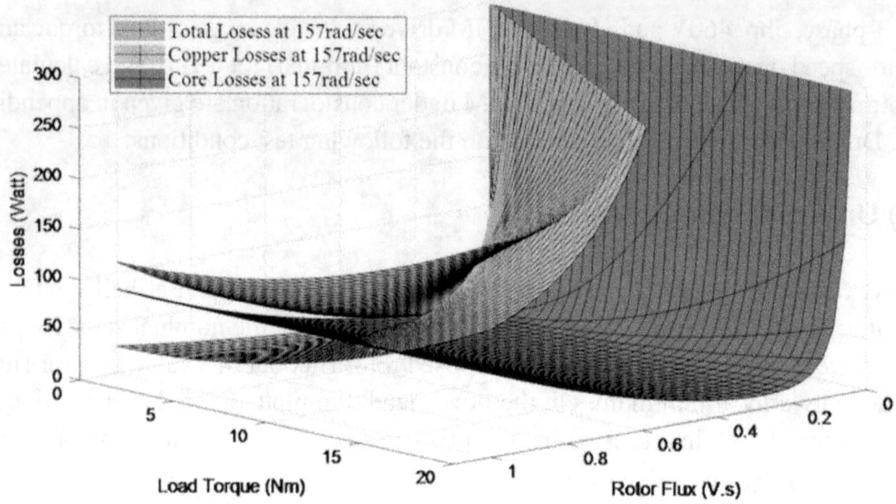

Table 1. Comparison of Nominal Vs Proposed rotor flux operation for load torque variation

Load Torque (Nm)	Nominal Rotor Flux Operation		Proposed Rotor Flux Operation	
	Flux (V.s)	Losses (watt)	Flux (V.s)	Losses (watt)
4.25	1.1	174.6624	0.585242	57.4040
8.5	1.1	186.345	0.790568	104.7480
12.75	1.1	206.3808	0.9517577	152.1922
17	1.1	232.564	1.09085	199.4360

The IFOC Simulink model was run at 157rad/sec and 4.25 Nm load was applied at 1 second. Drive was started and operated with nominal flux value up to 2 seconds. At 2 second, proposed strategy of loss minimization was initiated. Loss profile with both strategies is illustrated in figure 6.

Figure 6. Loss profile of the driveat 4.25 Nm load and 157rad/sec rad/sec speed

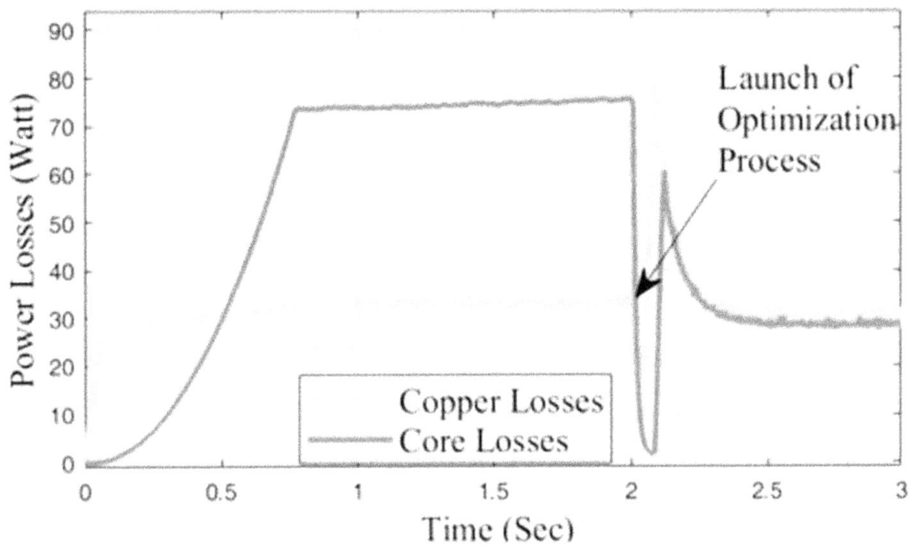

It is evident from the figure 6 that copper and core losses do not match with nominal flux operation, whereas proposed strategy forces them to be equal on the stated operating conditions. Figure 7 and 8 demonstrate the variations in stator current magnitude and input power during both the operation of the drive respectively. It is clear from the figures that during 1-2 seconds of operation the demand of stator current is high and hence the input power high as compared with performance after 2 seconds.

Figure 7. Stator current of the drive at 4.25 Nm load and 157rad/sec speed

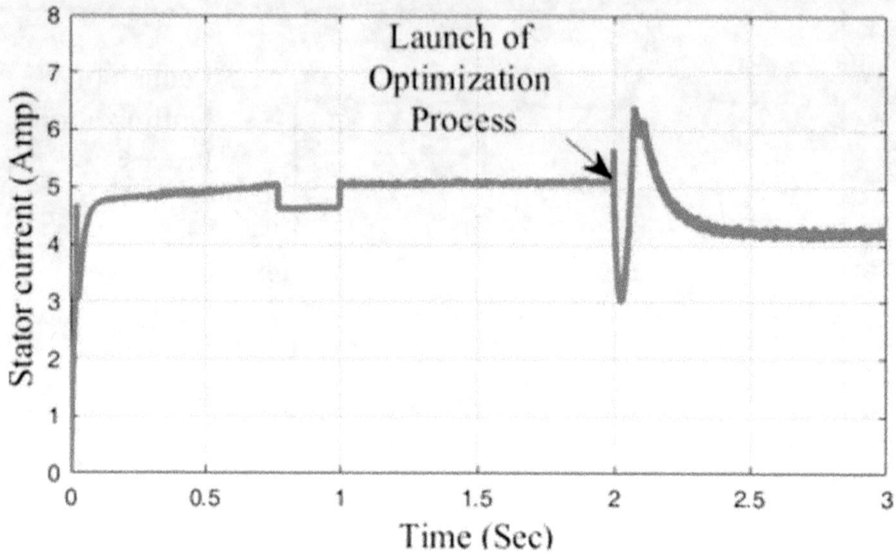

Figure 8. Input power of the drive at 4.25 Nm load and 157rad/sec speed

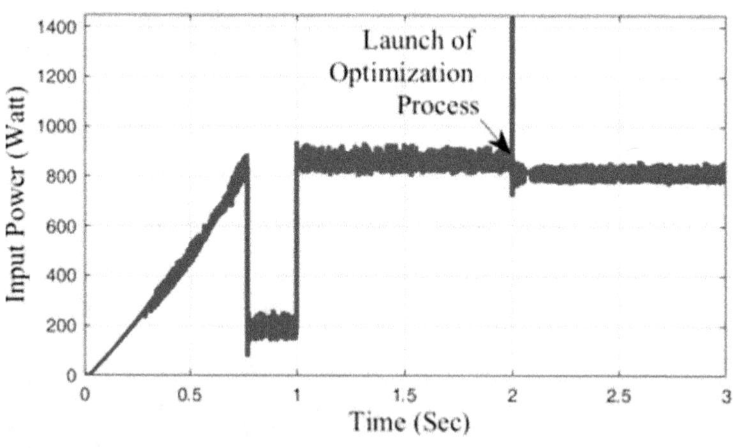

Figure 9 shows the efficiency curve of the drive with both the flux operation. The efficiency curve is at 88.5% between 1 to 2 second with nominal rotor flux opertion and between 2 to 3 second when the proposed rotor flux straegy is engagged the efficiency increases to 93%. The performance of the drive is also tested for proposed

LMC in figure 10. In both transiant state as well as steady state there is no abrupt increment in the stator current of the drive with proposed rotor flux operation.

Figure 9. Efficiency curve of the drive at 4Nm load and 157 rad/sec speed

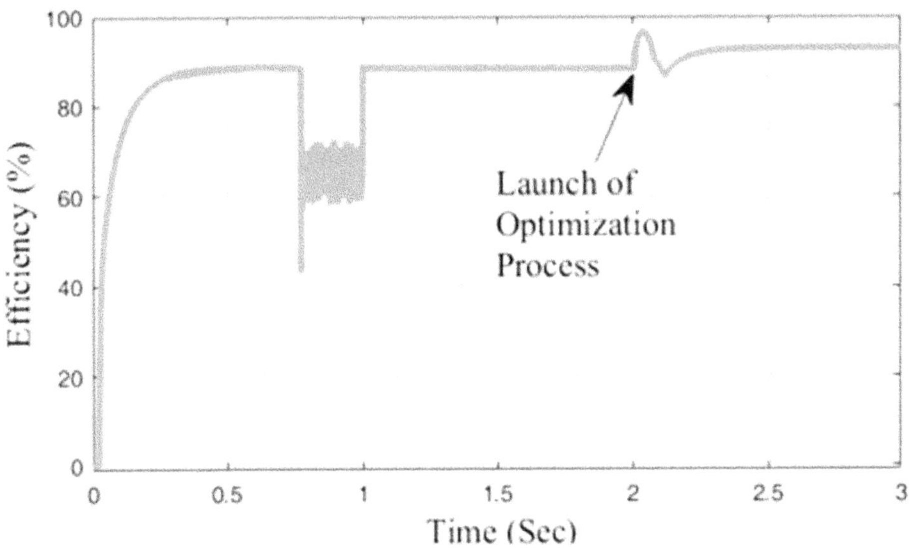

Figure 10. Stator current performance of the drive at 4Nm load and 157 rad/sec speed

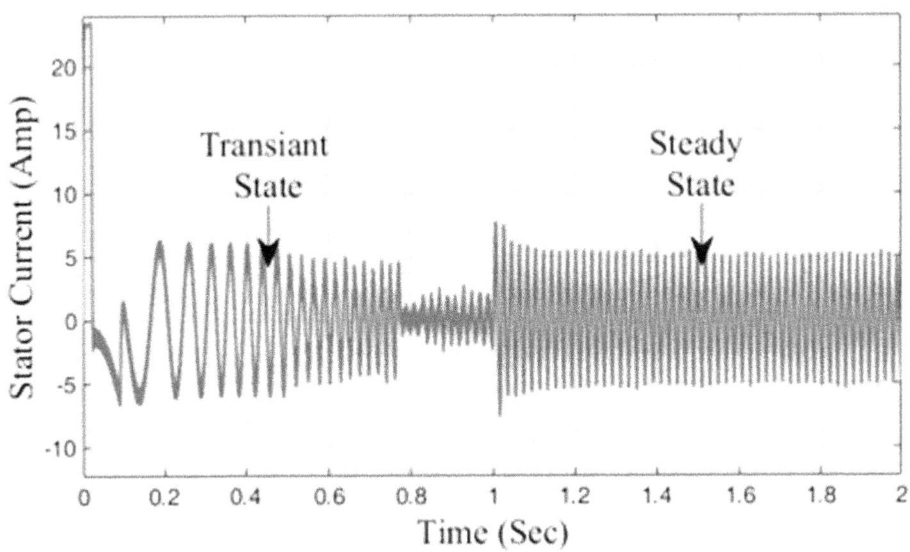

(ii) Under Varying Speed

Effect of variations in speed with fixed load is illustrated in figure 11. It is observed from the results that the variation in speed at fixed load causes slightly higher loss in the drive with the proposed strategy. But This extra amount of power ensures good performance of the drive during transient states. For various speed operations table 2 shows the comparison between nominal and proposed rotor flux operation. It is also observed from the table 2 that the proposed loss minimization strategy cannot work when the percentage applied load at the machine is equal to or greater than the percentage applied speed. Hence it is advisable not to use the loss minimization technique when speed variation is there.

Figure 11. Machine losses with variable speed at 4.25Nm Load

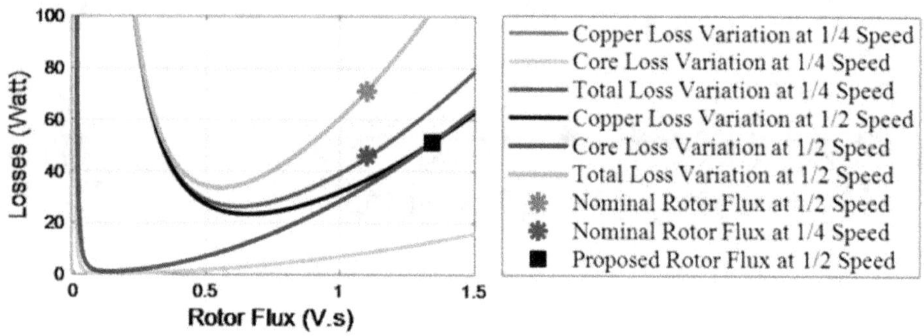

Table 2. Comparison of Nominal Vs Proposed rotor flux operation for speed variation

Rotor speed (rad/sec)	Nominal Rotor Flux Operation		Proposed Rotor Flux Operation	
	Flux (V.s)	Losses (watt)	Flux (V.s)	Losses (watt)
45.81	1.1	24.8548	NA	NA
91.63	1.1	31.7121	1.4494	119.54
137.44	1.1	40.7136	0.65754	55.4640
183	1.1	50.7279	0.531198	64.5510

VI. CONCLUSION

IM drive loss function is analysed and tested on different realistic operating conditions. Drive performance is examined under optimal rotor flux minimization and is compared with constant (nominal) flux operation. Simulation results confirm that the nominal rotor flux operation technique doesn't give the optimum value of flux for efficient condition of the drive, whereas the proposed rotor flux gives true rotor flux value that exactly matches the copper losses and core losses of the machine. Moreover, the proposed rotor flux strategy gives the stable operation in the transient mode of the drive. It is convenient for the electric vehicle driver not to remember or auto switch between the rated flux operation and optimized rotor flux operation. The efficiency of the drive is maintained at 93% as compared to 88.5% of nominal rotor flux operation. The efficiency in case of proposed rotor flux operation is best and supported with the simulation results in all aspects.

REFERENCES

Abootorabi Zarchi, H., Mosaddegh Hesar, H., & Ayaz Khoshhava, M. (2019). Online maximum torque per power losses strategy for indirect rotor flux-oriented control-based induction motor drives. IET Electric Power Applications, 13(2), 259-265. doi:10.1049/iet-epa.2018.5403

Ali, Hannan, & Mohamed. (2016). Improved indirect field-oriented control of induction motor drive based pso algorithm. *Jurnal Teknologi, 78*(6-2).

Bilgin, B., & Emadi, A. (2014). Electric motors in electrified transportation: A step toward achieving a sustainable and highly efficient transportation system. *IEEE Power Electronics Magazine, 1*(2), 10–17. doi:10.1109/MPEL.2014.2312275

Borisevich, A., & Schullerus, G. (2016). Energy efficient control of an induction machine under torque step changes. *IEEE Transactions on Energy Conversion, 31*(4), 1295–1303. doi:10.1109/TEC.2016.2561307

Bose, B. K. (2002). *Modern power electronics and AC drives* (Vol. 123). Prentice Hall.

Farhani, F., Zaafouri, A., & Chaari, A. (2017). Real time induction motor efficiency optimization. *Journal of the Franklin Institute, 354*(8), 3289–3304. doi:10.1016/j.jfranklin.2017.02.012

Hesari, S., & Hoseini, A. (2017). A New Approach to Improve Induction Motor Performance in Light-Load Conditions. *Journal of Electrical Engineering & Technology, 12*(3), 1195–1202. doi:10.5370/JEET.2017.12.3.1195

Kioskeridis, I., & Margaris, N. (1996, February). Loss minimization in induction motor adjustable-speed drives. *IEEE Transactions on Industrial Electronics*, *43*(1), 226–231. doi:10.1109/41.481429

Kumar, B., & Rani, A. (2018). Loss Minimization in Induction Motor Drive using Grey Wolf Optimization. In *2018 International Conference on Computing, Power and Communication Technologies (GUCON)* (pp. 770-774). IEEE.

Kumar, M. S., & Revankar, S. T. (2017). Development scheme and key technology of an electric vehicle: An overview. *Renewable & Sustainable Energy Reviews*, *70*, 1266–1285. doi:10.1016/j.rser.2016.12.027

Lim, S., & Nam, K. (2004). Loss-minimising control scheme for induction motors. *IEE Proceedings. Electric Power Applications*, *151*(4), 385–397. doi:10.1049/ip-epa:20040384

Saremi, S., Mirjalili, S., & Lewis, A. (2017). Grasshopper optimisation algorithm: Theory and application. *Advances in Engineering Software*, *105*, 30–47. doi:10.1016/j.advengsoft.2017.01.004

Shukla, S., & Singh, B. (2018). Solar powered sensorless induction motor drive with improved efficiency for water pumping. IET Power Electronics, 11(3), 416-426. doi:10.1049/iet-pel.2017.0452

Sreejeth, M., Singh, M., & Kumar, P. (2019). Efficiency enhancement for indirect vector-*controlled induction motor drive. International Journal of Electronics*, *106*(9), 1281–1294. doi:10.1080/00207217.2019.1584921

Sridharan, S., & Krein, P. T. (2016). Minimization of system-level losses in VSI-based induction motor drives: Offline strategies. *IEEE Transactions on Industry Applications*, *53*(2), 1096–1105. doi:10.1109/TIA.2016.2631513

Yin, S., Meng, D., Diao, L., Li, Y., & Dong, K. (2019). Improved hybrid loss control with optimized flux for traction induction motor under light load. *IEEJ Transactions on Electrical and Electronic Engineering*, *14*(3), 485–492. doi:10.1002/tee.22830

APPENDIX

Drive Parameters

Parameter	Value
Stator resistance (Rs)	1.115 Ω
Rotor resistance (Rr)	1.083 Ω
Stator inductance (Ls)	0.209 H
Rotor inductance (Lr)	0.209 H
Mutual inductance (Lm)	0.203 H
Pole (P)	4
Hysteresis constant (Kh)	1.9 10-5
Eddy current constant (Ke)	3.210-3

Chapter 10
Diversification of Agriculture and Impact of Industrial Applications on Farmer Income

Hemant Bhanawat
https://orcid.org/0000-0002-0321-8799
Amity Business School, Amity University, Jaipur, India

Hridaya Raj Bharti
Nirma University, India

Ambar Srivastava
https://orcid.org/0000-0002-7334-3421
Eternal University, India

ABSTRACT

A study carried out with a random sample of 105 beneficiary households under Japan International Cooperation Agency (JICA) project in Himachal Pradesh mainly to examine the extent of diversification and increase in income of the farmers reveals that on average about 68% of operational holding in the possession of farmers was covered under the culturable command area of the total cropped area of 0.88 ha per household, and around 47% was diversified to the cultivation of vegetable crops. On the whole, the implementation of JICA project in different sites under study has led to an increase in income of the target income of Rs 125000 to be accomplished by the end of the project. Furthermore, the detailed analysis carried out reveals that gross average annual farm income is expected to rise based on findings, and the study strongly suggests diversification towards vegetable crops to reduce risk since per hectare income from vegetable crops is expected to increase further as the process of diversification gains momentum in the next two years of the project.

DOI: 10.4018/978-1-6684-5871-6.ch010

1. INTRODUCTION

Risk is an integral part of agriculture as farmers face various types of risks that viciously drive many farmers out of agriculture. Due to change in weather, the incidence of pests and diseases, fluctuating production and prices, poor market connectivity, traders' dominance, defective policies, unmanageable post-harvest losses and poor infrastructure facilities are the issues related to risk in agriculture which directly or indirectly affect the marketing of crop produce and farmers' income. Managing risk in agriculture is particularly challenging as many risks are highly correlated affecting at times the whole community. Though several schemes are being operated by different states and union governments to mitigate the risk in agriculture, like INM-IPM, crop insurance, crop diversification, agriculture extension and so on, however, the impact at large is not satisfactory. As a result, many farm households are drifting from agriculture and migrating to urban areas or shifting to the non-farm sector. Fundamentally, the farmers should be made aware of the schemes and enabling environment should be created for them to avail the benefits of the schemes (Kurdyś-Kujawska et al. 2021).

Such an effort has been made successfully by the Government of Himachal Pradesh (GoHP) with the collaboration of the Japan International Cooperation Agency-Official Development Assistance (JICA-ODA) since 2011 to implement the most prestigious project entitled Himachal Pradesh Crop Diversification Promotion Project (HPCDP). This project is aimed at promoting crop diversification in the target area of five districts of Himachal Pradesh namely, Bilaspur, Hamirpur, Kangra, Mandi and Una through rehabilitation and development of infrastructures such as irrigation facilities, farm access roads supported by technical and capacity building programme for farmers on vegetable cultivation, foodgrain cultivation, post-harvest technology and strengthening of extension services functions. Resultantly, the vegetable-based crop diversification earlier confined to selected pockets and valleys in mid and high hills, descended onto low and mid hills of the state. At present Himachal Pradesh has now attained the status of off-season vegetable producing from the fruit-producing state of India, on account of rich natural resources and agro-climatically diversified niches (Aditya et al., 2017).Moreover, this has been rendered possible, among other things, by a well thought out and executed development strategy encompassing the creation of requisite infrastructure of road and communication network, the establishment of many research & development & extension institutions and above all the stable governments from time to time. At present, off-season vegetables like green pea, tomato, cabbage, cauliflower, French bean, capsicum, etc. and ginger, garlic, turmeric and onion are important spice crops have emerged as the money spinners in the state. Since the above-mentioned project has already been completed seven years, it was high time that its impact on crop diversification and increase in crop yields & farmers' income is examined (Shah et al., 2021). It is with this background and considering the baseline survey report of 2010, a study was undertaken with the following specific objectives:

2. OBJECTIVES OF THE STUDY

1. To study the extent of the shift in the area from traditional crops to vegetables after getting assured irrigation in the project area
2. To study the increase in annual farm income on per hectare basis after shifting to the cultivation of vegetables

3. RESEARCH METHODOLOGY

A study was carried out in eight randomly selected sub-project locations covering tube well schemes (1), lift irrigation schemes (1) and flow irrigation schemes (6) under JICA in five districts, namely, Bilaspur, Hamirpur, Kangra, Mandi and Una of Himachal Pradesh. A random sample of 105 beneficiary households was proportionally allocated to eight sub-project locations and three different irrigation systems developed under JICA viz tube well (10 beneficiary households), lift irrigation (10 beneficiary households) and flow irrigation (85 beneficiary households). Through tabular analysis, averages, percentages and ratios were computed to accomplish the objectives.

4. RESULTS AND DISCUSSION

The analysis of primary data collected through the survey method during April 2018 reveals that on average about 68 per cent of operational holding in the possession of farmers was covered under CCA. Of the total cropped area of 0.88 ha per household, around 47 per cent was diversified to the cultivation of vegetable crops. At the household level, the average area of 0.41 ha was under vegetable crops and it varied from 0.32 ha in Project Management Unit (PMU) Mandi to as high as 0.51 ha in PMU, Hamirpur (Table 4.1). The cropping intensity varied from 156 to as high as 209 per cent. Low cropping intensity in PMU Mandi was due to the temperate climate (from December to February the area remained buried under snowfall). In other project areas, the cropping intensity was above the state average. Another feature of the project area was that diversification did not take place at the cost of food grains security because still more than 45 per cent area was allocated to such crops and because of irrigation facilities and skill upgradation of farmers the production of food crops at household level did not affect.

Table 1. Cropping pattern of sample farms (Ha/hh)

Sr. No.	Particulars	PMU Hamirpur	PMU Palampur	PMU Mandi	Overall
1	Foodgrains	0.50 (45.05)	0.51 (53.68)	0.30 (46.87)	0.43 (48.86)
2	Nonfood crops	0.10 (9.01)	0.03 (3.16)	0.02 (3.13)	0.04 (4.55)
3	Vegetables	0.51 (45.94)	0.41 (43.16)	0.32 (50.00)	0.41 (46.59)
4	Cropped area	1.11 (100)	0.95 (100)	0.64 (100)	0.88 (100)
5	Sown area	0.53	0.50	0.41	0.48
6	Cropping intensity	209.43	190.00	156.10	183.33

Note: Figures in the parentheses indicate percentages
Source: Field survey, April 2018

Among various vegetable crops raised by the sample farmers in PMU, Hamirpur; potato, tomato, brinjal and cauliflower dominated the scene. In PMU, Palampur, cauliflower, cabbage, lady finger and brinjal were the important crops. Similarly, peas, tomatoes, potatoes and cauliflower occupied important positions in the cropping pattern in PMU, Mandi. At the overall level, potato (10.95%) followed by tomato (7.84%), green pea (7.68%), cauliflower (7.22%) and cabbage (3.42%) held dominance among 21 different crops raised by farmers (Table 4.2).

Table 2. Ranking of vegetables grown by farmers

Rank	PMU Hamirpur	PMU Palampur	PMU Mandi	Overall
	Crop & area	Crop & Area	Crop & area	Crop & area
First	Potato (22.95%)	Cauliflower (14.31%)	Pea (34.42%)	Potato (10.95%)
Second	Tomato (7.73%)	Cabbage (5.83%)	Tomato (21.34%)	Tomato (7.84%)
Third	Brinjal (4.42%)	Lady finger (4.98%)	Potato (9.45%)	Pea (7.68%)
Fourth	Cauliflower (3.60%)	Brinjal (4.35%)	Cauliflower (5.19%)	Cauliflower (7.22%)
Fifth	Lady finger (1.62%)	Radish (3.12%)	Garlic (2.69%)	Cabbage (3.42%)

Source: Field survey, April 2018

Average Yield and Targets Achieved

The average yield of a pea, potato, tomato, cabbage, brinjal and cauliflower was 9.34, 19.84, 21.10, 23.58, 19.75 and 24.58 t/ha, respectively (Table 4.3). In these crops, a yield gap ranging from 18 per cent to 50 per cent was noticed in comparison to the potential yields. In the case of root vegetables and cauliflower crops, per cent target achieved was quite higher. However, in case of tomato and pea the existing average yields were below target yields in some areas, *inter alia*, due to bacterial wilt and powdery mildew disease during the season (Table 4.4). This requires the introduction of resistant and suitable varieties.

Table 3. Gaps in average yield of important crops in study area as a whole (t/ha)

Crops (1)	Existing average farm yield (Yav) (2)	Exploitable yield (Yexp) (3)	Exploitable yield gap Col 3 - Col 2 (4)	Gap % (Col 4/Col 3) *100 (5)
Pea	9.34	12.50	3.16	25.28
Potato	19.84	40.00	20.16	50.40
Tomato	21.10	35.00	13.90	39.71
Cabbage	23.58	32.50	8.92	27.45
Brinjal	19.75	37.50	17.75	47.33
Cauliflower	24.58	30.00	5.42	18.07

Source: Field survey, April, 2018

Figure 1. Gaps in the average yield of important crops in the study area as a whole (t/ha)
Source: Field survey, April 2018

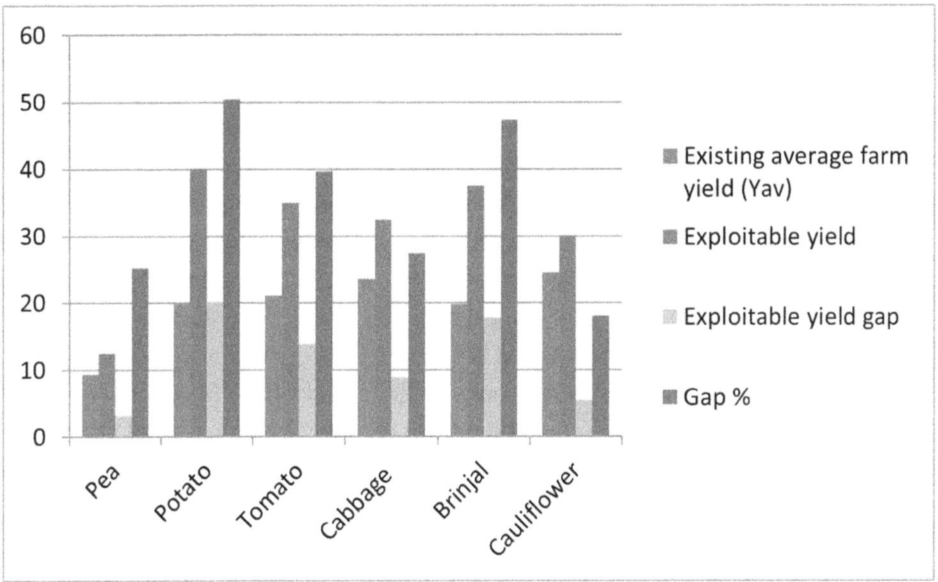

Table 4. Target and achievement for selected crop's average yields (t/ha)

Crops /income	Baseline average yield	Indicator yield as per baseline	Target to be achieved	% Target achieved by DPMU		
				Hamirpur	Palampur	Mandi
Tomato	19.00	30.00	+11.00	20.27 (21.23)	- 4.09 (18.55)	40.91 (23.50)
Root vegetables	6.90	11.50	+4.60	284.78 (20.00)	241.96 (18.03)	NA
Peas	6.20	10.40	+4.20	NA	90.48 (10.00)	-4.76 (6.18)
Cauliflower	9.50	15.90	+6.40	271.56 (26.88)	250.00 (25.50)	138.20 (18.35)

Source: Field survey, April 2018 and baseline report
Note: Figures in parentheses are existing average yields of vegetables in t/ha

Gross Annual Farm Income

The gross annual farm income emanating from foodgrains, non-food crops and vegetable crops has been depicted in Table 4.5. It is evident from the table that the contribution of foodgrains ranged from 13.03 per cent in PMU, Mandi to 25.28 per cent in PMU, Hamirpur. At the overall level, foodgrains accounted for 19.96 per cent of the total gross household income of Rs 1,23,850. The share of vegetables was as high as 85.90 per cent in PMU, Mandi. In other sub-project sites, it was 69.09 per cent in PMU, Hamirpur and 75.98 per cent in PMU, Palampur. Table 4.5 further shows that in absolute terms it was the highest of Rs 1,37,428 in PMU, Palampur wherein farming has been undertaken with great interest and zeal rather it was observed in the culture of Chaudharies and Sainies. Even in all the households where their family members are in a salaried job, they too including their school children contributed to vegetable farming. This shows that people have love, affection and respect for land possessed by them and brought under cultivation with innovations.

The findings of gross farm income computed per hectare basis have been compared with the baseline data. It can be observed from the table that the annual gross farm income from all crops varied from Rs. 1,01,174 in PMU, Hamirpur to as high as Rs. 1,28,785 in PMU, Mandi. For all crops, at the overall level, the annual gross farm income was assessed to be Rs. 1,38,923. The increase in this income due to JICA intervention at the overall level was 95.14 per cent. While comparing the data across PMUs, it can be seen that in PMU, Hamirpur and PMU, Mandi yet the target is to be achieved in terms of raising the level of annual gross farm income to the fixed target of Rs 1,25,000 per ha. However, this target has been achieved in PMU, Palampur, yet in PMU, Mandi and PMU, Hamirpur 13 to 35 per cent more efforts are needed to achieve the target. While vegetable crops accounted for 77.46 per cent of the gross average annual farm income of Rs 123850, the share of foodgrains and non-food crops was 19.96 and 2.58 per cent, respectively (Table 4.5).

Table 5. Gross annual farm income from crop production (Rs/hh)

Sr. No.	Particulars	PMU Hamirpur	PMU Palampur	PMU Mandi	Overall
1	Foodgrains	31335 (25.28)	29864 (21.73)	13600 (13.03)	24723 (19.96)
2	Nonfood crops	6975 (5.63)	3144 (2.29)	1115 (1.07)	3197 (2.58)
3	Vegetables	85640 (69.09)	104420 (75.98)	89681 (85.90)	95930 (77.46)
	Total	**123950 (100)**	**137428 (100)**	**104396 (100)**	**123850 (100)**

Note: Figures in parentheses are percentages of the total

Source: Field survey, April 2018

Figure 2. Gross annual farm income from crop production (Rs/hh)
Note: Figures in parentheses are percentages of the total
Source: Field survey, April 2018

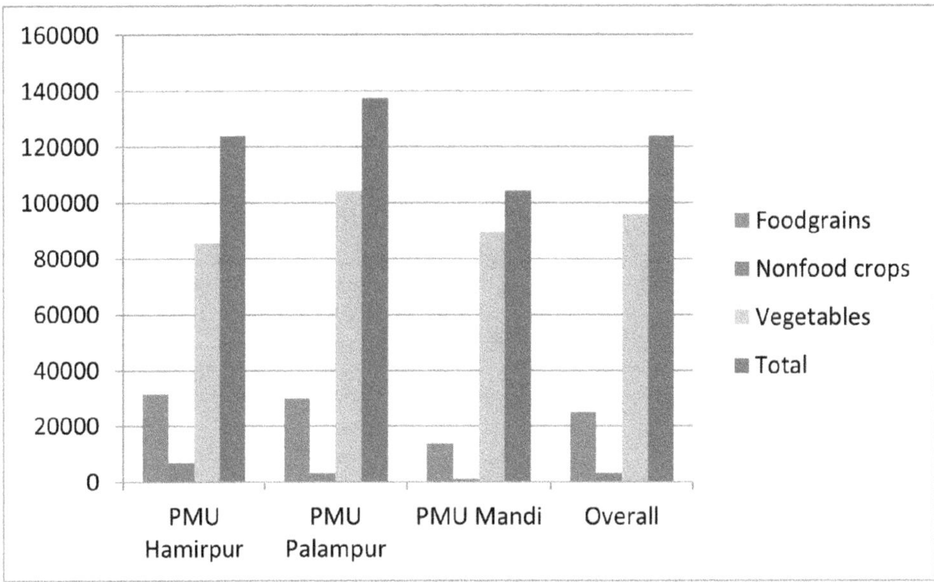

On the whole, the implementation of the project in the project sites under study has led to an increase in income to Rs. Rs 1, 18,923/ha which is 95.14 per cent of the target income of Rs 125000 which was sought to be accomplished by the end of the project (Table 4.6). Furthermore, the detailed analysis carried out over 1 per cent, 15 per cent and more than 40 per cent extent of diversification, reveals that gross average annual farm income on per ha basis is expected to rise from Rs 17492 to Rs 52284 to as high as Rs 137732, respectively (Table 4.7).

Table 6. Target and achievement for gross annual farm income

Baseline average income (Rs)	Indicator income as per baseline (Rs)	Target to be achieved (Rs)	% target achieved by DPMU		
			Hamirpur	Palampur	Mandi
20000	145000	+125000	64.94	112.90	87.03

Source: Field survey, April 2018 and baseline report

Table 7. Source-wise gross average annual farm income at different levels of diversification

Sr. No.	Particulars		Extent of diversification				
			<1%	10%	15%	30%	>40%
1	Foodgrains	Rs/hh	15830 (21.72)	14530 (19.80)	13980 (16.92)	11875 (11.65)	24723 (13.29)
2	Vegetables	Rs/hh	270 (0.37)	5190 (7.07)	21406 (25.91)	42816 (42.01)	95930 (51.57)
3	Livestock	Rs. /hh	56770 (77.91)	53664 (73.13)	47224 (57.17)	47232 (46.34)	65381 (35.14)
4	Total farm income with livestock (1+2+3)	Rs/hh	72872 (100)	73384 (100)	82610 (100)	101923 (100)	186034 (100)
5	Total farm income without livestock (1+2)	Rs/hh	16100 (22.09)	19720 (26.87)	35386 (42.83)	54691 (53.66)	120653 (64.86)
6	Total farm income with livestock	Rs/ha	79174	108428	122060	150595	212368
7	Total farm income without livestock	Rs/ha	17492	29137	52284	80808	137732

Note: Figures in parentheses are percentages of total farm income

Source: Field survey, April 2018 and report on the impact of crop diversification on food security and farmers' income in HPCDP area submitted by the department of agricultural economics, CSK HPKV Palampur to JICA in March 2017

Major Factors Responsible for An Increase in Yield and Gross Average Annual Farm Income

An attempt has been made to highlight the major factors responsible for the increase in yield and gross average annual farm income. The facts and figures have been shown in Table 8. Assured irrigation facilities, capacity building through training and demonstrations, the substitution of labour with farm power machinery, etc were noticed as the important factors enhancing average yields and income of farmers. Farmers could raise more radish and cauliflower crops consecutively in place of annual and seasonal crops like sugarcane and potato.

Table 8. Major impact indicators of an increase in yield and gross annual farm income

Sr. No.	Impact indicators	Facts & figures
1	Assured irrigation facility	0-30% to 90%
2	Enhancement in knowledge & expertise w. r t cultivation and type of varieties to be grown	10 to 70%
3	Correcting measures concerning usage of fertilizers (reducing use of urea and application of recommended fertilizers)	10 to 80%
4	Efficient use of farm power machinery, tools & implements in farm operations	4 days' work just in 1 day
5	Reduction in costs of labour for farm operations (harrowing/ploughing, sowing & transplanting)	From Rs 600 to Rs 100
6	Controlling insect pest attack	From 20/30 to 70%
7	The growing large number of commercial crops (sugarcane & potato to radish, cauliflower, peas, tomato, etc)	Four crops of radish and three of cauliflower

Source: Field survey, April 2018

5. PROBLEMS AND CONSTRAINTS

The shifting of farming from conventional crops to commercial ones such as vegetables has its travails. These come in way of successful transition due to several formidable constraints or problems. These can range from socio-economic to infrastructural to institutional like administrative and/or market-related. An in-depth analysis of such limitations not only helps in reorienting the course of the present project being implemented but also lays a sound foundation for well-designed future development projects. Hence, in the present investigation, efforts were made to examine the nature of problems faced by the farmers in different project sites. The constraints in the location-specific sub-projects are likely to be different; the details of these general problems and constraints are given in Table 9. One of the biggest threats to farming in general and vegetable farming, in particular, is the menace of stray and wild animals. This has cost escalation-related implications besides being a major deterrent for farming. The problem of insect pests and diseases was also reported in the areas wherein farmers have been raising vegetable cash crops since a few years ago. Likewise, the problem of disposing of perishable agricultural produce was also reported by the respondents in PMU, Palampur. Lack of awareness regarding commercial vegetable cultivation appeared more severe in PMU, Hamirpur. The problem of road connectivity was reported by respondents in PMU, Mandi. Since vegetable cultivation is labour intensive, therefore, the problem of labour scarcity was reported by the respondents in PMU, Palampur and PMU, Hamirpur. The lack of marketing avenues in the far-flung areas accompanied by the complete absence of value chain facilities was another problem reported by the sample farmers in PMU, Mandi. This problem was noticed more acute in SianjKothi project site of Mandi district.

Table 9. Problems and constraints faced by sample farmers

Constraint	Suggested solution
Attack of insects pests & incidence of root diseases like bacterial in crops (tomato and chillies, capsicum) and inadequate knowledge to control them	Farmers' training should be organized at the doorsteps of farmers regarding the package of practices in vegetable growing to upgrade skills in the application of chemical, and organic pesticides, producing/raising quality seed/seedlings, polyhouse cultivation, vermicomposting, new varieties; etc
Attack of wild and stray animals on crops	Provision of solar, chain-linked and barbed wire fencing as per the gravity of the attack of wild and stray animals
The farm access road to farms	Construction of farm access roads connecting the crop-producing areas amenable to the supply of inputs and disposal of produce through need-based transport means. Wherever feasible and land is available, the project has constructed roads.
Crops loss due to natural disasters/ calamities especially hail storms	Introduction of crop insurance schemes to compensate farmers against natural disasters in case of left out areas and vegetables also. Provision of crop safety nets.
Scarcity/ problem of labour for farm operations and harvesting. Also, costly labour.	Provision of affordable farm power machinery, tools and implements on an extensive scale for labour substitution and cost-effectiveness on a custom hiring/individual basis.
Problems in the marketing of produce	Crop produce collection centres near farms both private and public managed through the participation of farmers and the price of the product should be ensured to cover the cost of production and earn nominal profit to stay in farming. The provision of vegetable carts for local sale in Una district is a welcome step & needs replication in other areas as well.
Lack of adequate irrigation water when needed	The *KrishakVikas* Associations (KVAs) have to play a proactive role in ensuring the availability and distribution of water as and when needed by the stakeholders on a priority basis. Use of water-saving technological interventions like sprinkler and drip irrigation methods on an extensive scale be introduced although this is already being provided in the project area.

Source: Author Compilation

6. CONCLUSION AND POLICY INTERVENTIONS

To conclude it can be said that potatoes, followed by tomatoes, peas and cauliflower have occupied a prominent place in the cropping pattern of diversified agriculture in sample areas of JICA interventions as for as their ranking is concerned. It has also been observed that diversification has increased the on-farm employment opportunities in the project area. Thus, findings strongly suggest diversification towards vegetable crops since per hectare income from vegetable crops is expected to increase further as the process of diversification gains momentum in the next two years of the project. With the availability of assured irrigation in the study area, farmers can grow three to four vegetable crops in a year. This would result in enhancing their income per unit of land through intensive vegetable farming. Thus, in the times to come with an increase in cropping intensity and the extent of diversification beyond 40 per cent of the gross cropped area there is a huge scope to increase annual average farm income. Though the study found that an increase in the area under vegetable crops has led to a decrease in the area under foodgrain crops, the expected shortage of foodgrain production has been compensated by increased foodgrain productivity resulting in no loss in food grains production. However, to handle the resultant additional vegetable production, upgradation of the rural road network and augmentation of post-harvest, storage, processing, value addition, and market yards/ sub yards need to be scaled up. It was also reported by a few farmers that easy access to and use of modern farm machinery, tools & implements has not only helped them to complete farm operations quickly, it also led to a reduction in labour costs. This saving of time provides scope to raise more short-duration crop varieties of vegetables like, for example, raising radishes three to four times in DPMU, Palampur. The study, therefore, recommends the scaling up of such technologies on an extensive basis.

REFERENCES

Aditya, K. S., Subash, S. P., Praveen, K. V., Nithyashree, M. L., Bhuvana, N., & Sharma, A. (2017). Awareness about minimum support price and its impact on diversification decision of farmers in India. *Asia & the Pacific Policy Studies*, *4*(3), 514–526. doi:10.1002/app5.197

Anonymous. (2016). *Impact of crop diversification on food security and farmers' income in Himachal Pradesh crop diversification promotion project area lessons learnt and vision 2030.* Department of Agricultural Economics, Extension Education & Rural Sociology, College of Agriculture, CSK Himachal Pradesh Krishi Vishvavidyalaya.

Kurdyś-Kujawska, A., Strzelecka, A., & Zawadzka, D. (2021). The Impact of Crop Diversification on the Economic Efficiency of Small Farms in Poland. *Agriculture*, *11*(3), 250. doi:10.3390/agriculture11030250

Shah, K. K., Modi, B., Pandey, H. P., Subedi, A., Aryal, G., Pandey, M., & Shrestha, J. (2021). Diversified Crop Rotation: An Approach for Sustainable Agriculture Production. *Advances in Agriculture*.

Chapter 11
Integrating Systems and Design Thinking in Sustainable Innovation:
The Case of the Waste Management Sector

Lucky Diliza Madikiza
University of South Africa, South Africa

ABSTRACT

With large volumes of waste generated by increasing urbanisation and industrial activity, countries across the world are grappling with how to minimize or ideally prevent waste from being transported to increasingly dwindling landfill sites. The crisis of increasing waste as well as little landmass to allow for waste disposal is urging contemplations in waste disposal entities to consider ways in which waste can be eliminated. Recent thinking, in line with achieving sustainable ways of waste disposal, is to dispense with the linear approach of assuming a pathway from the production or manufacturing of products, their use, and ultimate disposal. Instead, a circular approach, in line with sustainability thinking, is beginning to gain traction. The chapter considers the merits of integrating systems thinking and design thinking in sustainable innovation within the waste management sector.

DOI: 10.4018/978-1-6684-5871-6.ch011

INTRODUCTION

Ways to reduce waste, normally destined for waste landfill sites, are being considered by various municipal entities or service providers discharged with waste management in city and town environments across the world. Recent thinking, in line with achieving sustainable ways of waste disposal, is to dispense with the old linear economy approach. In this approach, waste emanates after items having been used, which must then be destined for disposal in a specially zoned landfill site. In this approach, waste is considered an inevitable outcome when items are considered no longer useful. Such linear thinking is increasingly being challenged by the circular thinking approach imbued with the sustainability ethos. Contending the linear economy approach, the circular economy perspective considers how items can be used and circulated in society should they have other useful attributes. Hence, the emphasis is on product reuse initially. Should there be an inclination to eventually throw items away, they may be recycled as inputs into other useful products. Attuned to the circularity approach, design and systems thinking have been emerging paradigms to fuel innovative thinking to arrive at a circular sustainable innovative approach that aims to reduce and even avoid waste disposal.

Broadly systems thinking has been considered a favourable mindset tool for sustainable innovation. Owing to its tendency to consider component elements of a system and how it interrelates with its immediate environment, it is considered ideal in considering challenges holistically. Systems thinking allows for untangling and linking the myriad of complex interrelating factors. Design thinking, a creative problem-solving approach drawn from a recipient or user's perspective, has also attracted purchase as an approach to sustainable innovation. The discussion draws on literature in the waste management sector revolving around sustainable innovation. It agitates that for future sustainability in the sector, both design and systems thinking will be key to achieving sustainable waste management amidst land being considered a finite resource.

BACKGROUND OF SUSTAINABILITY INNOVATION

Innovation and sustainability are two important contemplations for contemporary businesses and organisations. It is not a case of choosing either but both. Innovation, whether it is about innovating processes, systems, products, services, or business models, presents organisations with an opportunity to improve or reinvent themselves to adjust their existence according to emerging threats or opportunities. Sustainability is an imperative in a world beset with climate change and environmental degradation.

Both these phenomena are attributable to a whole range of discordant human activities such as air and water pollution and unsustainable ways of producing goods.

The notion of innovation and sustainability interface along several fronts. Sustainability is considered a way of undertaking business, an innovation in itself as well as a key driver of innovation towards a less environmentally depleted planet (Gobble, 2015; Nidumolu et al., 2009). Innovation is seen as centrally important to achieve sustainability (Hansen & Grosse-dunker, n.d.). Conversely, sustainability has also been considered an important factor in business model innovation and a requirement for innovation broadly (Placet et al., 2015). Both sustainability and innovation have become important attributes companies would like to espouse for themselves for their business competitiveness image (Tunn & Dekoninck, 2016). In a sense, innovation is a factor in sustainability and vice versa. It can be expected that the two concepts will continue to intertwine as organisations and businesses navigate through sustainability as one of the imperatives of this century as the world grapples with climate change and the critical state of environmental depletion visited upon the earth.

With sustainability increasingly being seen as a way of innovation, discourse is emerging around the notions of sustainability-led innovation; sustainability-oriented innovation, and sustainability-driven, sustainability-informed, or sustainability-relevant innovation, among other configurations (Jay & Gerand, 2015). Yet it must be borne in mind that the concepts of sustainability and innovation, in their standalone sense, are also fraught with various definitional contestations which in turn leave room for various interpretations when applied. If we are then to invoke a twinning of the terms, such as in the notion of sustainability-oriented innovation, it does not become a straightforward process without some need to have a firm grasp of the underlying concepts embedded in the term. It will need to be accepted that we must deal with the complexity of integrating knowledge relating to planet-friendly economic growth, social responsibility, and environmental stewardship considerations as part of sustainability which would, in turn, present a sustainable approach to innovation as an information and learning challenge (Adams et al., 2016, p. 189). Again, the concept of innovation also presents its dilemmas when implementation is contemplated. Do we exert an incremental or radical variety of innovation, given the pressing circumstances of global climate change? Furthermore, who is supposed to be included or excluded in the innovation process? The latter question arises in the context of sustainability being considered as a way of transforming innovation and fashioning it to recognise and include grassroots actors, who are central to sustainability processes (Leach et al., 2012).

In a way, the relationship between sustainability and innovation, no matter how it can be integrated, may raise further questions as to how they can be effectively undertaken. To have some working grasp of sustainability, even as it may also relate to innovation, researchers and practitioners have sought to create frameworks or models that enable us to make sense of how sustainable innovations could be contemplated. Innovation processes themselves have been explained through frameworks and models to allow for a clearer handle on the multiple dimensions they sometimes entail (Beckman & Berry, 2007).

One of the most prevalent thinking constructs around sustainability has been systems thinking and design thinking, which we discuss in turn as we further contemplate them in a blended approach to innovating around sustainable waste management.

SYSTEMS THINKING AND SUSTAINABILITY INNOVATION IN WASTE MANAGEMENT

Systems thinking and theory have had a major footprint in sustainability science as well as in various transdisciplinary approaches to sustainability. The notion of systems thinking is undergirded by the idea of a 'system.' In scientific parlance, a 'system' entails a grouping of interlinking components and so systems thinking attempts to understand how such phenomena are interdependent over time (Bradbury, 2003, p. 176). Systems thinking enables people to see phenomena holistically instead of focusing simplistically only on cause-effect thinking (Palmberg et al., 2017, p. 4).

The systems approach has a long historical advent in various social sciences and is traceable in the initial decades of the twentieth century although some of its concepts are evident in the perspectives of ancient philosophers such as Aristotle's concept of form-substance dichotomy (Barile et al., 2018, p. 1198). With systems thinking focusing on the whole system including its parts and their interactions, it is considered an adequate framework for managing change and complexity (Nguyen & Bosch, 2013).

In delineating elements of systems thinking, it can be thought of as holistic and non-reductionist as well as non-linear in its approach. There are four underlying rules often considered in systems thinking conceptualized as the DSRP framework (distinction-making, organizing systems, inter-relating, and perspective-taking). In looking at each, in turn, the four elements as espoused in (Cabrera et al., 2008, pp. 304–305). are:

- Distinction-making: defining what is inside and outside that sets boundaries between externalities and internalities.
- Organizing systems: clustering elements as constituent parts or integrating them.
- Interrelating system elements such as how an idea relates to another.

- Perspective-taking or frame of reference entails viewing a concept through the perspective of another.

It is worthy of mention that various conceptual frameworks and theoretical streams are affiliated with systems thinking. However, these can hardly be exhausted enough within the confines of this chapter's contribution. For instance, (Porter, 2009) delineates three broad strands of systems thinking entailing functionalist, interpretive, and complex adaptive systems perspectives. This discussion does not wish to mine deeply the various discourses around systems thinking, already acknowledging that systems perspectives abound across disciplines and in sustainability topics as well.

As a framework for making sense of sustainability, systems thinking can be easily related to the notion of the earth as a system of component elements such as water, land, or biological life as well as for interrelating sustainability and sustainable development which are interconnecting systems of interest (Martin et al., 2007, p. 83). In terms of sustainability from a systems perspective, it entails "the ability is the ability of systems to persist, adapt, transform or transition in the face of constantly changing conditions"(Williams et al., 2017, p. 871).

With the notion of sustainability gaining traction in literature, there has been an assembly of an area of study termed sustainability science. Systems thinking has had a notable presence in sustainability science in that it is seen as a perspective that can be adopted as a lens for interpreting the inherent systemic nature of sustainability (Barile et al., 2018, p. 1199). The systems perspective in sustainability science is justified on several grounds. It is proffered that a simple analytical linear approach won't suffice to accord with sustainability issues that are considered complex, dynamic and multivariable whilst also involving multiple social, political, economic, and cultural aspects that interact with each other (Eli, 2018, p. 1338).

Systems thinking is also considered useful against reductionist thinking as sustainability tends to be more nuanced and embedded across various domains (Barile et al., 2018). This is because its assumptions of interdependence among phenomena make it useful in thinking about sustainability which requires a consciousness of natural and social systems surrounding and interacting with businesses or organisations (Bradbury, 2003, pp. 175–176). Besides untangling complexity, it is also considered to aid in the transdisciplinary nature of sustainability science which can be used to analyse problems and solutions by looking at interdependencies within its field and across other disciplines (Holling, 2001). Indeed, studies are beginning to explore the transdisciplinary domain of sustainability such as how systems thinking can be used as a bridging concept in transdisciplinary research on corporate sustainability matters (Williams et al., 2020). For sustainability management scholars keen to assess contexts of organisations through theories that reintegrate organisations with the socio-ecological systems in which they are embedded, systems theory has become a useful approach (Williams et al., 2017; Loorbach et al., 2010). Other inclinations are that it is even inconceivable to embark on education on sustainability issues without involving systems thinking (Palmberg et al., 2017, p. 4).

Systems thinking has also attracted purchase among innovation process thought leaders. Among the various theories of innovation as a generic process, notwithstanding a sustainability component, there is the 'systems of innovation' theory which considers the socioeconomic process creating innovation (Galanakis, 2006). Other areas in which the systems approach is contemplated include social innovation(Zenko & Sardi, 2014), diffusion of innovation approaches (Malgorzata, 2010), and service innovation (Jaaron & Backhouse, 2018). Within the stream of sustainability-related innovation approaches, even theoretically improvised versions of systems thinking have been applied. For instance, a mix between the systems of innovation approach and ecological economics is used to mobilise a 'sustainable systems of innovation' approach alluded to in the work of Altenburg and Pegels (2012, p. 10). So, Systems thinking has permeated both sustainability thinking and the generic innovation process itself as a theoretical framework.

Some important insights are yielded when invoking systems thinking concerning sustainable waste management. Waste management steps have been historically considered as discrete activities such as the generation of waste, collection, and disposal. By embracing systems thinking, we can revisit such a linear approach to waste management. Further continuing with the systems perspective, we can go beyond considering the three steps as independent operations and contemplate how they interlink or influence each other (Seadon, 2010, p. 1640). For instance, given the sustainability imperative, more generation of waste entails more volumes being collected which in turn means greater quantities being disposed of. Yet unfortunately, the dwindling land base to host the disposal of waste is not an infinite resource for most cities typically experiencing population growth through urbanisation. Furthermore, large quantities of waste, especially of the hazardous type, pose further social risks such as health risks and environmental concerns when hazardous substances permeate natural resources such as water. It could then be inferred that pressure in one component of the system – large volumes of waste collected – has implications further downstream in the waste system disposal. These implications would be felt when there are not enough landfill spaces to cater to unmitigated growth in waste. This implies that from the systems thinking perspective, waste generation and disposal cannot be decoupled from other considerations such as population dynamics and urban growth, land space, and environmental and health risks. It is precisely these aspects that Clark (1978) in his early work on solid waste management in Ohio, USA, considered in a systems approach to waste management. Clark uncovered that population trends, transportation networks, and densities had a bearing on solid waste management planning. The logic in this early attempt at systems thinking on waste management was that it could not be considered in its isolation and needed to be considered concerning other socio-economic interfacing contextual matters which may influence its inner workings. Indeed, a systems thinking-induced waste management approach, also advocated by (Marshall & Farahbakhsh, 2013), recognises sociocultural, political, and environmental spheres; engages with stakeholders, and considers a larger system in which waste is embedded through holistic methodologies.

However, in the latter years of sustainability being a pressing imperative, we ought to even think differently about waste itself in a systematic way. According to (Dijkema et al., 2000, p. 634), this would entail starting from dispensing with the notion of waste as something unwanted that needs to be discarded to a new paradigm whereby waste is labeled as something not yet used to its full potential. Such a paradigm begins to place to the fore a sustainability innovation mentality in which we seek to continuously improve phenomena and re-enter them into usefulness in lifestyles rather than disposing them. Waste would then become an object or substance which, through innovation potential, may be converted to usefulness. The consideration of handling waste management sustainably, has over the years, been to follow a sustainable logic of a three-pronged matrix of reduce-reuse-recycle. Initially, there should be an effort on the part of the consumer to reduce waste as much as possible. For instance, items such as old clothing or furniture need not be discarded as waste but donated or gifted to people who may still be able to use them. The reuse frame of thinking about waste is how certain items such as glass packaging for containers that have utility potential can still be used. The recycling approach investigates how objects which otherwise may have gone beyond their useful life could still serve as inputs to other products. A case in point of recycling would be to convert organic waste such as plant and tree shrubs into fertilizer for agricultural purposes.

The reduce-reuse-recycle (3Rs) approach, whilst attempting sustainability, has still been considered as needing further refinement through invoking further dimensions of systems thinking. Some opinions are that the 3Rs approach still reflects linear thinking and may be unbalanced when an effort is made to focus solutions such as incineration (converting waste to energy) at the downstream end of waste management whilst less focus is made on upstream solutions at the waste generation end (Conlon, 2021, p. 14). In a study conducted in Australia, a similar tendency was noted among industry efforts more focused on the recycling and composting aspect with lesser effort in the reuse or refurbishment of items being discarded as waste (Gertsakis & Lewis, 2003, p. 8). It is contended that a mixture of systems thinking, combined with design thinking, could offer value in proffering waste management solutions at the reduction end of the spectrum in terms of the reduce-reuse-recycle approach. The next section makes an overview of design thinking used in sustainability before an amalgamation of the two is presented to offer possible solutions for waste reduction.

DESIGN THINKING IN SUSTAINABILITY

Conceptually, it is important to delineate the difference between 'designerly' thinking and 'design' thinking, which are strands of thought that have been apparent in the design perspectives which have emerged as early as the sixties. Fischer (2015, p. 175) explains as follows: "designerly thinking focuses on the successful application and the theoretical discourse of design techniques for professionals, design thinking looks for possibilities to apply the method apart from professional design experiences." Stated differently, design thinking has been considered desirable for application beyond exclusive use by professional designers and is of value for innovation and change initiatives (Kimbell, 2015, p. 285). More succinctly, as a standalone concept, design thinking entails creative thinking which systematizes ideas with the aim of practical problem-solving or innovation, borrowing from designers' concepts, tools, or techniques (Leon et al., 2018; Fischer, 2015).

The characteristic features of design thinking that have been distilled in literature entail adaptive thinking, rather than inductive or deductive thinking: human-centeredness in its intention to alleviate human challenges; a problem-solving focus; and user-centeredness, in its ability to involve users (Gaziulusoy & Öztekin, 2019a; Micheli et al., 2019).

The typical process steps of design thinking, though not strictly to be invoked sequentially include:

- ***Empathizing:*** in line with human-centered, having the user's needs in mind as one tries to solve a problem
- ***Defining***: framing and defining the problem succinctly
- ***Ideation:*** bring forth ideas through creative thinking often using various techniques and tools
- ***Prototyping***: concept creation in which the envisaged product/service is being made as a tangible visualizable object
- ***Testing:*** taking the prototype to a sample of users to gauge its practical realisability and feasibility and to also allow for feedback for its refinement. (Tschimmel, 2012)

There may be an iterative process whereby there is a movement back and forth in these steps. For instance, testing may lead back to refining prototypes, which may invite another turn of ideation to call up new ideas based on the feedback from the testing. Regarding the second step of defining, this may further require rethinking in (re)defining the nature of the problem anew given a new appreciation of tested consumer use. To activate the various steps, among the tools that can be used include ethnographic methods and personas for advancing empathy and user-centeredness;

mind maps (which may advance collaboration with users); brainstorming tools that facilitate adaptive reasoning for ideation; and designing prototypes that allow for experimentation and iterative improvements (Micheli et al., 2019, p. 137).

Concerning sustainability, design thinking is concerned with the design of products or other items in a way that does not lead to adverse effects on the environment. The relationship between design thinking and sustainability has culminated in an emerging approach labeled Design for Sustainability Transitions (DfST) emerging in the 1990s which draws on systems innovation as a core term of sustainability transitions; product redesign; function innovation; transitions theory and design theory (Gaziulusoy & Öztekin, 2019b, p. 6). Interestingly, systems thinking has also been considered in design thinking begetting concepts such as systems-informed design thinking which intends to "fully honor the user-centered empathy of design thinking and a long-term perspective"(Jay & Gerand, 2015, p. 40).

A sustainability approach to design will entail embarking on "design practices while thinking green thoughts" (Faludi & A, 2017, p. 2). The various 'green thoughts' that may be informing the designer's thoughts as they embark on looking at sustainable product design as alluded to in Hopkins (2010, p. 76) could revolve around options such as how can one only use recyclable materials or design products using less packaging.

For design to lead to environmentally sustainable outcomes, Young (2010, p. 13) advocates approaches such as eco-design, which involves environmentally efficient materials use; design for purpose entailing designing that matches user needs; design for behaviour which promotes sustainable use and systems designs. The systems design approach resonates with systems thinking and according to Young (2010, p.13) may involve designing using whole systems thinking and being mindful of designing within a broader context or system. It is discernable that systems thinking has been embraced within design thinking. It should therefore not be too difficult to appreciate the value of design thinking in contributing to systems thinking as well. As a result, perspectives are emerging that suggest that design and systems thinking can be blended. It has also been made apparent by observers that design thinking is more ready to embrace systems thinking. According to (Buchanan, 2019, p. 85), the concept of a system has always been considered earlier on in the emergence of design theory and practice whilst on the other hand systems analysis tends to not provide clear identification of problems that designers may address. However, the yearning for fusing the two modes of thinking is being proposed particularly to reinforce each of the two perspectives. In one perspective vouching for merging systems and design thinking, the argument is that while design thinking has strengths in incubating ideas, it may not consider systemic complexity, which may lead to ideas being unused (Conway et al., 2017). This train of argument is reinforced by (Mugadza, 2015), who also highlights complementariness, asserting that the human-centered empathetic angle of design thinking stands to improve on the holism of systems thinking. Stated differently, it can be discerned that while design thinking is closer to the human experience in its innovative approach, systems thinking would look at the various revolving factors and stakeholders surrounding an innovation. We present a discussion in the next section on how dual design-systems thinking holds promising potential for innovation in sustainable waste management.

MERGING DESIGN AND SYSTEMS THINKING IN SUSTAINABLE WASTE MANAGEMENT AND ENTREPRENEURIAL SPIN-OFFS

The prognosis thus far made is that both systems thinking and design thinking hold prospects for application in sustainability innovation. This is even though design thinking has been considered to have relatively limited integration with sustainability science (Maher et al., 2018). Even before we invoke the two approaches that fuel creative thinking on sustainability innovation, it is important to first recap the waste architecture often followed, which has been alluded to in the preceding discussion. The various steps undertaken to deal with waste have been configured along a conceptual configuration of an inverted pyramid termed the Waste Hierarchy as visually illustrated below.

Figure 1. Typical Waste Hierarchy model
Source: Department of Environmental Affairs (DEA) Municipal Solid Waste Tariff strategy, 2012.

The first step, at the apex of the inverted pyramid, entails waste prevention or what may sometimes be referred to as waste avoidance. The second step is minimisation or reduction of the waste followed by re-use as the third. Recycling waste may be the fourth option before waste is finally destined to a waste processing facility to convert it as energy in terms of the energy recovery phase. The last option is waste disposal. As also denoted in the illustration, the initial options at the top of the inverted pyramid will be the most favoured whilst waste disposal is considered the least favoured one, and preferably to be avoided if possible. The waste hierarchy concept has been highly influential for most countries in handling waste management. The major drawback for waste managers is that they typically have little, if any control, over how waste may be generated and will have less capability to prevent waste.

In light of the waste management hierarchy, when we consider the two thinking approaches, the following steps can be suggested, in concert with the waste hierarchy model.

Apply Design Thinking More Strongly in the Waste Prevention or Avoidance Step

Design thinking should ideally be applied more strongly in the waste prevention or avoidance step of the waste hierarchy. What would be typically considered here is how can products or goods in the manufacturing phase be created to be sustainable to avoid them being thrown away as waste. One of the most innovative sustainable innovations emerging in recent years in South Africa is a second-year Chemical Engineering student's edible straw product, which is a substitute for environmentally polluting plastic straws, which can be used for drinking beverages (Etheridge, 2019).

Design thinking, being more human-centered and focused, is a key mindset that should be permeating sustainable product design with the guiding question as to how 'waste-free' products or goods can be created by the manufacturing sectors. One of the emergent thinking frameworks in waste management is that of achieving 'zero waste': an approach whereby there can be no waste generated in the first instance as the creation of any waste is considered environmentally detrimental (A. U. Zaman & Lehmann, 2013). This paradigm of achieving zero waste would be better achieved by invoking the design thinking mindset on how sustainable zero waste-inducing products could be achieved. In more recent work, design thinking has been invoked to reduce food waste during the recent Covid-19 pandemic period. In a technological development-related study, design thinking held the potential for designing new tools that could help consumers not to produce waste such as smart systems, interior design tools, and instruments for the kitchen (Massari et al., 2022). Design thinking is also going to be important for the zero-plastic and zero-toxic plastic waste agenda as is being contemplated in contemporary waste management discourse (Zaman & Newman, 2021).

Design thinking may also in turn be invoked in the subsequent initial options of waste product reuse and recycling. Among the prompting questions, as we have mentioned earlier being alluded to by Hopkins (2010, p.76), is how products can be designed in a way that uses recyclable materials or is customized for multiple uses so that they can remain reusable.

Apply Systems Thinking in Waste Minimization and the Latter End of the Least Favored Options

The waste minimization approach calls for systems thinking. This is because a range of options would need to be considered systems-wide in terms of the entire value chain that could be responsible for generating waste. Design thinking would initially have conceptualized the creation of products or items with the possibility of no residue of generating waste. For any remaining products that may be existing in the markets which still allow for waste to be generated, then systemic thinking can be relooked focusing on how much waste can be minimized. For instance, medical waste is one of the least recyclable waste categories and typically ends up for waste disposal amidst fears of it being one of the most toxic waste categories. The systems thinking approach would call for expanding the network of stakeholders involved or interfacing with the generation of medical waste and in the various steps of the value chain, exploring various options of at least minimizing possible adverse environmental and health conditions that may be introduced by medical waste. Given the limitations of medical waste in reuse or recycling efforts, attempts must be summoned to explore possibilities for energy recovery as the last option. Indeed, systemic thinking is much needed in medical waste considering how stakeholders in that fraternity have not been educated enough in managing waste. Some studies indicate how about only 41% of medical personnel are in-trained in medical waste disposal with at least 35% of materials used often using plastic materials (Singh et al., 2021). With incidences of Covid 19 and with increasing fears of the nature of health pandemics being increasingly global in scope, the need to seriously revisit medical waste management will be one of the key priorities regarding sustainable global waste management. Recent thinking, applying design thinking, has been how to alleviate the problem of infectious waste at the disposal level. Work in this regard includes applying design thinking to create a sustainable waste sterilization and sanitation system. This has been piloted in the Piedmont region in Italy to dispense with the traditional approaches of waste treatment such as incineration, which have potential risks to human health (Jimenez et al., 2021).

Overall, there would be a need for stronger exertion of systems thinking to fully exhaust the options preceding waste disposal. This may not also preclude the participation of design thinking.

Invoke Systems Thinking Within Design Thinking in the Most Favoured Options

Systems thinking should not necessarily be excluded in the options strongly weighted toward design thinking such as waste avoidance, reuse, or recycling. As alluded to earlier in the discussion, design thinking may always invoke a systems element such that 'systemic design thinking' is thought of as the paradigm merging both thinking approaches (Santi et al., 2022).

For instance, in a sector such as a vehicle tyre manufacturing, recycling has been considered as an option. However, in applying a systematic design framework, there could be a consideration of how tyres can be manufactured in a way that is customizable for use in other sectors besides the car industry. Indeed, even in their present designs, car tyres can make inputs in their present configuration for other uses thereby making them versatile in reuse. One of the most innovative uses of tyres in their customizable form has been demonstrated by Zola Ndema, an innovator in South Africa, based in the Eastern Cape province, who is converting discarded tyres into furniture (Jonas, 2020). Tyre products, in their contemporary form, would be reused for various purposes such as in domestic planting. For instance, planting on soil enclosed in tyres allows for less water use in watering plants while they are instrumental in heating the soil which allows plants to grow faster. So, in the case of tyres, a systems mindset shifts thinking to look at various other sectors that can make use of old tyres even beyond the vehicle industry.

SYNTHESIS

As the conceptual model in the diagram shows, the effort would be to blend systems thinking wherever possible with design thinking at all the options of waste management in the hierarchy. However, waste disposal, being an unsustainable way of handling waste, should be imbued into both systems and design thinking as a possibility and something that should be avoided. This would be in line to generate zero waste. Yet even the energy recovery phase, whereby waste is recast into energy, should endeavour to minimise socio-environmental impact.

Figure 2. Visual illustration of synthesized systems-design thinking approach in waste management

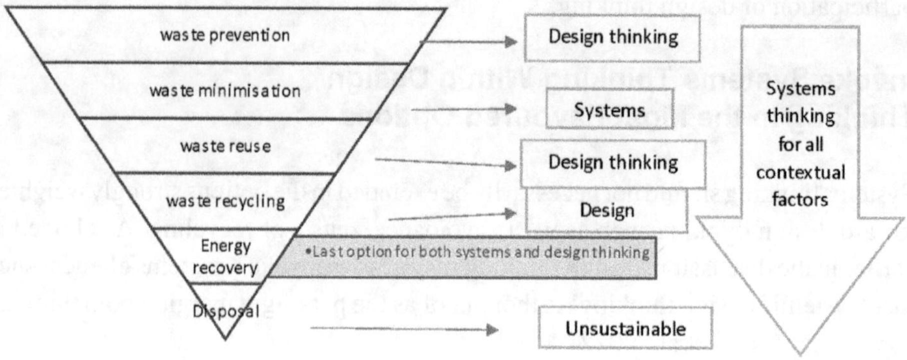

It is with the hindsight of the above conceptual model, infused with systems and design thinking, that lateral entrepreneurial opportunity may be continuously explored.

Starting at the level of waste prevention, an example was alluded to in the instance of a design-thinking-induced innovation of a young entrepreneur inventing edible straws. A range of entrepreneurial opportunities has already been evident in the waste prevention phase. The most obvious, though mostly centred on survivalist entrepreneurship, is the advent of individual waste pickers who embark on a door-to-door effort to excavate recyclable items such as plastic bottles, glass, or paper from domestic waste. However, there may still be more opportunities to be exploited within the waste prevention sphere. A redistributive type of economic activity in the waste prevention sphere may also chart an alternate route for items. This would be in line with creating a circular economy within the phase of waste prevention. For instance, Fischer (et al, 2015) advocate a 'leasing society' whereby goods such as jeans can be rented to people rather than people buying the goods. This would prevent clothing items from being discarded as waste. A similar effort has been documented in the case of a *Clean the World* campaign, a social entrepreneurship initiative entailing the collection of discarded shampoos and soaps which would be redistributed to impoverished communities (Parris & McInnes-Bowers, 2014).

In the same vein, from a design perspective, efforts could be undertaken to create a 'circular' approach in product usage such that products can circulate within the waste prevention phase. For instance, products could be designed for multiple uses that may be useful for a range of purposes. A case in point to draw from as an example is food waste. Organic food waste such as vegetables may be convertible to compost or can be reused for animal feed. Similarly in the instance of garden waste such as weeds and shrubs which can be converted into fertilizer products. The idea is to consider, in the instance of food waste or organic waste, how potential waste may be converted to other uses. A product more inclined to multiple uses, as alluded to before, is the vehicle tyre. It would be through invoking an innovative mindset and applying design thinking that an initial product is subsequently refashioned into use in another form such as when an old tyre could be used in the making of sandals.

In sum, the overall design thinking and systems thinking mindset is operable in the various phases of waste management starting from waste prevention, minimization, reuse, and recycling. It is within each of these layers that circular redistributive approaches to products can continuously be innovated. Though, the effort should be towards moving upstream towards the early stages of waste generation, specifically in the waste prevention end. In all the various phases of waste, entrepreneurial opportunities stimulated by innovative thinking may fuel ideas for products and product usage that prevents waste from moving to the next level towards its eventual disbandment.

CONCLUSION

Systems thinking and design thinking, paired together, present formidable sustainability innovation prospects for waste management. Whilst systems thinking has permeated much of sustainability science, including sustainability innovation, design thinking is beginning to emerge as the force to prompt creative innovation on sustainability. The two modes of thinking approaches need not necessarily be considered contradictory but more complementary if sustainability innovation is to gain more impetus. In the waste management sector, which faces a formidable challenge even going into the future with increasing urbanization and the resultant generation of large volumes of waste, the call for sustainability innovation is becoming as urgent given the increasing pace of urbanization and resultant growing human settlements. Pairing the two approaches will provide even more strength in the great challenge of confronting the question of whether the waste is even necessary at all. This is especially true in other non-human ecosystems such as in wildlife and nature where the natural ecosystem, left undisturbed, balances itself out without accumulating waste.

Systems and design thinking would even hold prospects in the very industry sectors such as manufacturing, which are pertinent if the quest for zero waste is to be attained. Yet both thinking approaches may still have to grapple with sectors such as the medical industry whose products are not always recyclable or reusable. However, the two perspectives when blended, hold great potential in tackling wicked problems. In the combined systems-design approach in sustainability innovation, the systems perspective provides a 'helicopter view' to map an issue complemented by the empathetic design approach which may form a more robust problem definition

(Wilkerson & Trellevik, 2021). Going forward, the two perspectives will increasingly be jointly applied in sustainable innovation more broadly. This tendency is already emerging. However, there would still be a need to agitate for and reinforce their complementarity in the waste management sector particularly in developing country contexts.

REFERENCES

Adams, R., Jeanrenaud, S., Bessant, J., Denyer, D., & Overy, P. (2016). Sustainability-oriented Innovation. *Systematic Reviews*, *18*, 180–205. doi:10.1111/ijmr.12068

Altenburg, T., & Pegels, A. (2012). *Sustainability-oriented innovation systems – Managing the green transformation.* doi:10.1080/2157930X.2012.664037

Barile, S., Orecchini, F., Saviano, M., & Farioli, F. (2018). People, technology, and governance for sustainability: The contribution of systems and cyber-systemic thinking. *Sustainability Science*, *13*(5), 1197–1208. doi:10.100711625-018-0621-y

Beckman, S. L., & Berry, M. (2007). Management. *California Management Review*, *50*(1), 25–56. doi:10.2307/41166415 PMID:19354009

Ben Eli, M. U. (2018). Sustainability: Definition and five core principles, a systems perspective. *Sustainability Science*, *13*(5), 1337–1343. doi:10.100711625-018-0564-3

Bradbury, H. (2003). *Sustaining inner and outer worlds : A whole-systems approach to developing sustainable business practices in management.* doi:10.1177/1052562903251414

Buchanan, R. (2019). Systems Thinking and Design Thinking: The Search for Principles in the World We Are Making. *She Ji*, *5*(2), 85–104. doi:10.1016/j.sheji.2019.04.001

Cabrera, D., Colosi, L., & Lobdell, C. (2008). Systems thinking. *Evaluation and Program Planning*, *31*(3), 299–310. doi:10.1016/j.evalprogplan.2007.12.001 PMID:18272224

Castiblanco Jimenez, I. A., Mauro, S., Napoli, D., Marcolin, F., Vezzetti, E., Rojas Torres, M. C., Specchia, S., & Moos, S. (2021). Design Thinking as a Framework for the Design of a Sustainable Waste Sterilization System: The Case of Piedmont Region, Italy. *Electronics (Basel)*, *10*(21), 2665. doi:10.3390/electronics10212665

Conlon, K. (2021). A social systems approach to sustainable waste management: Leverage points for plastic reduction in Colombo, Sri Lanka. *International Journal of Sustainable Development and World Ecology*, *00*(00), 1–19. doi:10.1080/13504509.2020.1867252

Conway, R., Masters, J., & Thorold, J. (2017). *From Design Thinking to Systems Change*. RSA Action and Research Centre.

Dijkema, G. P. J., Reuter, M. A., & Verhoef, E. V. (2000). *A new paradigm for waste management*. Academic Press.

Etheridge, J. (2019). *No more 'eating' paper? Maties student, 19, wins prize for edible straws*. Academic Press.

Faludi, J. A. (2017). *Golden Tools in Green Design: What drives sustainability, innovation, and value in green design methods?* [PhD dissertation]. Gradu.

Fischer, M. (2015). *Design It! Solving Sustainability Problems by Applying Design Thinking*. Academic Press.

Gaziulusoy, İ., & Öztekin, E. E. (2019). Design for sustainability transitions: Origins, attitudes and future directions. *Sustainability (Switzerland)*, *11*(13), 3601. Advance online publication. doi:10.3390u11133601

Gertsakis, J., & Lewis, H. (2003). Sustainability and the Waste Management Hierarchy. *EcoRecycle Victoria*.

Hansen, E. G., & Grosse-dunker, F. (n.d.). *Sustainability Innovation Cube – A framework to evaluate sustainability of product innovations*. Academic Press.

Holling, C. S. (2001). Understanding the complexity of economic, ecological, and social systems. *Ecosystems*, *4*(5), 390–405. doi:10.100710021-001-0101-5

Hopkins, M. S. (2010). How sustainability fuels design innovation. *MIT Sloan Management Review*, *52*(1), 75–81.

Jaaron, A. A. M., & Backhouse, C. J. (2018). Operationalisation of service innovation: A systems thinking approach. *Service Industries Journal*, *38*(9–10), 561–583. doi:10.1080/02642069.2017.1411480

Jay, J., & Gerand, M. (2015). *MIT Sloan School of Management Accelerating the Theory and Practice of Sustainability-Oriented Innovation Accelerating the Theory and Practice of Sustainability-Oriented Innovation*. Academic Press.

Jonas, S. (2020, Sept. 9). Discarded tyres turned into treasured furniture. *New Frame*.

Kimbell, L. (2015). *Rethinking Design Thinking: Part I Thinking: Part I.* doi:10.2752/175470811X13071166525216

Leach, M., Rockström, J., Raskin, P., Scoones, I., Stirling, A. C., Smith, A., Thompson, J., Millstone, E., Ely, A., Arond, E., & Folke, C. (2012). *Transforming Innovation for Sustainability*. Academic Press.

Leon, N. De, Sun, Q., Utriainen, T., Nordberg, M., & Jones, R. (2018). *Future states: Design and science for sustainability*. Academic Press.

Loorbach, D., van Bake, J. C., Whiteman, G., & Rotmans, J. (2010). Business strategies for transitions towards sustainable systems. *Business Strategy and the Environment*, *19*(2), 133–146. doi:10.1002/bse.645

Maher, R., Maher, M., Mann, S., & McAlpine, C. A. (2018). Integrating design thinking with sustainability science: A Research through Design approach. *Sustainability Science*, *13*(6), 1565–1587. doi:10.100711625-018-0618-6 PMID:30546488

Malgorzata, B. (2010). Diffusion of Innovations in the Systems Thinking Approach. *Management Business Innovation*, *6*(6), 16–24.

Marshall, R. E., & Farahbakhsh, K. (2013). Systems approaches to integrated solid waste management in developing countries. *Waste Management (New York, N.Y.)*, *33*(4), 988–1003. doi:10.1016/j.wasman.2012.12.023 PMID:23360772

Martin, S., Brannigan, J., Hall, A., Martin, S., Brannigan, J., Sustainability, A. H., Martin, S., Brannigan, J., & Hall, A. (2007). Sustainability, Systems Thinking and Professional Practice Sustainability. *Systems Thinking and Professional Practice.*, *8265*. Advance online publication. doi:10.1080/03098260500030389

Massari, S., Principato, L., Antonelli, M., & Pratesi, C. A. (2022). Learning from and designing after pandemics. CEASE: A design thinking approach to maintaining food consumer behaviour and achieving zero waste. *Socio-Economic Planning Sciences*, *82*, 101143. doi:10.1016/j.seps.2021.101143

Micheli, P., Wilner, S. J. S., Bhatti, S. H., Mura, M., & Beverland, M. B. (2019). *Doing Design Thinking: Conceptual Review, Synthesis, and Research Agenda.* doi:10.1111/jpim.12466

Mugadza, G. (2015). Systems Thinking and Design Thinking: Complimentary Approaches. *Systems Thinking World Journal. Reflection in Action*, *4*(February), 1–7.

Nguyen, N. C., & Bosch, O. J. H. (2013). *A Systems Thinking Approach to identify Leverage Points for Sustainability: A Case Study in the Cat Ba Biosphere Reserve, Vietnam.* Academic Press.

Nidumolu, R., Prahalad, C. K., & Rangaswami, M. R. (2009). *Why Sustainability Is Now the Key Driver of Innovation*. Academic Press.

Palmberg, I., Hofman-bergholm, M., Jeronen, E., & Yli-panula, E. (2017). *education sciences Systems Thinking for Understanding Sustainability? Nordic Student Teachers' Views on the Relationship between Species Identification, Biodiversity and Sustainable Development*. doi:10.3390/educsci7030072

Placet, M., Anderson, R., Fowler, K. M., Placet, M., Anderson, R., & Fowler, K. M. (2015). *Strategies for Sustainability*. doi:10.1080/08956308.2005.11657336

Porter, T. (2009). *Three Views of Systems Theories and their Implications for Sustainability Education*. Academic Press.

Santi, R., Sossini, L., Italia, M., D'Ambrosio, S., Zurlo, F., & Del Curto, B. (2022). Materials for SDGs: A Synergy Towards Sustainable Development. *DIID*, *76*(76). Advance online publication. doi:10.30682/diid7622i

Seadon, J. K. (2010). Sustainable waste management systems. *Journal of Cleaner Production*, *18*(16–17), 1639–1651. doi:10.1016/j.jclepro.2010.07.009

Singh, N., Ogunseitan, O. A., & Tang, Y. (2021). Medical waste: Current challenges and future opportunities for sustainable management. *Critical Reviews in Environmental Science and Technology*, *0*(0), 1–23. doi:10.1080/10643389.2021.1885325

Tschimmel, K. (2012). Design Thinking as an effective Toolkit. *Proceedings of the XXIII Conference: Action for Innovation: Innovation from Experience*, 1–20.

Tunn, V., & Dekoninck, E. (2016). *How Does Sustainability Help or Hinder Innovation? A Study of Successful Companies Founded on Sustainability Principles*. doi:10.1007/978-3-319-32098-4

Wilkerson, B., & Trellevik, L.-K. L. (2021). Sustainability-oriented innovation: Improving problem definition through combined design thinking and systems mapping approaches. *Thinking Skills and Creativity*, *42*, 100932. doi:10.1016/j.tsc.2021.100932

Williams, A., Kennedy, S., Philipp, F., & Whiteman, G. (2017). Systems thinking: A review of sustainability management research. *Journal of Cleaner Production*, *148*, 866–881. doi:10.1016/j.jclepro.2017.02.002

Williams, A., Sagen, S., & Ahlstr, H. (2020). *Enhancing systems thinking in corporate sustainability through a transdisciplinary research process*. doi:10.1016/j.jclepro.2020.120691

Young, G. (2010). *Design thinking and sustainability*. Academic Press.

Zaman, A., & Newman, P. (2021). Plastics: Are they part of the zero-waste agenda or the toxic-waste agenda? *Sustainable Earth*, *4*(1), 4. doi:10.118642055-021-00043-8

Zaman, A. U., & Lehmann, S. (2013). The zero waste index: A performance measurement tool for waste management systems in a 'zero waste city'. *Journal of Cleaner Production*, *50*, 123–132. doi:10.1016/j.jclepro.2012.11.041

Zenko, Z., & Sardi, V. (2014). Systemic thinking for socially responsible innovations in social tourism for people with disabilities. *Kybernetes*, *43*(3), 652–666. doi:10.1108/K-09-2013-0211

Chapter 12
Remote Code Execution:
A Major Threat to Data Loss

Sanskar Raizada
Amity University, Jaipur, India

Likshit Girish Matwani
Amity University, Jaipur, India

Yudhveer Singh
Amity University, Jaipur, India

ABSTRACT

Data needs to be protected first and foremost these days. The biggest threat to any organization is when someone has access to its data, credentials, or sensitive information. Every firm is establishing its services online as we move toward a digital future, and for those services, data loss, disruption, or corruption pose a serious hazard . Web apps are becoming more and more popular because of their ability to meet both consumer and commercial needs. The most effective and efficient way to deliver business services to stakeholders is now possible with web applications. Many services are now offered through web apps, and the efficiency of those services is gauged by the speed at which they are processed and their informational capabilities. However, because of incorrect validation, those services may also be threatened. Currently, cyber-attacks are a serious concern for any global digital transition. This chapter presents a case study on a critical criteria vulnerability named RCE.

DOI: 10.4018/978-1-6684-5871-6.ch012

I. INTRODUCTION

Remote code execution is one of the most critical vulnerabilities in today's era. A security flaw that enables attackers to connect to a remote system via public or private networks and execute arbitrary code on it. In simple terms, your device is accessible by someone remotely without your knowledge (Internet World Stats, 2017). When such personal information about you is made public, there is a good probability that hackers will target you. Cyberattacks have escalated at an astonishing rate in

recent years, particularly in India. This is a result of India's internet user population growing significantly. Multinational corporations employ bug bounty programs all around the world to deter hacking, offering rewards to security experts who uncover vulnerabilities in the company's software. It is the responsibility of devoted security researchers to identify security flaws in the applications of the business that manages the bug bounty program.

The introduction of bug bounty programs significantly decreased the hacks that businesses experienced. However, Black Hat hackers continue to hack for financial gain. For simplicity of access and to allow for accessibility from anywhere in the world, all sensitive data is stored online. But the security of the data that is stored online is where developers fall short. The main cause of data theft is that the developer never considers the perspective of the attacker. In the information age that we currently live in, every piece of information is valued highly. Sensitive data includes more than just passwords. Sensitive information is any information about you that other people don't know, such as your email address, mobile number, or birthday. More than 3.88 billion people all over the world are using the Internet as well as several service provider web applications because of the friendly usability and easy accessibility to anywhere at any time (Cavusoglu et al., 2004).

Due to the aforementioned reasons, modern online applications store sensitive data from both customers and organizations. The likelihood of those web apps being exploited by online attackers is growing daily. A significant system flaw that could have an impact on an organization's assets is web application vulnerability. A survey reveals that more than 82.8% of web service providers are using the PHP platform to build their web applications for easier code practice (Madan et al., 2002). However, in recent years, "Remote code execution" (RCE) has emerged as a prominent cyber threat that can take advantage of web server features by storing scripts or files on the server" (Homer et al., 2009).

This paper is organized into five sections. Introduction and Literature Review are discussed in sections 1& 2 Methodology is discussed in section 3. RCE Impact is explained in section 4. This paper is concluded with the outcome of the study, limitations, and future work in section 5.

II. FOLLINA (CVE-2022-30190)

Remote code execution is a critical vulnerability that has been found recently in Microsoft's zero-day vulnerability named Follina as a main key algorithm, on 30 May 2022, Microsoft issued *CVE-2022-30190* regarding Microsoft Support diagnostic Tool in Windows Vulnerability (Stepankin, 2015). The Microsoft Support Diagnostic Tool will be discussed first. Information is gathered and sent to Microsoft Support using the Microsoft Support Diagnostic Tool. After reviewing this data, Microsoft support decides how to fix any issues you might be having with your machine. When MSDT is contacted through the URL protocol from a calling program like word, it is possible for remote code execution to occur, according to a new zero-day vulnerability that Microsoft has disclosed (Shcherbakov & Musard, 2021).

If the vulnerability is successfully exploited, an attacker might execute any code with the caller application's permissions. In the context permitted by the user's privileges, the attacker can then install applications, read, modify, remove the data, or create new accounts.

Figure 1. Follina vulnerability Methodology

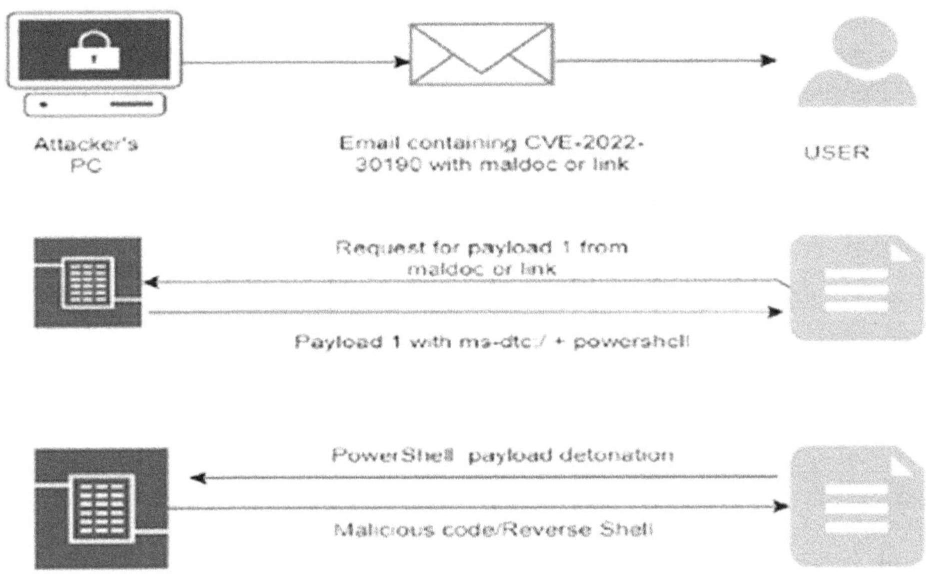

We can see the working process of how the attacker got access to the victim's machine using the **Follina** vulnerability. The attacker sent the victim a phishing email with a word attachment. When the victim clicked the malicious link, a payload request was sent to an external source. Once the external connection was made, the attacker was able to run additional commands on the victim's computer by successfully exploiting the Follina vulnerability (CVE-2022-30190, n.d.).

III. EXPLOITATION TECHNIQUE

Remote command execution occurs when an attacker is able to execute server instructions on a distant server. The goal of many exploitation techniques is to grant client-level access to a computer's root-level access. As a result, using exploits is also possible. To advance in privileges until one reaches the root, it is crucial to first obtain low-level access (Takamatsu et al., 2012). A web application's request-based field, such as a URL base parameter or input field-based parameter request, can be used by an attacker to create an RCE vulnerability. The server is expected to carry out instructions as verified users and respond to the attacker when the attacker sends a request to the server through any middleman. The main goal of remote arbitrary code execution is to provide remote user control over a susceptible machine. Typically, the assault is preceded by a data collection attack, in which the attacker utilizes a tool like an automated scanning tool to find the software version that is susceptible (Mahmoud et al., 2017). Once the application has been discovered, the attacker runs the script against it to acquire local administrative access to the host.

The procedure is started after the attacker has achieved local administrative access to the system. The attacker will make every effort to go undetected inside the system. After that, he may execute remote arbitrary code execution attacks against other hosts using the compromised host (Mohammad & Pourdavar, 2010).

Figure 2. Process of Remote Code Execution

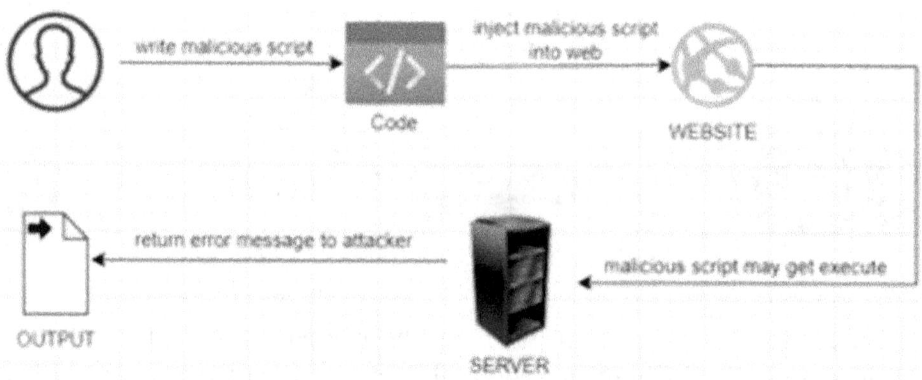

Exploitation in Public v/s Private Sectors-

The table demonstrates that 73% of web applications in the public sector are vulnerable to remote code execution, while only 27% of applications in the private sector have the same flaws. The combined percentage of the two sectors is therefore 27% of the private sector and 73% of the public sector (Alam et al., 2015).

Figure 3. Exploitation in Sectors

SECTOR	FREQUENCY	PERCENT	CUMULATIVE PERCENTAGE
PUBLIC	101	73	73%
PRIVATE	37	27	100%
TOTAL	138	100%	

The data mentioned above indicates that public sector web application owners are more focused on the functions and services of their hosted applications than they are on doing adequate security testing and enforcing security measures prior to hosting. Alternatively, private-sector online applications

Remote Code Execution on Web Application

The Remote Code Execution vulnerability in web applications is a well-known one. This kind of vulnerability allows an attacker to execute any code on a server that has the relevant hole with system-level privileges. When a server is sufficiently infiltrated, an attacker may be able to access all information within, even databases that hold data that unwary customers submitted. (Sommestad et al., 2012)

This type of attack commonly targets PHP-based applications like WordPress, Joomla, and Drupal. This means that you can hack into remote systems and execute programs to steal data or create havoc with just one click.

Most of these attacks are executed by injection of malicious web shells into the target server and subsequently executing this web shell to gain control over the system.

NETCAT

Linux has a tool called Netcat that may be used for network testing, port listening, port redirection, and port checking. The Swiss Army Knife of networking tools is another name for Netcat. Another purpose for this command is to build a reverse shell. Before delving further into the reverse shell, one needs to understand the precise nature of the Netcat tool. You can read the article on the netcat command to learn more.

Figure 4. Net cat Reverse Shell on Listening port

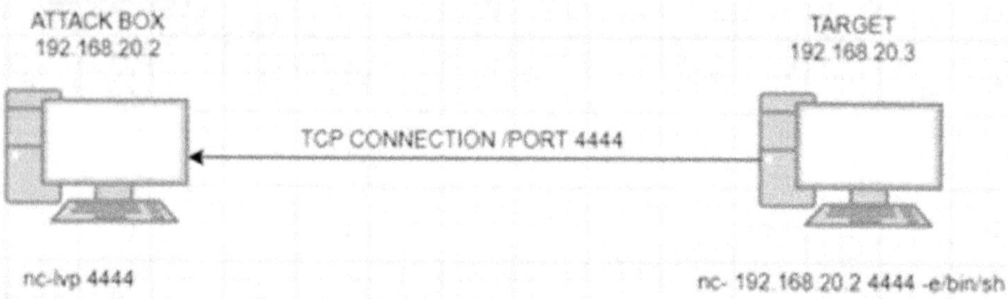

A hacker often tries to get shell access to a system in order to run malicious payload commands. The obtained shell is known as the reverse shell, and an attacker might use it to execute any code while posing as the root user (Wu et al., 2014).

To construct a reverse shell and serve as a server from which we can access all resources and issue commands to access our victim's data and compromise his confidentiality and integrity, we set up a listener port on our attacker's system. We send our payload to the victim's computer from a reverse shell that was generated in the backend after our listener's connection is established (Huluka & Popov, 2012). The attacker will be able to run any command and can also escalate privileges after the reverse shell has been built.

IV. IMPACT

The impact of this vulnerability is the lack of resources, the compromise of the assets' confidentiality and integrity, and massive data loss. If the attacker increases his level of access, he will have full control over their resources and be able to do anything he pleases (Zhang et al., 2007).

Privilege escalation, data corruption, data loss, and resource unavailability are the major effects of remote code execution. Due to these numerous significant effects, this vulnerability meets the critical standard.

Once a reverse shell has been successfully established, an attacker can use your service to distribute any malware, which poses a significant risk to both your assets and users. Users won't be able to tell if the services they are accessing are legitimate or not. It will grow to be a serious threat to the entire community's users. They will download the malicious software and get the attacker's ransom demand. Malware and ransomware pose a danger to any business, its resources, and its people in the form of remote code execution.

V. CONCLUSION

One of the most dangerous flaws in online applications is remote code execution. The delivery or insertion of malicious code into a susceptible program causes harm to the application and its users. Malicious users always find a way to break the target application's security. So, we must analyze more RCE vulnerable patterns, and then we can use prevention techniques efficiently. This paper was conducted on System based, Web-based and server- based RCE of web application vulnerability, and an Examination has been conducted on 357 real-world web applications where we are successfully able to identify 138 RCE vulnerabilities during our examination time.

REFERENCES

Alam, D., Bhuiyan, T., Kabir, M. A., & Farah, T. (2015). SQLi vulnerability in education sector websites of Bangladesh. *2015 Second International Conference on Information Security and Cyber Forensics (InfoSec)*, 152-157. 10.1109/InfoSec.2015.7435521

Cavusoglu, H., Mishra, B., & Raghunathan, S. (2004). The effect of internet security breach announcements on market value: Capital market reactions for breached firms and internet security developers. *International Journal of Electronic Commerce*, *9*(1), 70–104. doi:10.1080/10864415.2004.11044320

CVE-2022-30190. (n.d.). https://msrc-blog.microsoft.com/2022/05/30/guidance-for-cve-2022-30190-microsoft-support- diagnostic-tool-vulnerability/

Homer, J., Manhattan, K., Ou, X., & Schmidt, D. (2009). *A Sound and Practical Approach to Quantifying Security Risk in Enterprise Networks*. Citeseer.

Huluka, D., & Popov, O. (2012). Root cause analysis of session management and broken authentication vulnerabilities. *World Congress on Internet Security (WorldCIS-2012)*, 82-86.

Internet World Stats. (2017, December). *Internet global Stats*. https://www.internetworldstats.com/stats.htm

Madan, B. B., Gogeva-Popstojanova, K., Vaidyanathan, K., & Trivedi, K. S. (2002). Modelling, and quantification of security attributes of software systems. In *International Conference on Dependable Systems and Networks*. IEEE Computer Society. 10.1109/DSN.2002.1028941

Mahmoud, Q. H., Kauling, D., & Zanin, S. (2017). *Hidden android permissions: Remote code execution and shell access using a live wallpaper. In 2017 14th IEEE Annual Consumer Communications & Networking Conference*. CCNC.

Mohammad, S., & Pourdavar, S. (2010). Penetration test: A case study on remote command execution security hole. *2010 Fifth International Conference on Digital Information Management (ICDIM)*, 412-416. 10.1109/ICDIM.2010.5664671

Shcherbakov, M., & Musard, B. (2021). Serial Detector: Principled and Practical Exploration of Object Injection Vulnerabilities for the Web. *Network and Distributed System Security Symposium (NDSS'21)*. 10.14722/ndss.2021.24550

Sommestad, T., Holm, H., & Ekstedt, M. (2012). Estimates of success rates of remote arbitrary code execution attacks. *Information Management & Computer Security*, *20*(2), 107–122. doi:10.1108/09685221211235625

Stepankin, M. (2015). *Remote Code Execution Vulnerability*. Retrieved 2022 from https://artsploit.blogspot.com/2016/01/paypal-rce.html

Takamatsu, Y., Kosuga, Y., & Konno, K. (2012). Automated detection of session management vulnerabilities in web applications. *2012 Tenth Annual International Conference on Privacy, Security and Trust*, 112-119. 10.1109/PST.2012.6297927

Wu, J., Arrott, A., & Osorio, F. C. C. (2014). Protection against remote code execution exploits of popular applications in Windows. *2014 9th International Conference on Malicious and Unwanted Software: The Americas (MALWARE)*, 26-31. 10.1109/MALWARE.2014.6999416

Zhang, L., Zhang, H., Zhang, X., & Chen, L. (2007). A New Mechanism for Trusted Code Remote Execution. *2007 International Conference on Computational Intelligence and Security Workshops (CISW 2007)*, 574-578. 10.1109/CISW.2007.4425561

Chapter 13
Women Entrepreneurship and the Road to Success: A Review

Navmi Arora
Manipal University Jaipur, India

Prashasti Jain
Manipal University Jaipur, India

ABSTRACT

Human behaviour is a result of personal and environmental factors. People who exhibit exceptional qualities are the ones who have the fire within them to achieve something different and exceptional in life. Creating something new is a task that requires spark within one's personality. Observing or perceiving the need for change, planning for bringing about the change, and implementing the strategies to accomplish the target is what can be called entrepreneurship, which involves exploitation of opportunities, evaluation, and discovery.

1. INTRODUCTION

Human behaviour is a result of personal and environmental factors. People who exhibit exceptional qualities are the ones who have the fire within them to achieve something different and exceptional in life. Creating something new is a task that requires spark within one's personality. Wanting something to create is not solely required, action, along with intention is that which is effective. Observing or perceiving the need for change, planning for bringing about the change and implementing the strategies

DOI: 10.4018/978-1-6684-5871-6.ch013

to accomplish the target is what can be called entrepreneurship, which involves exploitation of opportunities, evaluation, and discovery (Shane & Venkataraman, 2000). Opposingly, entrepreneurship is not only discovering the existing opportunities, but also creating opportunities for oneself. Creating and developing opportunities for entrepreneurial endeavours and exploring the undefined and unknown parameters and acting upon the lines may be defined as opportunity creation (Sarasvathy, 2001). For society to flourish economically and socially, innovative practices and entrepreneurial ventures need to be promoted and embraced. Entrepreneurship is based on the establishment of new ventures via innovative thinking. Most crucially, the entrepreneur is seen as someone who can seize market possibilities (Nieman & Nieuwenhuizen, 2014; Balhara & Singh, 2015).

Entrepreneurship and entrepreneur have two definitions in the literature (Van Praag & Versloot, 2008). The first is an occupational category that centers on entrepreneurs. Entrepreneurs are defined in this context to include business owner-managers and self-employed individuals (Rauch & Frese, 2000), as opposed to those who are employed by others or are jobless. Thus, entrepreneurship includes both, control and ownership which means being the owner/manager of a business. Entrepreneurs are perceived as business owner-managers who coined their organisation. Gorgievski (2016) suggests that because of the simplicity with which entrepreneurs may be categorised using this framework, it is the "occupational category" method which tends to be constantly prevalent in research published in psychological publications on entrepreneurship (for instance, "self-employed" has been included in the occupational category as iterated by most household panel). In addition, the second type of categorization inculcates the business operations and processes. Processes related to the discovery, production, and identification of opportunities are seen as crucial to entrepreneurship, in existing literature (Venkatraman & Shane, 2000). The idea of identifying/creating opportunities generally involves the production of "new things", i.e. the integration of creativity into market sectors through entrepreneurial action (Lumpkin & Dess, 1996). This demonstrates an important economic function of entrepreneurship. Innovations in technology, services, processes, or business practices help markets and economies remain competitive and prosper (Schumpeter, 1934).

In summation, entrepreneurship is associated with trying something new that brings value to both the entrepreneur and the client. It entails taking risks. The vulnerability might be financial, social, or emotional, or a mix of these (Nwaoga & Omeke, 2012).

1.1 Phases of Entrepreneurial Development

Baron (2007) describes the three stages of entrepreneurial development. The first phase is the pre-launch phase, which identifies plausible possibilities. The second phase comprises execution and resource gathering, eventually leading to the postlaunch phase wherein the entrepreneur strives to nurture the enterprise, ensuring its development and survival in the market. In the pre-launch phase, in an effort to enable the launch, the entrepreneur gathers resources. In order to accomplish this, the entrepreneur must be initiative-taking, otherwise if they don't attempt to do things in a novel way, it will turn out to be a complete mock-up of incumbent companies. This approach will not be effective because fellow competitors already have a first-mover advantage (Lieberman and Montgomery, 1998). Entrepreneurs must take the lead and overcome pre-launch challenges. They must have a long-term vision that can be translated into goals through the OTIUM (Opportunity, Time, Importance, Urgency and Means) process. Opportunities must be identified and evaluated. Temporary and financial resources must be amassed for future releases. The substance must be viewed as both necessary and urgent. During these actions, the founder(s) are prone to undergo a variety of mishaps and inconsistencies, which the future entrepreneur must handle.

1.2 Barriers to Entrepreneurial Phases

There are obstacles to be overcome at every stage of this procedure. The phase of launch is defined by establishing the company, accomplishing the very first sale(s), and surviving. Handling different and sometimes competing needs (the latter indicates that the entrepreneur is constantly overwhelmed by the demands and must be able to make rapid judgments), grappling with blunders, defeats, and impediments, and creating long and short goals (strategy). During this phase, the entrepreneur must be self-starting since fresh and exciting answers to issues are required, and they will decide if the entrepreneur is successful or not. In the next phase there exists a time of expansion, which can be followed by a stable period (or of stagnation). Growth, as opposed to stagnation, may need a more proactive strategy. The final stage of corporate life is often a period of decline. The company could inevitably disintegrate, at least in its present form (although there are a few organizations that are over 2,000 years old). Institutional collapse and appeals to profitability may be leaving early or falling gracefully. Selling or leaving an organization requires a high level of active engagement.

1.3 Overcoming Barriers

Behavioral theory and experimental studies show that extensive, proactive planning increases the likelihood that people will begin to turn goals into actions and mobilize additional effort (Gollwitzer, 1996), thereby reducing distraction or increasing persistence (Diefendorff and Lord, 2004). This can be achieved by reducing the amount of work during an activity because parts of the activity are planned in advance so that the activity goes more smoothly, and it inspires people to solve unexpected problems and set up an immediate response if something happens. turned out to be bad. Extensive and anticipatory planning enables an individual to manage with the inherent anxieties of being an owner of the business by making optimal use of constrained resources. Planning allows individuals to maintain the course of action they're on and guarantees the avoidance of neglect (Latham and Locke, 2002), and it reduces the likelihood of an action being triggered prematurely (Kazen and Kuhl, 1999). In addition, the proactive nature of planning encourages exploration and helps individuals learn more effectively (Bruner, 1966), which reinforces the psychological model of the problem. Strategic planning strengthens knowledge of situational situations and time spent on tasks and leads to greater focus on goals (Tripoli, 1998). It also helps clients develop innovative methodologies and shamelessly ignore them when they don't work. As a result, knowledge of the initial conditions of the theoretical and empirical literature is improved.

2. GENDER DIFFERENCES IN ENTREPRENEURSHIP

Female and male entrepreneurs have diverse personal and professional profiles: they establish and operate firms in various industries, produce assorted products, seek goals that are different in nature, and organize their enterprises in different ways (Verheul, Stel, Thurik, 2004). Despite women being risen in professional and management positions, as well as their economic potential, the gender disparity continues to remain substantial in entrepreneurship (Minniti, 2003 & Verheul, 2004). Although data from "The Global Entrepreneurship Monitor" (2007) show that female engagement in company is expanding, the persistently lower rate of female engagement reveals that certain inequalities exist. Foreign scientists argue that women confront several challenges while starting their own businesses. Some of these obstacles have been found as being more difficult for women than males. Obtaining cash, receiving suitable skills, opposition from relatives, friends, and family, and conquering societal conditioning and prejudice are among the hurdles (McKay, 2001). According to the European Economic and Social Committee (2007), the obstacles highlighted are caused by sociocultural barriers along with a lack of knowledge regarding leaning opportunities and education, as well as extra difficulty in getting finance for business ideas. However, both theoretical and empirical evaluations show that women are effective in founding and growing businesses.

Malaya (2006) describes the low participation of women in entrepreneurship as a result of differing value systems. For example, women don't start companies just for monetary benefits (McClelland, Swail, Bell, Ibbotson, 2005; Kuratko, Hornsby,

1997). Additionally, economic success just might be secondary to fulfilment of the self and other non-financial aims (Buttner and Moore, 1997; Kyro, 2001; Scott, 1986; Chaganti, 1986). Meanwhile, the increase of revenue and firm is not always the most fundamental determinant of profitability for men. They work to improve self-actualization, professional success and progress, a harmonious microclimate of business and employee satisfaction, recognition and skill advancement, balancing household duties, and so forth. Other writers (Watson, 2002) use two approaches to understanding the gender gap: social feminist theory and liberal feminist theory. Watson (2002) proposes Reuber, Fischer, and Dyke (1993) liberal feministic theory suppositions that women-owned small and medium-sized enterprises (SMEs) will perform worse as women are blatantly discriminated against, for instance, by systematic factors that divest women of vital resources (i.e. business education and experience) or by lending institutions. As per the social feminist theory, women and men are different inherently by nature, and as compared to men, women are no less appropriate for business. They just pick alternative means of growing entrepreneurship, which may be less effective in contrast to techniques used by men.

2.1 Factors Contributing to Gender Gap in Entrepreneurship

In a 2008 study, Grazina Startiene identified and classified the elements that raise, lessen, or neutralise the gender difference in entrepreneurship. Wage disparities in the labour market (group of economic factors), unemployment, marriage, parenting, redundancy, emigration, and accessibility of capital, social security, and business licences (group of institutional and political factors), employment history (group of demographic factors), and finally inspiration and personal value system (group of psychological factors). In order to close the gender gap, the most significant factors are education, service market share, psychological characteristics of a person and motivation. The availability of finance, social security, and company licencing have the greatest effect on the gender gap among organizational and governmental intervention variables. Several studies (Rosti & Chelli, 2005; Alsos et al., 2006) show that money collecting is more difficult for women than for men, and persuading capitalists is somewhat more onerous for women. In the domain of psychological variables, notably drive and personal sense of morality, tend to widen the gender difference in entrepreneurship in one way or another (Buttner and Moore, 1997; Cliff, 1998; Verheul et al., 2001). Male entrepreneurs, for example, are more incentivised by a desire to improve their status in the society for themselves and their families, whereas female entrepreneurs are involved in efforts for good fortune, self-fulfillment, or dissatisfaction. Female entrepreneurs are determined by the perceived fulfilment and great interpersonal ties, whereas male entrepreneurs are motivated by status, riches, and achievement.

Yes, being a homemaker is also like running a business. But how did women come to realise they wanted to go out into the world and run their own businesses or work? It was and is still the norm that the man of the house 'provides' for the family, which does not only include spending money on their children's education or paying the bills and bringing the bread home. It also includes miscellaneous expenses, like giving pocket money to the children and the wife too. The whole purpose of pocket money is so that an individual is that someone who is not eligible to earn for themselves can fulfill their personal wishes with that money. Children at some point in their life start earning for themselves via the career they make and that is how they achieve autonomy. But women of the household would always have to depend on that 'pocket money' from their partners and that is something that never lets them have the feeling of 'autonomy' which is a crucial part of one's self-esteem and also there always remains a certain level of accountability towards the provider for where the money has been spent. That destroys the purpose of having money for "personal" expenses.

3. FEMALE ENTREPRENEURSHIP

According to Buttner and Moore (1997), initially only males chose to create their own businesses, but as time passed, women began to experience gender discrimination at work and opted to start their own. Avoiding gender discrimination has emerged as the most prominent reason for women to pursue business. Males seek to be entrepreneurs because they want to push themselves or develop in their careers. There is a connection between female entrepreneurs and numerous motivators; these motivators work as driving forces for them, allowing them to explore uncharted territory and new business chances. These factors combine personal and societal obligations, allowing women to choose their path and prioritize their needs. Individual motivation aspects differ; as a woman, a combination of variables, as well as an entrepreneurial spirit, function as motivators. Several factors influence female entrepreneurs' decision to start a firm.

3.1 Factors Responsible for Female Entrepreneurship

There are various factors that influence women to become entrepreneurs. These are known as the push and pull factors. While the push factors revolve around addressing one's basic requirements, the pull elements involve strong motivation and a sense of self-sufficiency.

The motives for entering this sector differ between men and women. There is a significant gap between the motivations for becoming an entrepreneur. Women, on the other hand, have various expectations, such as bringing more cash to the family or achieving a sense of accomplishment, whereas males expect profitability and advancement in their professional lives. There are various factors that influence women to become entrepreneurs. These are known as the push and pull factors. While the push factors revolve around addressing one's basic requirements, the pull elements involve strong motivation and a sense of self-sufficiency. In reality, many women start their businesses as a result of a traumatic or upsetting occurrence in their life, such as the loss of a male family member, divorce, and so on. However, regardless of the scenario, financial independence is unquestionably important. Women have particular demands and traits when it comes to surviving the business activity (Nawang et al., 2018). Ismail N. et al. (2021) found that the desires for success, affiliation, and power were the motivating elements that lead women to be active in entrepreneurship based on prior results.

3.1.1 Motivational Factors

Emotional intelligence is one of the important factors that encourage women entrepreneurs to succeed. Rhee and White (2017) studied that emotional intelligence is useful in leadership and women's entrepreneurship in the twenty-first century. This attribute is key to a successful and continued growth in the wide range of sectors. Thus, solid family support is essential for every female entrepreneur to develop balanced emotional intelligence. As per Abbas et al. (2016), social capital and familial support systems are crucial variables in women's sustainable entrepreneurship. To be a successful woman entrepreneur in the twenty-first century, the novice must have increased flexibility and self-control toward work-home obligations, as well as emotional equilibrium (Agarwal & Shah, 2014).

Following that, education has emerged as the most important factor in driving women to pursue careers in entrepreneurship. Kavitha (2014) concluded that women with educational degrees are more interested in becoming entrepreneurs. The most fundamental elements influencing a woman's decision to establish a business and the company's overall profitability are education and relevant expertise. Furthermore, Welsh et al. (2018) discovered that an individual's past experience, motivation for learning, and workplace challenges are some of the imperative factors that play a significant role in their decision to become an entrepreneur.

3.1.2 Push and Pull Factor

The pull factor may inspire and drive entrepreneurs to begin investing. It stresses the good and desirable factors for starting a business and draws entrepreneurs to their respective choices (Tandir & Džananović, 2020). The element This element motivates people to embark on new endeavours. The pull motivation stems from an inner drive to improve abilities in order to venture into entrepreneurship. This occurs when a suitable incentive is provided to entice individuals toward the achievement of a successful entrepreneurial objective. This element is based on an inherent component to encourage entrepreneurs to boost productivity levels instead of an external force to lead a firm, but rather. The pull motivation guarantees that entrepreneurs maintain the energy required to achieve the success that lies ahead of them. Some aspiration variables, on the other hand, do not always motivate persons to engage in the activities. The push forces sometimes urge a person to take the necessary steps to ensure the success of their business and establish it. As a result, the circumstances that compels people to establish a business are referred to as push factors. To reiterate, people are naturally drawn away from things that threaten their security and comfort. Human dread drives push motivation, and individuals take action to combat the threat. Women are motivated to start their own businesses by psychological needs such as self-satisfaction (Džananović & Tandir, 2020). Women become entrepreneurs due to a lack of stability in their profession. Patil and Deshpande (2019) add to this by stating that the need to accomplish more motivates women towards business. The necessity considerations are related with the push elements for female entrepreneurship. These variables include financial situation, lack of family financial gain, unemployment, redundancy, dissatisfaction with current job, and the need to accommodate work and home duties (Amit & Muller, 1995). Businesswomen choose to be self-employed because of the pull forces of a booming economy. Entrepreneurial opportunities are exemplified by factors such as the need for challenge, the flexibility of balancing family and work, increased financial opportunity, the desire for independence, self-realization, the decision to be the head of an entrepreneur, achieving personal success, and serving as a role model (Amit, & Muller, 1995).

Job security and unemployment is a national issue in the current times. But for women, these issues have been present for a long time. Women who are in their 40s and 50s presently, did not have the kind of access to education that women do today. Hence, unemployment and lack of experience went hand in hand, making unemployment a persistent issue. If a woman who is in her 40s or 50s right now, is to go to out to find jobs, she will find only disappointment and a slap in the face from the harsh reality that their time to succeed just never arrives. Meanwhile, women who did have access to education during the 80s and 90s don't even think about going into the market to find themselves work because they've imbibed learned helplessness to a level where the harsh reality now aligns with it. Their reasons to not join work immediately after completing their education include - a lack of support from their respective families, the choice to get married at the "right age" and raise a family, give undivided attention to their children, etc. And by the time they finally realize they do have the time and need to make a living for themselves, learned helplessness has been set in. They are on the mental track that they are inexperienced women with degrees, so no one is going to give them a job; even the youth (including maybe their children even) are getting rejections everyday with their fancy degrees. Gaining work experience by this time, seems too much effort and they give up trying to find a job and work for someone else. Another reason for this learned helplessness is that they don't want to work 'under' someone else, as the age for working 'for' someone else and obliging with their orders has surpassed. Hence, they make use of their degrees and think of making the most out of them, by starting their own ventures. That's one of the ways how women entrepreneurship in startups has emerged.

Nor and Ramli (2016) summated that, the primary motivation for women's engagement in entrepreneurship is to generate income; however, past job experiences, family and friends also play an important part in igniting women's interest in entrepreneurship. Ramadani et al. (2015) iterated that, women pursue entrepreneurship in order to increase their family's household income. As per the study of five respondents on a semi-structured interview, the findings indicate that one of the most important elements influencing women's participation in entrepreneurial activities is, family.

3.1.3 Family Support

Previous research has found that family has always been a priority for women. Majority of women become entrepreneurs because of the crucial assistance they receive from their families. Mustapha and Subramanian (2016) summated, family support is critical and is seen as the most essential factor to the success of female entrepreneurs. As per Zikmund et al. (2013), family is an important motivator for female entrepreneurs.

Some women have supportive family members and motivate their women of the house to learn business skills from the family business as there's no better way to gain hands-on training and experience. These women go on to have a grateful and optimistic outlook towards their ventures as their family has their back. They may not go on to join the family business, but the skills they have assimilated over the years, helps them in running their own ventures or at their position in an organization. Other aspects like as innovation, talents, and self - motivation help them attract clients. Ismail N. et al. (2021) concluded that, the support of families and spouses is also highly crucial to female entrepreneurs.

An external aspect that encourages women to start their own businesses is family support. In certain families, the father's engagement in business is a primary motivator for individuals to participate in business (Overbeke et al., 2015).

3.1.4 Family Level of Income

Daud and Idris (2014) described how businesswomen operating in markets discovered that doing business in the market itself may give a way out of poverty. Many female entrepreneurs feel obligated to change their way of life, boost their income, and improve their level of living (Nor & Ramli, 2016). On the other hand, by pursuing business, they are capable of managing their household, children, and time. It allows individuals more flexibility in carrying out business from home, like managing internet company using social media and e-commerce platforms, as long as they can maintain their presence online (Nasir, 2020).

3.1.5 Self-Independence

The desire to be self-sufficient and to run a business are both pull forces and environmental variables. As per Alam, et al. (2012), businesswomen believe that they do not have equal opportunities in their previous jobs, hence they seek employment for themselves. Simultaneously time, many people feel they are capable of generating more money than they are.

Finally, the push factors have a bigger impact on female entrepreneurs than the pull aspects. The revealed push factors include family aspect, family history, opportunity to change family lifestyle, whereas self-independence is the suggested pull factor. These two attributes have a significant influence on women's decision to start their own businesses.

We have seen women in households since time immemorial, being creative with whether it's budget management or how to serve a family when the resources are lacking.

One discovers that developing strategic flexibility via connections is crucial and necessary for women's entrepreneur resilience. Some of the well-known benefits of women's entrepreneur groups is that they generate partners out of otherwise would-be rivals, allowing for and collaborative growth and interdependence for all members. Members have access to expertise from more resilient and successful members of their associations in this manner. Notwithstanding from family members' and personal savings, the apparent consolidation of assets by these connotations, information transfers well as their collaboration of member actions, price caps, create an excellent process that effectively encapsulates entrepreneurial actions with environmental variables and thereby helps boost resilient outcomes.

During evolution, men used to be the hunters whereas women were gatherers. Women have shown excellence in the field of business as they have always been involved in making the most out of what the men used to hunt and bring home. This is parallel with a research published in the British Journal of Psychology that found males were better at concentrating solely on items at a distant range while women were faster and more efficient at putting their focus on regions near to hand. Women had to make do with whatever was hunted by the men and make it into an edible, nutritious and tasteful dish. Not just this, they had the responsibility to make utensils out of whatever material was available to them in the nature. Women have always been criticised for indulging themselves in kitty parties but what most people do not understand is that it's more than just a party. It's about building resilience within the community and strengthening sisterhood. As times moved on, husbands started earning money and giving some part of it to run the household. The amount was fixed and the mouths to feed kept increasing. But women came forward with their resource management and social skills; conceptualized 'committee' where a few women who were in a closely knit network would pool in a certain amount of money and one fine day they would pick out a name randomly (like a lucky draw) and that woman would get the whole pool of that money. This would continue quarterly so every woman got a chance to win and then participate again, and also fulfill the financial demands of the family without making the 'man of the house' realise what he's earning is not enough.

4. RESILIENCE

Resilience, in studies related to mental health, has been regarded as a method of overcoming obstacles in which people recuperate from considerable stress by employing learnable and developable attitudes and behaviours (APA, 2012). As per Bonnano (2004) it is the ability to maintain happiness throughout time. Masten (2010) reworded it as the ability to endure, a cascade of events naturally when individuals are making an attempt to interacting with their respective environments and adapting to them. Resilience is viewed as a personal process that is affected by settings and unique circumstances; individuals discover strategies to cope as best they can in their surroundings (Ungar et al., 2013; Patterson, 2002; Southwick et al., 2014). Resilience is recognized as a key component for victory in entrepreneurship, at times as an intellectual function or behavioural trait (Bullough et al., 2013; Ayala & Manzano, 2014; Bullough & Renko, 2013), at other times as a method illustrated by business owners or organisations, analogous to keeping faith through adversity (McNaughton & Korber, 2018).

4.1 Factors Contributing to Psychological Resilience

There are a few factors that contribute to an entrepreneur's psychological resilience which are divided into personal and contextual factors.

4.1.1 Personal Factors

Personality, educational opportunities, life experiences, commitment, attitudes, and behaviours are examples of these, as are contextual elements such as the social networks and support, external and internal environment and resources.

Several studies have been conducted to investigate the personal characteristics and personality traits connected with entrepreneurial resilience. A favourable association between self-efficacy in detecting entrepreneurial possibilities and university students' resilience was discovered by Pérez-López et al., (2016). Furthermore, it was discovered that persistence of effort and constancy of interest, both characteristics of the changeable personality trait grit, were positively connected to resilience (Salisu et al., 2020)

A quasi-experimental study discovered that students who took an entrepreneurship business class established more resilience, and that the process is mediated by perceived behavioural control, attitudes, and normative beliefs (González-López et al., 2019), though Okolie et al. (2021) found no support for this relationship. Several studies have demonstrated that learning from earlier bad experiences and business failures may aid in recovery and develop resilience in succeeding entrepreneurial ventures, emphasising the importance of learning (Doern, 2016; Lafuente et al., 2018; Crick & Crick, 2016; Stephens et al., 2021). Furthermore, individual entrepreneurial experiences in entrepreneurial environments and private have been demonstrated to bring an increase in resilience. Duchek (2018) discovered that businessmen whose parents offered learning opportunities for their children or gave their children responsibility for dealing with difficult and unpleasant circumstances were more likely to be resilient. Positive attitudes toward entrepreneurship were associated with resilience and provided individuals with the tenacity necessary in uncertain conditions (Pérez-López et al., 2016; González-López et al., 2019). Similarly, research discovered that entrepreneurs' resilience was positively connected with entrepreneurial preparedness (Muoz et al., 2019), a growth mind-set or a positive mind-set (Billingsley et al., 2021).

4.2.2 Contextual Factors

Entrepreneurs usually operate in highly volatile and dynamic environments, and exposure to dynamic environmental variables, such as unexpected shifts in competitors and consumer bases, has been associated to the resourcefulness feature of entrepreneurial resilience (Franco et al., 2021). Academics have sought to question these explanatory variables that foster entrepreneur resilience. Researchers have also investigated how organisational characteristics influence entrepreneurial resilience. As an illustration, Franco et al. (2021) discovered that entrepreneurs who had greater control over their businesses' operational problems (like raw materials and technical requirements) were more resilient. Entrepreneurs who invest in resource development prior to the commencement of a crisis are more likely to get financial and emotional support, helping them to be more resilient, as per Doern (2016). Furthermore, following the crisis, these companies were better equipped to aggressively organise resources.

5. ROLE OF RESILIENCE IN FEMALE ENTREPRENEURSHIP

Women have always been warriors. They've had to fight for everything they've ever wanted, even basic rights like the right to vote or have a say in the family by expressing their own opinions. Patriarchy has existed since forever, and even though the society is becoming aware of it, the process is slow, hence, meanwhile, women continue to fight for everything they want to do. Because of the continuous struggle they've had to face, they've developed resilience in the face of stress, because they are aware that their life is not going to be easy. Nothing is going to come easy and it's imperative to keep fighting, building yourself and not backing out in this world, if they want to move forward. Families have now become a tad more acceptable of the women of the household going out to work, but whenever a woman is in a more powerful position than a man, she has to again fight to keep her position and justify it constantly.

The only constant in a woman's life is the fight for her autonomy and growth. In India, it actually begins from birth itself. The fight to be born and not be killed in the womb, to have the same freedom as her brother to go out with her friends, to wear clothes that she feels comfortable in rather than the clothes that are "safe", to go for higher studies/open her own business instead of getting married at the "right age" and finally, to work after marriage (which should not be something one should need to ask consent for) but women do.

Entrepreneurial activities demonstrate several features that characterise continuous changes in the workplace, like time pressure, responsibility, greater uncertainty, flexibility, and insecurity, all of which must be tackled by individual proactivity. Furthermore, there are few or no norms and procedures in job positions in the early stages of a corporation (Gorgievski, 2016). Covid-19 was something that was completely unpredictable. Women who were not working, began working from the comfort of their homes, opened new ventures that they could create from their talent alone, in fact, it was a major struggle for the housewives to handle the household chores with their whole family sitting at home. Yet, they managed everything. Work was now not just limited to performing household chores but also staying with the family 24x7 and adjusting own personal goals along with them. Women perceived

Covid as a challenge and came stronger out of it. Nutritional care was an additional responsibility on the women of the house. Making healthy drinks as preventative measures, making healthy and leafy food, avoiding outside junk food with minimum number of rounds to the market to avoid infection.

Notice, when a mother is teaching her child, she keeps on finding out new ways of teaching him/her, and the same goes for when the child is resisting to eat. Whereas when this responsibility falls on a father, he gives up after a while. This behaviour is representative of how a woman is more open to challenges, finding out novel ways to solve a problem and attain the goal, by being patient, resilient and novel.

Let's take another example, where when a child does not score well, the mother's attitude is always around "you did your best", "you'll do better next time" - when really, she's planning on what changes she can make to the process of teaching so the child scores better the next time. She talks to the child's teachers for feedback, speaks with the parents of classmates and finds out what resources they're referring to and if they're open to sharing them, finding out new ways to make the child comprehend the information more easily and perform better next time. Whereas a father mostly expresses anger and disappointment in the same situation, with no plan of action for the future success.

Entrepreneurial resilience, involves managing the stress caused by the ongoing tug-of-war between the domestic and commercial spheres (Hamilton, 2013). Disparities in family work activities in which women balance caregiving, company management and home demands were highlighted (St-Arnaud & Giguère, 2018). This process (McGowan et al., 2012) of reconciling duties as a mother, caregiver, and business owner has been described as "wearing different hats" at times. All these factors imply that the weight of caring influences how women develop and operate their businesses, as well as how they feel resilience, reinforcing feminist researchers' stance that gender is a setting that matters a great lot in entrepreneurship (Cukier et al., 2020; Brush et al., 2018; Brush et al., 2009). This study also found that intimate relationships had the greatest impact on the resilience of women entrepreneurs, validating the influence of proximal processes which most impede or facilitate resilience (Bronfenbrenner, 2007)

6. CRITICAL EVALUATION

Female emotional intelligence, which is a necessary managerial talent (Flory, et al, 2021; Miliopoulou, et al., 2021), facilitates the promotion of important competences in companies such as skill development, cooperation, and involvement. They can manage their emotions, and their distinguishing features include self-control, empathy, self-awareness and self-motivation, all of which translate into a great capacity to form positive connections with others. In short, they have a high ability for healthy professional relationships due to their intrapersonal and interpersonal intelligence (Sterbenk, et al., 2021). On the other hand, other studies suggest that female leadership may be a barrier to meeting corporate objectives (Bozhinov, et al., 2021) and that the execution of their tasks may take on negative characteristics. Other scholars, such as (Hossain, et al., 2021) place greater emphasis on the positive perception of female leadership, which is defined by personal stability, independence, altruism, the enterprising woman capable of making change, and the ability to convert work into a passion.

REFERENCES

Abbas, T., Abrar, M., Saleem, R., & Iqbal, A. (2016). What Leads to Success for Women Entrepreneurs? An Empirical Study of Southern Punjab in Pakistan. *Academic Research International*, *7*, 120–130.

Agarwal, R., & Shah, S. K. (2014). Knowledge sources of entrepreneurship: Firm formation by academic, user and employee innovators. *Research Policy*, *43*(7), 1109–1133. doi:10.1016/j.respol.2014.04.012

Alam, S. S., Senik, Z. C., & Jani, F. M. (2012). An Exploratory Study of Women Entrepreneurs in Malaysia: Motivation and Problems. *Journal of Management Research*, *4*(4). Advance online publication. doi:10.5296/jmr.v4i4.2377

Alsos, G. A., Isaksen, E. J., & Ljunggren, E. (2006). New Venture Financing and Subsequent Business Growth in Men- and Women-Led Businesses. *Entrepreneurship Theory and Practice*, *30*(5), 667–686. doi:10.1111/j.1540-6520.2006.00141.x

American Psychological Association. (2012, January 1). *2012 Impact of Stress.* https://www.apa.org/news/press/releases/stress/2012/impact

Amit, R., & Muller, E. (1995). "Push" and "pull" entrepreneurship. *Journal of Small Business and Entrepreneurship*, *12*(4), 64–80. doi:10.1080/08276331.1995.10600505

Ayala, J.-C., & Manzano, G. (2014). The resilience of the entrepreneur. Influence on the success of the business. A longitudinal analysis. *Journal of Economic Psychology*, *42*, 126–135. doi:10.1016/j.joep.2014.02.004

Balhara, S., & Singh, D. A. (2015). Women Entrepreneurship: A Big Motivation. *Business and Economic Review*, *5*(2), 207–216.

Baron, D. P. (2007). Corporate Social Responsibility and Social Entrepreneurship. *Journal of Economics & Management Strategy*, *16*(3), 683–717. doi:10.1111/j.1530-9134.2007.00154.x

Billingsley, J., Lipsey, N. P., Burnette, J. L., & Pollack, J. M. (2021). Growth mindsets: Defining, assessing, and exploring effects on motivation for entrepreneurs and non-entrepreneurs. *Current Psychology (New Brunswick, N.J.)*. Advance online publication. doi:10.100712144-021-02149-w

Bonanno, G. A. (2004). Loss, Trauma, and Human Resilience: Have We Underestimated the Human Capacity to Thrive After Extremely Aversive Events? *The American Psychologist*, *59*(1), 20–28. doi:10.1037/0003-066X.59.1.20 PMID:14736317

Bosma, N., Jones, K., Autio, E., & Levie, J. D. (2007). *Global Entrepreneurship Monitor*. https://pureportal.strath.ac.uk/en/publications/global-entrepreneurship-monitor-2007

Bozhinov, V., Joecks, J., & Scharfenkamp, K. (2021). Gender spillovers from supervisory boards to management boards. *Managerial and Decision Economics*, *42*(5), 1317–1331. Advance online publication. doi:10.1002/mde.3311

Bronfenbrenner, U., & Morris, P. A. (2007). Handbook of Child Psychology: Vol. 1. *The Bioecological Model of Human Development*. doi:10.1002/9780470147658.chpsy0114

Bruner, J. S. (1966). *Toward a theory of instruction*. Harvard University Press.

Brush, C., Edelman, L. F., Manolova, T., & Welter, F. (2018). A gendered look at entrepreneurship ecosystems. *Small Business Economics*, *53*(2), 393–408. doi:10.100711187-018-9992-9

Brush, C. G., de Bruin, A., & Welter, F. (2009). A gender-aware framework for women's entrepreneurship. *International Journal of Gender and Entrepreneurship*, *1*(1), 8–24. doi:10.1108/17566260910942318

Bullough, A., & Renko, M. (2013). Entrepreneurial resilience during challenging times. *Business Horizons*, *56*(3), 343–350. doi:10.1016/j.bushor.2013.01.001

Bullough, A., Renko, M., & Myatt, T. (2013). Danger Zone Entrepreneurs: The Importance of Resilience and Self-Efficacy for Entrepreneurial Intentions. *Entrepreneurship Theory and Practice*, *38*(3), 473–499. doi:10.1111/etap.12006

Buttner, E. H., & Moore, D. (1997). *Women's Organizational Exodus to Entrepreneurship: Self-Reported Motivations and Correlates with Success*. Academic Press.

Chaganti, R. (1986). *Management in Women-Owned Enterprises*. https://www.semanticscholar.org/paper/Management-in-Women-Owned-Enterprises-Chaganti/bdee407ae1009bb88eb9cf2c231b5801e8d79155

Cliff, J. E. (1998). Does one size fit all? exploring the relationship between attitudes towards growth, gender, and business size. *Journal of Business Venturing*, *13*(6), 523–542. doi:10.1016/S0883-9026(97)00071-2

Crick, J. (2016). *The facets, antecedents and consequences of coopetition: An entrepreneurial marketing perspective*. doi:10.1108/QMR-11-2016-0109

Cukier, W., & Hassannezhad Chavoushi, Z. (2020). Facilitating women entrepreneurship in Canada: the case of WEKH. *Gender in Management: An International Journal*. doi:10.1108/gm-11-2019-0204

Diefendorff, J. M., & Lord, R. (2004). Examination of the Roles of Action-State Orientation and Goal Orientation in the Goal-Setting and Performance Process. *Human Performance*, *17*(4), 375–395. doi:10.120715327043hup1704_2

Doern, R. (2016). Entrepreneurship and crisis management: The experiences of small businesses during the London 2011 riots. *International Small Business Journal: Researching Entrepreneurship*, *34*(3), 276–302. doi:10.1177/0266242614553863

Duchek, S. (2018). Entrepreneurial resilience: A biographical analysis of successful entrepreneurs. *The International Entrepreneurship and Management Journal*, *14*(2), 429–455. doi:10.100711365-017-0467-2

Džananović, Đ., & Tandir, N. (2020). Motivational and Limiting Factors for Female Entrepreneurship. *Open Journal for Research in Economics*, *3*(1), 1–8. doi:10.32591/coas.ojre.0301.01001d

Fischer, E. M., Reuber, A. R., & Dyke, L. S. (1993). A theoretical overview and extension of research on sex, gender, and entrepreneurship. *Journal of Business Venturing*, *8*(2), 151–168. doi:10.1016/0883-9026(93)90017-Y

Flory, J. A., Leibbrandt, A., Rott, C., & Stoddard, O. (2021). Increasing Workplace Diversity: Evidence from a Recruiting Experiment at a Fortune 500 Company. *The Journal of Human Resources*, *56*(1), 73–92. doi:10.3368/jhr.56.1.0518-9489R1

Franco, P. L., & Christie, L. M. (2021). Effectiveness of a one day self-compassion training for pediatric nurses' resilience. *Journal of Pediatric Nursing, 61*, 109–114. doi:10.1016/j.pedn.2021.03.020 PMID:33839602

Gollwitzer, P. M. (1996). The volitional benefits of planning. In P. M. Gollwitzer & J. A. Bargh (Eds.), *Linking cognition and motivation to behavior* (pp. 287–312). The psychology of action. The Guilford Press.

González-López, M. J., Pérez-López, M. C., & Rodríguez-Ariza, L. (2019). Clearing the Hurdles in the Entrepreneurial Race: The Role of Resilience in Entrepreneurship Education. *Academy of Management Learning & Education, 18*(3), 457–483. doi:10.5465/amle.2016.0377

Gorgievski, M. J., & Stephan, U. (2016). Advancing the psychology of entrepreneurship: A review of the psychological literature and an introduction. *Applied Psychology, 65*(3), 437–468. doi:10.1111/apps.12073

Hamilton, E. (2013). The discourse of entrepreneurial masculinities (and femininities). *Entrepreneurship and Regional Development, 25*(1-2), 90–99. doi:10.1080/08985626.2012.746879

Hossain. (2021). A Study of Women Manager's Success Factors in Multinational Organisation from Bangladesh Perspective. *Bangladesh Journal of Multidisciplinary Scientific Research*, 28–40. doi:10.46281/bjmsr.v3i2.1196

Idris, N. A., & Daud, N. A. (2014). Aktiviti hilirin di kawasan FELDA: Analisis faktor pendorong penglibatan wanita dalam aktiviti perniagaan. *Prosiding PERKEM ke,* (9), 467-476.

Ismail, N. N. H. M., Nasir, M. K. M., & Rahman, R. S. A. R. A. (2021). Factors That Influence Women to Be Involved in Entrepreneurship: A Case Study in Malaysia. *Creative Education, 12*(04), 837–847. doi:10.4236/ce.2021.124060

Kavitha, G. (2014). Attitude of Youth towards Entrepreneurship—An Exploratory Study among the College Students in Coimbatore District. *Zenith International Journal of Multidisciplinary Research,* (4), 170-180.

Korber, S., & McNaughton, R. (2018). *Resilience and Entrepreneurship: A Systematic Literature Review*. https://papers.ssrn.com/sol3/papers.cfm?abstract_id=3993485

Kuhl, J., & Kazén, M. (1999). Volitional facilitation of difficult intentions: Joint activation of intention memory and positive affect removes Stroop interference. *Journal of Experimental Psychology. General, 128*(3), 382–399. doi:10.1037/0096-3445.128.3.382

Kuratko, D., Hornsby, J., & Naffziger, D. W. (1997). *An Examination of Owner's Goals in Sustaining Entrepreneurship*. https://www.semanticscholar.org/paper/An-Examination-of-Owner%27s-Goals-in-Sustaining-Kuratko-Hornsby/d08fb48489400903e66f25cf8df5ea0eec38cf25

Kyro. (2001). *Annual Report 2001 - Euroland*. https://www.yumpu.com/en/document/view/19569465/annual-report-2001-euroland

Lafuente, E., Vaillant, Y., Vendrell-Herrero, F., & Gomes, E. (2018). Bouncing Back from Failure: Entrepreneurial Resilience and the Internationalisation of Subsequent Ventures Created by Serial Entrepreneurs. *Applied Psychology*, *68*(4), 658–694. doi:10.1111/apps.12175

Lieberman, M. B., & Montgomery, D. B. (1998). First-mover (dis)advantages: Retrospective and link with the resource-based view. *Strategic Management Journal*, *19*(12), 1111–1125. doi:10.1002/(SICI)1097-0266(1998120)19:12<1111::AID-SMJ21>3.0.CO;2-W

Locke, E. A., & Latham, G. P. (2002). Building a practically useful theory of goal setting and task motivation: A 35-year odyssey. *The American Psychologist*, *57*(9), 705–717. doi:10.1037/0003-066X.57.9.705 PMID:12237980

Lumpkin, G. T., & Dess, G. G. (1996). Clarifying the Entrepreneurial Orientation Construct and Linking It To Performance. *Academy of Management Review*, *21*(1), 135–172. doi:10.2307/258632

Malaya, M. F. (2006). *A Gender-based Analysis of Performance of Small and Medium Printing Firms in Metro Manila*. https://www.semanticscholar.org/paper/A-Gender-based-Analysis-of-Performance-of-Small-and-Malaya/6f470562a24185cf7be018bdd5371394fdb88ac0

Masten, A. S., & Wright, M. O. (2010). Resilience over the lifespan: Developmental perspectives on resistance, recovery, and transformation. In J. W. Reich, A. J. Zautra, & J. S. Hall (Eds.), *Handbook of adult resilience* (pp. 213–237). The Guilford Press.

McClelland, E., Swail, J., Bell, J., & Ibbotson, P. (2005). *Following the Pathway of Female Entrepreneurs: A Six-Country Investigation*. https://papers.ssrn.com/sol3/papers.cfm?abstract_id=1500896

McGowan, P., Redeker, C. L., Cooper, S. Y., & Greenan, K. (2012). Female entrepreneurship and the management of business and domestic roles: Motivations, expectations and realities. *Entrepreneurship and Regional Development*, *24*(1-2), 53–72. doi:10.1080/08985626.2012.637351

McKay, S. (2001). Between Flexibility and Regulation: Rights, Equality and Protection at Work. *British Journal of Industrial Relations*, *39*(2), 285–303. doi:10.1111/1467-8543.00200

Miliopoulou, G., & Kapareliotis, I. (2021). The toll of success: Female leaders in the "women-friendly" Greek advertising agencies. *Gender, Work and Organization*, *28*(5), 1741–1765. Advance online publication. doi:10.1111/gwao.12636

Minniti, M., & Bygrave, W. D. (2003). *Global Entrepreneurship Monitor (Gem) - National Entrepreneurship Assessment United States of America - 2003 Executive Report*. https://papers.ssrn.com/sol3/papers.cfm?abstract_id=1509254

Muñoz, P., Kimmitt, J., Kibler, E., & Farny, S. (2019). Living on the slopes: Entrepreneurial preparedness in a context under continuous threat. *Entrepreneurship and Regional Development*, *31*(5-6), 413–434. doi:10.1080/08985626.2018.1541591

Mustapha, M., & Subramaniam, P. A. (2016). Challenges and Success Factors of Female Entrepreneurs: Evidence from a Developing Country. *International Review of Management and Marketing*, *6*(4S), 224–231. https://econjournals.com/index.php/irmm/article/view/2492

Nasir, M. (2020). The Influence of Social Presence on Students' Satisfaction toward Online Course. *Open Praxis*, *12*(4), 485. doi:10.5944/openpraxis.12.4.1141

Nawang, W. M. Z. W., Mamat, I., & Sa'at, N. H. (2018). The Relationship between Predictor Factors and Career Inclination of Entrepreneurship among Program Tunas Niaga Members. *Akademika.*, *88*, 19–31.

Nieman, G. (2014). *Entrepreneurship: A SouthAfrican Perspective* (3rd ed.). Van Schaik.

Nor, Z. M., & Ramli, Z. (2016). A Glimpse at Women Entrepreneurs in Penang. *Akademika,* (86), 79-86. 1 doi:0.17576/akad-2016-8602-06

Nwaoga, C. T., & Omeke, F. C. (2012). Entrepreneurship and Employability Among Nigerian Graduates. *Mediterranean Journal of Social Sciences*, *3*(16), 68.

Okolie, U. C., Igwe, P. A., Ayoola, A. A., Nwosu, H. E., Kanu, C., & Mong, I. K. (2021). Entrepreneurial competencies of undergraduate students: The case of universities in Nigeria. *International Journal of Management Education, 19*(1), 100452. doi:10.1016/j.ijme.2021.100452

Overbeke, K. K., Bilimoria, D., & Somers, T. (2015). Shared vision between fathers and daughters in family businesses: The determining factor that transforms daughters into successors. *Frontiers in Psychology, 6*. Advance online publication. doi:10.3389/fpsyg.2015.00625 PMID:26074830

Patil, P., & Deshpande, Y. (2019). Why Women Enter into Entrepreneurship? An Exploratory Study. *Journal of Organisational Studies and Innovation,* (6), 30-40. https://www.researchgate.net/publication/334389192_Why_Women_Enter_Into_Entrepreneurship_An_Exploratory_Study#fullTextFileContentiv

Patterson, J. M. (2002). Understanding family resilience. *Journal of Clinical Psychology, 58*(3), 233–246. doi:10.1002/jclp.10019 PMID:11836706

Pérez-López, M. C., González-López, M. J., & Rodríguez-Ariza, L. (2016). Competencies for entrepreneurship as a career option in a challenging employment environment. *Career Development International, 21*(3), 214–229. doi:10.1108/CDI-07-2015-0102

Ramadani, V., Hisrich, R. D., & Rashiti, S. G. (2015). Female entrepreneurs in transition economies: Insights from Albania, Macedonia and Kosovo. *World Review of Entrepreneurship, Management and Sustainable Development, 11*(4), 391. doi:10.1504/WREMSD.2015.072066

Rauch, A., & Frese, M. (2000). Psychological approaches to entrepreneurial success. *International Review of Industrial and Organizational Psychology*, 101–142. https://research.rug.nl/en/publications/psychological-approaches-to-entrepreneurial-success

Rhee & White. (2017). The relationship between the emotional intelligence of entrepreneurs and the new venture creation: The role of age, gender and motive. *Arab Economic and Business Journal, 12*(2), 99–108. doi:10.1016/j.aebj.2017.10.002

Rosti, L., & Chelli, F. (2005). Gender Discrimination, Entrepreneurial Talent and Self-Employment. *Small Business Economics, 24*(2), 131–142. doi:10.100711187-003-3804-5

Salisu, A. A., Sikiru, A. A., & Vo, X. V. (2020). *Pandemics and the emerging stock markets*. Borsa Istanbul Review. doi:10.1016/j.bir.2020.11.004

Sarasvathy, S. D. (2001). Causation and Effectuation: Toward a Theoretical Shift from Economic Inevitability to Entrepreneurial Contingency. *Academy of Management Review*, *26*(2), 243–263. doi:10.2307/259121

Schumpeter, J., & Opie, R. (1934). *The theory of economic development; an inquiry into profits, capital, credit, interest, and the business cycle*. Harvard University Press.

Scott, J. W. (1986). Gender: A Useful Category of Historical Analysis. *The American Historical Review*, *91*(5), 1053–1075. doi:10.2307/1864376

Shane, S., & Venkataraman, S. (2000). The Promise of Enterpreneurship as a Field of Research. *Academy of Management Review*, *25*(1), 217–226. doi:10.2307/259271

Southwick, S. M., Bonanno, G. A., Masten, A. S., Panter-Brick, C., & Yehuda, R. (2014). Resilience definitions, theory, and challenges: Interdisciplinary Perspectives. *European Journal of Psychotraumatology*, *5*(1), 25338. doi:10.3402/ejpt.v5.25338 PMID:25317257

St-Arnaud, L., & Giguère, É. (2018). Women entrepreneurs, individual and collective work–family interface strategies and emancipation. *International Journal of Gender and Entrepreneurship*, *10*(4), 198–223. doi:10.1108/IJGE-09-2017-0058

Startienė, G., & Remeikienė, R. (2008). Gender Gap in Entrepreneurship. *The Engineering Economist*, *60*(5). https://inzeko.ktu.lt/index.php/EE/article/view/11596

Stephens, W. D. (2021). *Arranging Resilience: The role of social actors in preventing violent extremism.* https://research.vu.nl/en/publications/arranging-resilience-the-role-of-social-actors-in-preventing-viol

Sterbenk, Y., Champlin, S., Windels, K., & Shelton, S. (2021). Is Femvertising the New Greenwashing? Examining Corporate Commitment to Gender Equality. *Journal of Business Ethics*. Advance online publication. doi:10.100710551-021-04755-x

Tripoli, A. M. (1998). Planning and allocating: Strategies for managing priorities in complex jobs. *European Journal of Work and Organizational Psychology*, *7*(4), 455–476. doi:10.1080/135943298398501

Ungar, M. (2013). Resilience, Trauma, Context, and Culture. *Trauma, Violence & Abuse*, *14*(3), 255–266. doi:10.1177/1524838013487805 PMID:23645297

Value and Supply Chain Development. (2007). European Economic and Social Committee.

Van Praag, M., & Versloot, P. H. (2008). *The Economic Benefits and Costs of Entrepreneurship: A Review of the Research.* https://papers.ssrn.com/sol3/papers.cfm?abstract_id=1625828

Verheul, I., & Thurik, R. (2001). Start-Up Capital: "Does Gender Matter? *Small Business Economics, 16*(4), 329–346. doi:10.1023/A:1011178629240

Verheul, I., van Stel, A., & Thurik, R. (2004, February 1). *Explaining female and male entrepreneurship across 29 countries.* https://ideas.repec.org/p/esi/egpdis/2004-08.html

Watson, T. J. (2002). Reviews. *Management Learning, 33*(3), 407–410. doi:10.1177/1350507602333009

Welsh, D. H. B., Kaciak, E., & Shamah, R. (2018). Determinants of women entrepreneurs' firm performance in a hostile environment. *Journal of Business Research, 88*, 481–491. doi:10.1016/j.jbusres.2017.12.015

Zikmund, W. G., Babin, B. J., Carr, J. C., & Griffin, M. (2013). *Business Research Methods*. Cengage Learning.

Compilation of References

Mohammad, S., & Pourdavar, S. (2010). Penetration test: A case study on remote command execution security hole. *2010 Fifth International Conference on Digital Information Management (ICDIM)*, 412-416. 10.1109/ICDIM.2010.5664671

Alam, D., Bhuiyan, T., Kabir, M. A., & Farah, T. (2015). SQLi vulnerability in education sector websites of Bangladesh. *2015 Second International Conference on Information Security and Cyber Forensics (InfoSec)*, 152-157. 10.1109/InfoSec.2015.7435521

Sommestad, T., Holm, H., & Ekstedt, M. (2012). Estimates of success rates of remote arbitrary code execution attacks. *Information Management & Computer Security*, *20*(2), 107–122. doi:10.1108/09685221211235625

Wu, J., Arrott, A., & Osorio, F. C. C. (2014). Protection against remote code execution exploits of popular applications in Windows. *2014 9th International Conference on Malicious and Unwanted Software: The Americas (MALWARE)*, 26-31. 10.1109/MALWARE.2014.6999416

Huluka, D., & Popov, O. (2012). Root cause analysis of session management and broken authentication vulnerabilities. *World Congress on Internet Security (WorldCIS-2012)*, 82-86.

Zhang, L., Zhang, H., Zhang, X., & Chen, L. (2007). A New Mechanism for Trusted Code Remote Execution. *2007 International Conference on Computational Intelligence and Security Workshops (CISW 2007)*, 574-578. 10.1109/CISW.2007.4425561

Internet World Stats. (2017, December). *Internet global Stats*. https://www.internetworldstats.com/stats.htm

Cavusoglu, H., Mishra, B., & Raghunathan, S. (2004). The effect of internet security breach announcements on market value: Capital market reactions for breached firms and internet security developers. *International Journal of Electronic Commerce*, *9*(1), 70–104. doi:10.1080/10864415.2004.11044320

Madan, B. B., Gogeva-Popstojanova, K., Vaidyanathan, K., & Trivedi, K. S. (2002). Modelling, and quantification of security attributes of software systems. In *International Conference on Dependable Systems and Networks*. IEEE Computer Society. 10.1109/DSN.2002.1028941

Homer, J., Manhattan, K., Ou, X., & Schmidt, D. (2009). *A Sound and Practical Approach to Quantifying Security Risk in Enterprise Networks*. Citeseer.

Stepankin, M. (2015). *Remote Code Execution Vulnerability*. Retrieved 2022 from https://artsploit.blogspot.com/2016/01/paypal-rce.html

Shcherbakov, M., & Musard, B. (2021). Serial Detector: Principled and Practical Exploration of Object Injection Vulnerabilities for the Web. *Network and Distributed System Security Symposium (NDSS'21)*. 10.14722/ndss.2021.24550

CVE-2022-30190. (n.d.). https://msrc-blog.microsoft.com/2022/05/30/guidance-for-cve-2022-30190-microsoft-support- diagnostic-tool-vulnerability/

Takamatsu, Y., Kosuga, Y., & Konno, K. (2012). Automated detection of session management vulnerabilities in web applications. *2012 Tenth Annual International Conference on Privacy, Security and Trust*, 112-119. 10.1109/PST.2012.6297927

Mahmoud, Q. H., Kauling, D., & Zanin, S. (2017). *Hidden android permissions: Remote code execution and shell access using a live wallpaper. In 2017 14th IEEE Annual Consumer Communications & Networking Conference*. CCNC.

Abbas, T., Abrar, M., Saleem, R., & Iqbal, A. (2016). What Leads to Success for Women Entrepreneurs? An Empirical Study of Southern Punjab in Pakistan. *Academic Research International*, *7*, 120–130.

Abdulazeez, D. A., Ndibe, L., & Mercy, A. M. (2016). Corporate governance and financial performance of listed deposit money banks in Nigeria. *Journal of Account Mark*, *5*(1), 1–6.

Abdullah, H., & Valentine, B. (2009). Fundamental and ethics theories of corporate governance. *Middle Eastern Finance, and Economics*, *4*, 89–96.

Abdulshaheed, A., Mustapha, F., & Ghavamian, A. (2017). A pressure-based method for monitoring leaks in a pipe distribution system: A Review. *Renewable & Sustainable Energy Reviews*, *69*, 902–911. doi:10.1016/j.rser.2016.08.024

Abilasha, N. (2019). Impact of CSR on the financial performance of top 10 performing CSR companies in India. *Journal of Economics and Finance*, *10*(2), 49–55.

Abootorabi Zarchi, H., Mosaddegh Hesar, H., & Ayaz Khoshhava, M. (2019). Online maximum torque per power losses strategy for indirect rotor flux-oriented control-based induction motor drives. IET Electric Power Applications, 13(2), 259-265. doi:10.1049/iet-epa.2018.5403

About – Sutrakaar Creations. (n.d.). Retrieved December 13, 2022, from https://sutrakaar.in/about-sutrakaar/

Adams, R., Jeanrenaud, S., Bessant, J., Denyer, D., & Overy, P. (2016). Sustainability-oriented Innovation. *Systematic Reviews*, *18*, 180–205. doi:10.1111/ijmr.12068

Aditya, K. S., Subash, S. P., Praveen, K. V., Nithyashree, M. L., Bhuvana, N., & Sharma, A. (2017). Awareness about minimum support price and its impact on diversification decision of farmers in India. *Asia & the Pacific Policy Studies*, *4*(3), 514–526. doi:10.1002/app5.197

AdrieReinders, M. (2019). *The E factor, entrpreneurship in the social media age.* BenBella.

Agarwal, R., & Shah, S. K. (2014). Knowledge sources of entrepreneurship: Firm formation by academic, user and employee innovators. *Research Policy*, *43*(7), 1109–1133. doi:10.1016/j.respol.2014.04.012

Ahmad. (2012). Relationship between employability and graduates' skill. *International Business Management, 6*(4), 440-445.

Ahmed, S. (2004). Affective Economies. *Social Text, 22*(2), 117-139.

Ahmed, E., & Hamdan, A. (2015). The effect of corporate governance on firm performance: Evidence from Bahrain Exchange. *European Journal of Business and Innovation Research*, *3*(5), 25–48.

Ajala, O. A., Amuda, T., & Arulogun, L. (2012). Evaluating the effects of corporate governance on the performance of Nigerian banking sector. *Review of Contemporary Business Research*, *1*(1), 32–42.

Ajit, V. (2013). Factors Impacting Employability Skills of Engineers. *International Journal of Science and Research.*

Akingunola, R. O., Olusegun, B., & Adedipe, E. (2013). Corporate governance and banks performance in Nigeria (post bank consolidation). *European Journal of Business and Social Sciences*, *2*(8).

Al Qahtani, T., Yaakob, M. S., Yidris, N., Sulaiman, S., & Ahmad, K. A. (2020). A Review on Water Leakage Detection Method in the Water Distribution Network. *J. Adv. Res. Fluid Mech. Therm. Sci*, *68*(2), 152–163. doi:10.37934/arfmts.68.2.152163

Alam, S. S., Senik, Z. C., & Jani, F. M. (2012). An Exploratory Study of Women Entrepreneurs in Malaysia: Motivation and Problems. *Journal of Management Research*, *4*(4). Advance online publication. doi:10.5296/jmr.v4i4.2377

Albort-Morant, G., Hervas-Oliver, J. L., & Roig-Tierno, N. (2019). Artificial intelligence and blockchain: A multidisciplinary exploration for future sustainable cities. *Journal of Cleaner Production*, *214*, 799–808.

Alexander, V. N., & Matts, R. (2003). *Corporate governance mechanisms and firm performance: Evidence from Finland.* Working Papers 497, Hanken School of Economics.

Ali, Hannan, & Mohamed. (2016). Improved indirect field-oriented control of induction motor drive based pso algorithm. *Jurnal Teknologi, 78*(6-2).

Allen, J. P. (2019). *Digital Entrepreneurship*. Taylor & Francis. doi:10.4324/9780429506567

AL-Najjar, D. (2015). The effects of institutional ownership on firm performance: Evidence from Jordanian listed firms. *International Journal of Economics and Finance*, *7*(12), 97–105. doi:10.5539/ijef.v7n12p97

Alsos, G. A., Isaksen, E. J., & Ljunggren, E. (2006). New Venture Financing and Subsequent Business Growth in Men- and Women-Led Businesses. *Entrepreneurship Theory and Practice*, *30*(5), 667–686. doi:10.1111/j.1540-6520.2006.00141.x

Altenburg, T., & Pegels, A. (2012). *Sustainability-oriented innovation systems – Managing the green transformation.* doi:10.1080/2157930X.2012.664037

American Psychological Association. (2012, January 1). *2012 Impact of Stress.* https://www.apa.org/news/press/releases/stress/2012/impact

Amit, R., & Muller, E. (1995). "Push" and "pull" entrepreneurship. *Journal of Small Business and Entrepreneurship*, *12*(4), 64–80. doi:10.1080/08276331.1995.10600505

Amu, C. U., Nwezeaku, N. C., Akujuobi, L. E., Ozurunba, B. A., Njie, S. N., Wogu, I. A., & Misra, S. (2019). The Politics of Public Debt Management Among Rising Hegemonies and the Role of ICT: Implications for Theory and Practice for 21st Century Polities. *International Journal of Electronic Government Research*, *15*(3), 72–83. doi:10.4018/IJEGR.2019070105

Andrei, S., & Robert, W. V. (1997). A survey of corporate governance. *The Journal of Finance*, *52*(2), 737–783. doi:10.1111/j.1540-6261.1997.tb04820.x

Anonymous. (2016). *Impact of crop diversification on food security and farmers' income in Himachal Pradesh crop diversification promotion project area lessons learnt and vision 2030.* Department of Agricultural Economics, Extension Education & Rural Sociology, College of Agriculture, CSK Himachal Pradesh Krishi Vishvavidyalaya.

Arellano, M., & Bond, S. (1991). Some test of specification for panel data: Monte Carlo evidence and an application to employment equations. *The Review of Economic Studies*, *58*(2), 277–297. doi:10.2307/2297968

Arora, B., Nambisan, S., & Sebastian, I. M. (2020). Coordinating innovation in digital ecosystems: A strategic perspective. *The Academy of Management Perspectives*, *34*(2), 169–186.

Arunmozhi, M., Venkatesh, V. G., Arisian, S., Shi, Y., & Sreedharan, V. R. (2022). Application of blockchain and smart contracts in autonomous vehicle supply chains: An experimental design. *Transportation Research Part E, Logistics and Transportation Review*, *165*, 102864. doi:10.1016/j.tre.2022.102864

Arun, T. G., Almahrog, Y. E., & Ali-Aribi, Z. (2015). Female directors and earnings management: Evidence from UK companies. *International Review of Financial Analysis*, *39*, 137–146. doi:10.1016/j.irfa.2015.03.002

Ayala, J.-C., & Manzano, G. (2014). The resilience of the entrepreneur. Influence on the success of the business. A longitudinal analysis. *Journal of Economic Psychology*, *42*, 126–135. doi:10.1016/j.joep.2014.02.004

Babatunde, M. A., & Olaniran, O. (2009). The effects of internal and external mechanisms on governance and performance of corporate firms in Nigeria. *Corporate Ownership and Control*, *7*(3), 330–344. doi:10.22495/cocv7i2c3p1

Bach, P. M., & Kodikara, J. K. (2017). Reliability of infrared thermography in detecting leaks in buried water reticulation pipes. *IEEE Journal of Selected Topics in Applied Earth Observations and Remote Sensing*, *10*(9), 4210–4224. doi:10.1109/JSTARS.2017.2708817

Balakrishnan Selvakumaran, S., & Hall, D. M. (2022). From crowd to cloud: Simplified automatic reconstruction of digital building assets for facility management. *Journal of Facilities Management*, *20*(3), 401–436. doi:10.1108/JFM-02-2021-0017

Balhara, S., & Singh, D. A. (2015). Women Entrepreneurship: A Big Motivation. *Business and Economic Review*, *5*(2), 207–216.

Bamgbade, J. A., Nawi, M. N. M., Kamaruddeen, A. M., Adeleke, A. Q., & Salimon, M. G. (2022). Building sustainability in the construction industry through firm capabilities, technology and business innovativeness: empirical evidence from Malaysia. *International Journal of Construction Management, 22*(3), 473-488.

Bardhi, F., & Eckhardt, G. M. (2012). Access-Based Consumption: The Case of Car Sharing. *The Journal of Consumer Research*, *39*(4), 881–898. doi:10.1086/666376

Barile, S., Orecchini, F., Saviano, M., & Farioli, F. (2018). People, technology, and governance for sustainability: The contribution of systems and cyber-systemic thinking. *Sustainability Science*, *13*(5), 1197–1208. doi:10.100711625-018-0621-y

Barnes, S. J., & Mattsson, J. (2016). Understanding current and future issues in collaborative consumption: A four-stage Delphi study. *Technological Forecasting and Social Change*, *104*, 200–211. doi:10.1016/j.techfore.2016.01.006

Barney, J. B. (2002). Strategic management: From informed conversation to academic discipline. *The Academy of Management Perspectives*, *16*(2), 53–57. doi:10.5465/ame.2002.7173521

Baron, D. P. (2007). Corporate Social Responsibility and Social Entrepreneurship. *Journal of Economics & Management Strategy*, *16*(3), 683–717. doi:10.1111/j.1530-9134.2007.00154.x

Barrett, A., & Beeson, J. (2002). *Developing leaders for 2010*. The Conference Board.

Beckman, S. L., & Berry, M. (2007). Management. *California Management Review*, *50*(1), 25–56. doi:10.2307/41166415 PMID:19354009

Belk, R., & Llamas, R. (2012). The nature and effects of sharing in consumer behavior. *Transformative Consumer Research for Personal and Collective Well-Being*, 625–646.

Belk, R. (2014a). Sharing versus pseudo-sharing in web 2.0. *Anthropologist*, *18*(1), 7–23. doi:10.1080/09720073.2014.11891518

Belk, R. (2014b). You are what you can access: Sharing and collaborative consumption online. *Journal of Business Research, 67*(8), 1595–1600. doi:10.1016/j.jbusres.2013.10.001

Ben Eli, M. U. (2018). Sustainability: Definition and five core principles, a systems perspective. *Sustainability Science, 13*(5), 1337–1343. doi:10.100711625-018-0564-3

Benoit, S., Baker, T. L., Bolton, R. N., Gruber, T., & Kandampully, J. (2017). A triadic framework for collaborative consumption (CC): Motives, activities and resources & capabilities of actors. *Journal of Business Research, 79*(May), 219–227. doi:10.1016/j.jbusres.2017.05.004

Berghe, V. D., & Baelden, T. (2005). The complex relation between director independence and board effectiveness. *Corporate Governance, 5*(5), 61–83.

Berle, G. (1991). *The Green Entrepreneur: Business Opportunities that Can Save the Earth and Make You Money* (1st ed.). Liberty Hall Press.

Bernard, A. B., & Jensen, J. B. (1999). Exceptional exporter performance: Cause, effect, or both? *Journal of International Economics, 47*(1), 1–25. doi:10.1016/S0022-1996(98)00027-0

Bhattacharyya, N., Mawani, A., & Morrill, C. (2008). Dividend payout and executive compensation: Theory and evidence. *Accounting and Finance, 48*(4), 521–541.

Bilgin, B., & Emadi, A. (2014). Electric motors in electrified transportation: A step toward achieving a sustainable and highly efficient transportation system. *IEEE Power Electronics Magazine, 1*(2), 10–17. doi:10.1109/MPEL.2014.2312275

Billingsley, J., Lipsey, N. P., Burnette, J. L., & Pollack, J. M. (2021). Growth mindsets: Defining, assessing, and exploring effects on motivation for entrepreneurs and non-entrepreneurs. *Current Psychology (New Brunswick, N.J.)*. Advance online publication. doi:10.100712144-021-02149-w

Blesa, J., & Pérez, R. (2018). Modelling uncertainty for leak localization in water networks. *IFAC-PapersOnLine, 51*(24), 730–735. doi:10.1016/j.ifacol.2018.09.656

Böcker, L., & Meelen, T. (2017). Sharing for people, planet or profit? Analysing motivations for intended sharing economy participation. *Environmental Innovation and Societal Transitions, 23*, 28–39. doi:10.1016/j.eist.2016.09.004

Bok, D. (2006). Our Underachieving Colleges. Princeton University Press.

Bonanno, G. A. (2004). Loss, Trauma, and Human Resilience: Have We Underestimated the Human Capacity to Thrive After Extremely Aversive Events? *The American Psychologist, 59*(1), 20–28. doi:10.1037/0003-066X.59.1.20 PMID:14736317

Boretti, A., & Rosa, L. (2019). Reassessing the projections of the world water development report. *NPJ Clean Water, 2*(1), 1–6. doi:10.103841545-019-0039-9

Borisevich, A., & Schullerus, G. (2016). Energy efficient control of an induction machine under torque step changes. *IEEE Transactions on Energy Conversion, 31*(4), 1295–1303. doi:10.1109/TEC.2016.2561307

Bose, B. K. (2002). *Modern power electronics and AC drives* (Vol. 123). Prentice Hall.

Bosma, N., Jones, K., Autio, E., & Levie, J. D. (2007). *Global Entrepreneurship Monitor*. https://pureportal.strath.ac.uk/en/publications/global-entrepreneurship-monitor-2007

Botsman, R., & Rogers, R. (2010). *What's Mine Is Yours: The Rise of Collaborative Consumption*. Academic Press.

Boudreau, K. J., & Jeppesen, L. B. (2021). Digital innovation: Creating shared value in low-resource settings. *Journal of International Business Studies*, *52*(4), 583–602.

Bozhinov, V., Joecks, J., & Scharfenkamp, K. (2021). Gender spillovers from supervisory boards to management boards. *Managerial and Decision Economics*, *42*(5), 1317–1331. Advance online publication. doi:10.1002/mde.3311

Bradbury, H. (2003). *Sustaining inner and outer worlds : A whole-systems approach to developing sustainable business practices in management*. doi:10.1177/1052562903251414

Brem, Behrens, & Baierl. (2019). Digital Entrepreneurship (Interfaces Between Digital Technologies and Entrepreneurship). Springer International Publishing.

Bronfenbrenner, U., & Morris, P. A. (2007). Handbook of Child Psychology: Vol. 1. *The Bioecological Model of Human Development*. doi:10.1002/9780470147658.chpsy0114

Bruner, J. S. (1966). *Toward a theory of instruction*. Harvard University Press.

Brush, C. G., de Bruin, A., & Welter, F. (2009). A gender-aware framework for women's entrepreneurship. *International Journal of Gender and Entrepreneurship*, *1*(1), 8–24. doi:10.1108/17566260910942318

Brush, C., Edelman, L. F., Manolova, T., & Welter, F. (2018). A gendered look at entrepreneurship ecosystems. *Small Business Economics*, *53*(2), 393–408. doi:10.100711187-018-9992-9

Buchanan, R. (2019). Systems Thinking and Design Thinking: The Search for Principles in the World We Are Making. *She Ji*, *5*(2), 85–104. doi:10.1016/j.sheji.2019.04.001

Buczynski, B. (n.d.). *Sharing is Good: How to Save Money*. Time and Resources Through Collaborative Consumption.

Bullough, A., & Renko, M. (2013). Entrepreneurial resilience during challenging times. *Business Horizons*, *56*(3), 343–350. doi:10.1016/j.bushor.2013.01.001

Bullough, A., Renko, M., & Myatt, T. (2013). Danger Zone Entrepreneurs: The Importance of Resilience and Self-Efficacy for Entrepreneurial Intentions. *Entrepreneurship Theory and Practice*, *38*(3), 473–499. doi:10.1111/etap.12006

Bushra, K., & Rabia, T. (2017). Corporate social responsibility impact on the financial performance of Islamic and conventional banks: Evidence from Asian countries. *Research Journal of Finance and Accounting, 8*(7), 20-28. www.iiste.org

Buttner, E. H., & Moore, D. (1997). *Women's Organizational Exodus to Entrepreneurship: Self-Reported Motivations and Correlates with Success*. Academic Press.

Cabrera, D., Colosi, L., & Lobdell, C. (2008). Systems thinking. *Evaluation and Program Planning*, *31*(3), 299–310. doi:10.1016/j.evalprogplan.2007.12.001 PMID:18272224

Cadbury, A. (1992). Report of the committee on the financial aspects of corporate governance. Gee Gee Ltd. (Professional Publishing Ltd.).

Cameron, A. C., & Trivedi, P. K. (2005). *Microeconometrics: Methods and applications*. Cambridge University Press. doi:10.1017/CBO9780511811241

Cappelli, P. (2008). Talent management for the twenty-first century. *Harvard Business Review*, (March), 74–81. PMID:18411966

Carroll, A. B. (1979). A three-dimensional conceptual model of corporate social performance. *Academy of Management Review*, *4*(4), 491–509. doi:10.2307/257850

Carsrud, L. S. (2020). Exploring diversity in enterpreneurship (M. E. Carsrud, Ed.). Springer.

Castaldi, C. (2021). *Sustainable innovation and intellectual property rights: friends, foes or perfect strangers?* (No. 2021/11). LEM Working Paper Series.

Castiblanco Jimenez, I. A., Mauro, S., Napoli, D., Marcolin, F., Vezzetti, E., Rojas Torres, M. C., Specchia, S., & Moos, S. (2021). Design Thinking as a Framework for the Design of a Sustainable Waste Sterilization System: The Case of Piedmont Region, Italy. *Electronics (Basel)*, *10*(21), 2665. doi:10.3390/electronics10212665

Chadha. (2014). Industry's Requirement for Employability of Management Student in Present Scenario. *International Journal of Business Quantitative Economics and Applied Management Research, 1*(3).

Chaganti, R. (1986). *Management in Women-Owned Enterprises*. https://www.semanticscholar.org/paper/Management-in-Women-Ow ned-Enterprises-Chaganti/bdee407ae1009bb88eb9cf2c231b5801e8d 79155

Chan, T. K., Chin, C. S., & Zhong, X. (2018). Review of current technologies and proposed intelligent methodologies for water distributed network leakage detection. *IEEE Access: Practical Innovations, Open Solutions*, *6*, 78846–78867. doi:10.1109/ACCESS.2018.2885444

Chaudhry, S., & Garg, S. (2019). Smart irrigation techniques for water resource management. In *Smart Farming Technologies for Sustainable Agricultural Development* (pp. 196–219). IGI Global. doi:10.4018/978-1-5225-5909-2.ch009

Cheng, M. (2016). Sharing economy: A review and agenda for future research. *International Journal of Hospitality Management*, *57*, 60–70. doi:10.1016/j.ijhm.2016.06.003

Cheng, X., Fu, S., Sun, J., Bilgihan, A., & Okumus, F. (2019). An investigation on online reviews in sharing economy driven hospitality platforms: A viewpoint of trust. *Tourism Management, 71*, 366–377. doi:10.1016/j.tourman.2018.10.020

Chen, Y. (2009). Possession and access: Consumer desires and value perceptions regarding contemporary art collection and exhibit visits. *The Journal of Consumer Research, 35*(6), 925–940. doi:10.1086/593699

Chen, Y.-J., Shanthikumar, J. G., & Shen, Z.-J. M. (2015). Incentive for Peer-to-Peer Knowledge Sharing among Farmers in Developing Economies. *Production and Operations Management, 24*(9), 1430–1440. doi:10.1111/poms.12328

Chesbrough, H. (2018). The future of open innovation: Perspectives on research and practice. *Research Technology Management, 61*(1), 17–26.

Chithra, R. (2013). Employability Skills-A Study on the Perception of the Engineering Students and their Prospective Employers. *Global Journal of Management and Business Studies, 3*(5).

Chung, K. H., & Pruitt, S. W. (1994). A Simple Approximation of Tobin's q. *Financial Management, 23*(3), 70–74. doi:10.2307/3665623

Cliff, J. E. (1998). Does one size fit all? exploring the relationship between attitudes towards growth, gender, and business size. *Journal of Business Venturing, 13*(6), 523–542. doi:10.1016/S0883-9026(97)00071-2

Cody, R., Harmouche, J., & Narasimhan, S. (2018). Leak detection in water distribution pipes using singular spectrum analysis. *Urban Water Journal, 15*(7), 636–644. doi:10.1080/1573062X.2018.1532016

Commission on Sustainable Development, Department of Economic and Social Affairs. (2007). *Indicators of Sustainable Development: Guidelines and Methodologies* (3rd ed.). United Nations.

Conlon, K. (2021). A social systems approach to sustainable waste management: Leverage points for plastic reduction in Colombo, Sri Lanka. *International Journal of Sustainable Development and World Ecology, 00*(00), 1–19. doi:10.1080/13504509.2020.1867252

Conway, R., Masters, J., & Thorold, J. (2017). *From Design Thinking to Systems Change.* RSA Action and Research Centre.

Crick, J. (2016). *The facets, antecedents and consequences of coopetition: An entrepreneurial marketing perspective.* doi:10.1108/QMR-11-2016-0109

Cukier, W., & Hassannezhad Chavoushi, Z. (2020). Facilitating women entrepreneurship in Canada: the case of WEKH. *Gender in Management: An International Journal.* doi:10.1108/gm-11-2019-0204

Cusumano, M. A. (2014). How traditional firms must compete in the sharing economy. *Communications of the ACM, 58*(1), 32–34. doi:10.1145/2688487

Dana, L. P., Salamzadeh, A., Mortazavi, S., & Hadizadeh, M. (2022). Investigating the impact of international markets and new digital technologies on business innovation in emerging markets. *Sustainability*, *14*(2), 983. doi:10.3390u14020983

Dar, L. A., Naseem, M. A., Rehman, R. U., & Niazi, G. S. K. (2011). Corporate governance and firm performance: A case study of Pakistan Oil and Gas Companies listed in Karachi Sick Exchange. *Global Journal of Management and Business Research*, *11*(8).

Deakin, S. A., & Hughes, J. (1997). Board of directors and corporate financial performance: A review and integrative model. *Journal of Management*, *76*(13), 291–334.

Dhall, S., Dwivedi, A. D., Pal, S. K., & Srivastava, G. (2021). Blockchain-based framework for reducing fake or vicious news spread on social media/messaging platforms. *Transactions on Asian and Low-Resource Language Information Processing*, *21*(1), 1–33.

Dhawan, V. (2017, January). Water and agriculture in India. In *Background paper for the South Asia expert panel during the Global Forum for Food and Agriculture (GFFA)* (p. 15). Academic Press.

Diefendorff, J. M., & Lord, R. (2004). Examination of the Roles of Action-State Orientation and Goal Orientation in the Goal-Setting and Performance Process. *Human Performance*, *17*(4), 375–395. doi:10.120715327043hup1704_2

Dijkema, G. P. J., Reuter, M. A., & Verhoef, E. V. (2000). *A new paradigm for waste management*. Academic Press.

Dixon, S. E. A., & Clifford, A. (2007). Ecopreneurship- A new approach to managing the triple bottom line. *Journal of Organizational Change Management*, *20*(3), 326–345. doi:10.1108/09534810710740164

Doern, R. (2016). Entrepreneurship and crisis management: The experiences of small businesses during the London 2011 riots. *International Small Business Journal: Researching Entrepreneurship*, *34*(3), 276–302. doi:10.1177/0266242614553863

Duchek, S. (2018). Entrepreneurial resilience: A biographical analysis of successful entrepreneurs. *The International Entrepreneurship and Management Journal*, *14*(2), 429–455. doi:10.100711365-017-0467-2

Džananović, Đ., & Tandir, N. (2020). Motivational and Limiting Factors for Female Entrepreneurship. *Open Journal for Research in Economics*, *3*(1), 1–8. doi:10.32591/coas.ojre.0301.01001d

Eccles, R. G., & Krzus, M. P. (2010). Integrated reporting for a sustainable strategy: One Report has the potential to significantly change how companies operate and investors think, shifting the focus from meeting short-term financial goals to developing a long-term business strategy that not only commits to corporate social responsibility but also to a sustainable society. *Financial Executive*, *26*(2), 28-33.

Ecoplore - Book your eco-hotel now ! (n.d.). Ecoplore. Retrieved November 13, 2022, from https://ecoplore.com/

EE-HUB. (2017, APRIL). *Policy recommendation*. Retrieved from The Europeon entrpreneurship education network: http://ee-hub.eu/component/attachments/?task=download&id=492:EE-HUB-Policy-Recommendations-web

Effiok, S. O., Effiong, C., & Usoro, A. A. (2012). Corporate governance, corporate strategy, and corporate performance: Evidence from the financial institutions listed on the Nigerian Stock Exchange. *European Journal of Business and Management*, *4*(18), 84–95.

Elavarasan, R. M., Pugazhendhi, R., Shafiullah, G. M., Irfan, M., & Anvari-Moghaddam, A. (2021). A hover view over effectual approaches on pandemic management for sustainable cities–the endowment of prospective technologies with revitalization strategies. *Sustainable Cities and Society*, *68*, 102789. doi:10.1016/j.scs.2021.102789 PMID:35004131

Elia, G., Margherita, A., Ciavolino, E., & Moustaghfir, K. (2021). Digital society incubator: Combining exponential technology and human potential to build resilient entrepreneurial ecosystems. *Administrative Sciences*, *11*(3), 96. doi:10.3390/admsci11030096

Elizabeth, F. A., (2018). Corporate social responsibility and financial performance: An examination of the Dow Jones Sustainability North American Index. *Applied Economics Theses*, 33.

El-Zahab, S., & Zayed, T. (2019). Leak detection in water distribution networks: An introductory overview. *Smart Water*, *4*(1), 5. doi:10.118640713-019-0017-x

Ertz, M., Durif, F., & Arcand, M. (2019). A conceptual perspective on collaborative consumption. *AMS Review*, *9*(1), 27–41. doi:10.100713162-018-0121-3

Etheridge, J. (2019). *No more 'eating' paper? Maties student, 19, wins prize for edible straws*. Academic Press.

European Comission. (2016). Communication from the Commission to the European Parliament, the European Economic and Social Committee of the Regions: A European agenda for the collaborative economy. *Europe Commission*, 16. https://ec.europa.eu/germany/news/kollaborative-wirtschaft-eu-kommission-will-rechtliche-klarheit-für-neue-geschäftsmodelle_de?newsletter_id=188&utm_source=representations_newsletter&utm_medium=email&utm_campaign=EU-Aktuell&utm_content=Kollaborat

Eyenubo, A. S. (2013). The impact of bigger board size on financial performance for firms: The Nigerian experience. *Journal of Research in International Business and Management*, *3*(3), 85–90.

Faludi, J. A. (2017). *Golden Tools in Green Design: What drives sustainability, innovation, and value in green design methods?* [PhD dissertation]. Gradu.

Fama, E., & Jensen, M. (2012). Separation of ownership and control. *The Journal of Law & Economics*, *26*(12), 1–32.

Famogbiele, A. (2012). Failure of the universal banking system in Nigeria: The role of corporate governance. Paper Presented at the *1st Annual International Conference on Accounting, Finance and Management*, Obafemi Awolowo University, Ile Ife.

Fanta, A. B., Kemal, K. S., & Waka, Y. K. (2013). Corporate governance and impact on bank performance. *Journal of Finance and Accounting*, *1*(1), 19–26. doi:10.11648/j.jfa.20130101.12

Farhani, F., Zaafouri, A., & Chaari, A. (2017). Real time induction motor efficiency optimization. *Journal of the Franklin Institute*, *354*(8), 3289–3304. doi:10.1016/j.jfranklin.2017.02.012

Fischer, M. (2015). *Design It! Solving Sustainability Problems by Applying Design Thinking*. Academic Press.

Fischer, E. M., Reuber, A. R., & Dyke, L. S. (1993). A theoretical overview and extension of research on sex, gender, and entrepreneurship. *Journal of Business Venturing*, *8*(2), 151–168. doi:10.1016/0883-9026(93)90017-Y

Flory, J. A., Leibbrandt, A., Rott, C., & Stoddard, O. (2021). Increasing Workplace Diversity: Evidence from a Recruiting Experiment at a Fortune 500 Company. *The Journal of Human Resources*, *56*(1), 73–92. doi:10.3368/jhr.56.1.0518-9489R1

Franco, P. L., & Christie, L. M. (2021). Effectiveness of a one day self-compassion training for pediatric nurses' resilience. *Journal of Pediatric Nursing*, *61*, 109–114. doi:10.1016/j.pedn.2021.03.020 PMID:33839602

Freeman, R. E., Wicks, A. C., & Parmar, B. (2004). Stakeholder theory and corporate objective revisited. *Organization Science*, *15*(3), 364–369. doi:10.1287/orsc.1040.0066

Frenken, K., & Schor, J. (2017). Putting the sharing economy into perspective. *Environmental Innovation and Societal Transitions*, *23*, 3–10. doi:10.1016/j.eist.2017.01.003

Fugate, D. L., & Jefferson, R. W. (2001). Preparing for globalization: Do we need structural change for our academic programs? *Journal of Education for Business*, *76*(3), 160–166. doi:10.1080/08832320109601304

Ganguli, S. K., & Agrawal, S. (2009). Ownership structure and firm performance : An empirical study on listed mid-cap Indian companies. *The IUP Journal of Applied Finance*, *15*(12), 37–52.

García Lara, J. M., García Osma, B., Mora, A., & Scapin, M. (2017). The monitoring role of female directors over accounting quality. *Journal of Corporate Finance*, *45*, 651–668. doi:10.1016/j.jcorpfin.2017.05.016

Garriga, E., & Melé, D. (2004). Corporate social responsibility theories: Mapping the territory. *Journal of Business Ethics*, *53*(1/2), 51–71. doi:10.1023/B:BUSI.0000039399.90587.34

Gavetti, G., & Abecassis-Moedas, C. (2019). Learning and adapting in platform ecosystems: The rise of new technologies and entrepreneurial ventures. *Academy of Management Journal*, *62*(4), 1090–1099.

Gaziulusoy, İ., & Öztekin, E. E. (2019). Design for sustainability transitions: Origins, attitudes and future directions. *Sustainability (Switzerland)*, *11*(13), 3601. Advance online publication. doi:10.3390u11133601

George, T. P., & Karibo, B. B. (2014). Corporate governance mechanisms and financial performance of listed firms in Nigeria: A Content Analysis. *Global Journal of Contemporary Research in Accounting, Auditing and Business Ethics*, *1*(2).

Germann Molz, J. (2013). Social networking technologies and the moral economy of alternative tourism: the case of couchsurfing.org. *Annals of Tourism Research*, *43*, 210–230. doi:10.1016/j.annals.2013.08.001

Gertsakis, J., & Lewis, H. (2003). Sustainability and the Waste Management Hierarchy. *EcoRecycle Victoria*.

Gerwe, O., & Silva, R. (2020). Clarifying the sharing economy: Conceptualization, typology, antecedents, and effects. *The Academy of Management Perspectives*, *34*(1), 65–96. doi:10.5465/amp.2017.0010

Ghasemkhani, H., Li, Y.-M., Moinzadeh, K., & Tan, Y. (2018). Contracting Models for P2P Content Distribution. *Production and Operations Management*, *27*(11), 1940–1959. doi:10.1111/poms.12718

Ghazinoory, S., Yousefi, M., & Ghazinoori, S. S. (2020). The role of social media in entrepreneurial ecosystems: A systematic literature review. *Technology in Society*, *62*, 101315.

Göcke, Soltanifar, & Hughes. (2020). *Digital Entrepreneurship*. Springer International Publishing.

Godelnik, R. (2017). Millennials and the sharing economy: Lessons from a 'buy nothing new, share everything month' project. *Environmental Innovation and Societal Transitions*, *23*, 40–52. doi:10.1016/j.eist.2017.02.002

Gollwitzer, P. M. (1996). The volitional benefits of planning. In P. M. Gollwitzer & J. A. Bargh (Eds.), *Linking cognition and motivation to behavior* (pp. 287–312). The psychology of action. The Guilford Press.

Gompers, P., Ishii, J., & Metric, A. (2003). Corporate governance and prices. *The Quarterly Journal of Economics*, *118*(1), 107–155. doi:10.1162/00335530360535162

González-López, M. J., Pérez-López, M. C., & Rodríguez-Ariza, L. (2019). Clearing the Hurdles in the Entrepreneurial Race: The Role of Resilience in Entrepreneurship Education. *Academy of Management Learning & Education*, *18*(3), 457–483. doi:10.5465/amle.2016.0377

Gopalakrishnan, S., & Matthews, D. (2018). Collaborative consumption: A business model analysis of second-hand fashion. *Journal of Fashion Marketing and Management*, *22*(3), 354–368. doi:10.1108/JFMM-05-2017-0049

Gorgievski, M. J., & Stephan, U. (2016). Advancing the psychology of entrepreneurship: A review of the psychological literature and an introduction. *Applied Psychology*, *65*(3), 437–468. doi:10.1111/apps.12073

Goudin, P. (2016). The Cost of Non-Europe in the Sharing Economy: Economic, Social and Legal Challenges and Opportunities. European Parliamentary Research Service.

Griffiths, R. (2013). *The great sharing economy*. Co-Operatives UK.

Gul, F. A., Srinidhi, B., & Tsui, J. (2007). *Do female directors enhance corporate board monitoring? Some evidence from earnings quality*. Working Paper, the Hong Kong Polytechnic University.

Gull, A. A., Nekhili, M., Nagati, H., & Chtioui, T. (2018). Beyond gender diversity: How specific attributes of female directors affect earnings management. *The British Accounting Review*, *50*(3), 255–274. doi:10.1016/j.bar.2017.09.001

Guyader, H., & Kienzler, M. (2019). "True Sharing" or "Sharing Economy" Fad? In A. G. B. Edvardsson Mary Jo Bitner & R. Verma (Eds.), *QUIS16 symposium: "Advancing Service Research and Practice", 10-13 June 2019*. CTF Service Research Center, Karlstad University. http://urn.kb.se/resolve?urn=urn:nbn:se:liu:diva-160319

Habbash, M. (2010). *The effectiveness of corporate governance and external audit on constraining earnings management practice in the UK* [Doctoral thesis]. Durham University.

Habibi, M. R., Kim, A., & Laroche, M. (2016). From sharing to exchange: An extended framework of dual modes of collaborative nonownership consumption. *Journal of the Association for Consumer Research*, *1*(2), 277–294. doi:10.1086/684685

Hamari, J., Sjöklint, M., & Ukkonen, A. (2016). The sharing economy: Why people participate in collaborative consumption. *Journal of the Association for Information Science and Technology*, *67*(9), 2047–2059. doi:10.1002/asi.23552

Hamilton, E. (2013). The discourse of entrepreneurial masculinities (and femininities). *Entrepreneurship and Regional Development*, *25*(1-2), 90–99. doi:10.1080/08985626.2012.746879

Hansen, E. G., & Grosse-dunker, F. (n.d.). *Sustainability Innovation Cube – A framework to evaluate sustainability of product innovations*. Academic Press.

Hari Prasad, N. (2014). Alarming Employability Skills Deficiency among Budding Engineering Graduates – A study on engineering graduates in Chittoor district. *SAMZODHANA – Journal of Management Research, 3*(1).

Harvey, J., Smith, A., Goulding, J., & Illodo, I. B. (2020). Food sharing, redistribution, and waste reduction via mobile applications: A social network analysis. *Industrial Marketing Management*, *88*, 437–448. doi:10.1016/j.indmarman.2019.02.019

Heinrichs, H. (2013). Sharing economy: A potential new pathway to sustainability. *GAIA - Ecological Perspectives for Science and Society, 22*(4), 228–231. doi:10.14512/gaia.22.4.5

Hermalin, B. E., & Weisback, M. S. (2003). *Board of Directors as an Endogenously Determined Institution: A Survey of the Economic Literature*. Center for Responsible Business. Working Paper Series; Paper 3.

Hesari, S., & Hoseini, A. (2017). A New Approach to Improve Induction Motor Performance in Light-Load Conditions. *Journal of Electrical Engineering & Technology*, *12*(3), 1195–1202. doi:10.5370/JEET.2017.12.3.1195

Hockerts, K., & Wüstenhagen, R. (2021). The role of innovation in creating a sustainable future. *Nature Reviews Sustainable Business*, *4*(1), 7–9.

Holling, C. S. (2001). Understanding the complexity of economic, ecological, and social systems. *Ecosystems*, *4*(5), 390–405. doi:10.100710021-001-0101-5

Holzmann, P., & Gregori, P. (2023). The promise of digital technologies for sustainable entrepreneurship: A systematic literature review and research agenda. *International Journal of Information Management*, *68*, 102593. doi:10.1016/j.ijinfomgt.2022.102593

Hopkins, M. S. (2010). How sustainability fuels design innovation. *MIT Sloan Management Review*, *52*(1), 75–81.

Horst, S.-O. (n.d.). *Digital Media Entrepreneurship: Implications for Strategic Identity Work and Knowledge Sharing of Beginning*. Academic Press.

Hossain. (2021). A Study of Women Manager's Success Factors in Multinational Organisation from Bangladesh Perspective. *Bangladesh Journal of Multidisciplinary Scientific Research*, 28–40. doi:10.46281/bjmsr.v3i2.1196

Humanising fashion. (n.d.). Retrieved August 12, 2022, from https://www.ecokaari.org/

Huynh, H. X., Huynh, N. T., Huynh, T. P., Van Tran, S., & Nguyen, L. T. T. (2018). Simulating the Irrigation Operations with Cellular Automata. In *Context-Aware Systems and Applications, and Nature of Computation and Communication* (pp. 195–210). Springer.

Idris, N. A., & Daud, N. A. (2014). Aktiviti hilirin di kawasan FELDA: Analisis faktor pendorong penglibatan wanita dalam aktiviti perniagaan. *Prosiding PERKEM ke,* (9), 467-476.

Imam, M.O. (2006). *Firm Performance and Corporate Governance through Ownership Structure: Evidence from Bangladesh Stock Market*. Academic Press.

Irshad, R., Hashmi, S. H., Kausar, S., & Nazir, M. I. (2015). Board effectiveness, ownership structure, and corporate governance: Evidence from Pakistan. *Journal of Business Studies Quarterly*, *7*(2), 46–60.

Isaak, R. (2002). The Making of the Ecopreneur. In *Greener Management International* (pp. 81–91). Greenleaf Publishing Limited.

Iskander, M. O., & Chamlou, N. (2000). *Corporate governance: A framework for implementation*. The World Bank Group. doi:10.1596/0-8213-4741-1

Ismail, N. N. H. M., Nasir, M. K. M., & Rahman, R. S. A. R. A. (2021). Factors That Influence Women to Be Involved in Entrepreneurship: A Case Study in Malaysia. *Creative Education*, *12*(04), 837–847. doi:10.4236/ce.2021.124060

Jaaron, A. A. M., & Backhouse, C. J. (2018). Operationalisation of service innovation: A systems thinking approach. *Service Industries Journal*, *38*(9–10), 561–583. doi:10.1080/02642069.2017.1411480

Jain. (2013). Globalization and Developing Employability Skills: Challenges and their Solutions with Reference to NPSD & Government's Action Plan and role of Life Long Learning and Extension Departments. *Journal of Business Management & Social Sciences Research, 2*(5).

Javadiha, M., Blesa, J., Soldevila, A., & Puig, V. (2019, April). Leak localization in water distribution networks using deep learning. In *2019 6th International Conference on Control, Decision and Information Technologies (CoDIT)* (pp. 1426-1431). IEEE. 10.1109/CoDIT.2019.8820627

Jay, J., & Gerand, M. (2015). *MIT Sloan School of Management Accelerating the Theory and Practice of Sustainability-Oriented Innovation Accelerating the Theory and Practice of Sustainability-Oriented Innovation*. Academic Press.

Jensen, M. C. (1993). The modern industrial revolution, exit the failure of internal control systems. *The Journal of Finance, 48*(3), 831–880. doi:10.1111/j.1540-6261.1993.tb04022.x

Jensen, M. C., & Meckling, W. H. (1976). Theory of the firm: Managerial behavior, agency costs, and ownership structure. *Journal of Financial Economics, 3*(4), 305–360. doi:10.1016/0304-405X(76)90026-X

Johari, N. H., Saleh, N. M., Jaafar, R., & Hassan, M. S. (2008). The Influence of Board Independence, Competency and Ownership on Earnings Management in Malaysia. *International Journal of Economics and Management, 2*(2), 281–306.

Jonas, S. (2020, Sept. 9). Discarded tyres turned into treasured furniture. *New Frame.*

Jose, M. L., Nichols, L. M., & Stevens, J. L. (1986). Contributions of diversification, promotion, and research &development to the value of multiproduct firms: A Tobin's q Approach. *Financial Management, 15*(4), 33–42. doi:10.2307/3665778

Kajola, S. O. (2008). Corporate governance and firm performance: The case of Nigerian listed firms. *European Journal of Economics, Finance, and Administrative Sciences, 14.*

Kakabadse, N. K., Yang, H., & Sanders, R. (2010). The effectiveness of non-executive directors in Chinese state-owned enterprises. *Management Decision, 48*(7), 1063–1079. doi:10.1108/00251741011068770

Kamrani, A. K., & Parast, M. M. (2021). A systematic review of the Industry 4.0 framework: Research directions and challenges. *International Journal of Production Research, 59*(5), 1285–1306.

Kapoor, E. (2022, September 12). *This Amazon grant-winning startup is saving the environment, one tote bag at a time*. Business Insider. Retrieved September 15, 2022, from https://www.businessinsider.in/sustainability/news/this-amazo n-grant-winning-startup-is-saving-the-environment-one-tote-b ag-at-a-time/articleshow/94071570.cms

Kapoor, A. P., & Vij, M. (2021). Want it, rent it: Exploring attributes leading to conversion for online furniture rental platforms. *Journal of Theoretical and Applied Electronic Commerce Research, 16*(2), 188–207. doi:10.4067/S0718-18762021000200114

Karamanou, I., & Vafeas, N. (2005). The association between corporate boards, audit committees, and management earnings forecasts: An empirical analysis. *Journal of Accounting Research, 43*(3), 453–486. doi:10.1111/j.1475-679X.2005.00177.x

Kavitha, G. (2014). Attitude of Youth towards Entrepreneurship—An Exploratory Study among the College Students in Coimbatore District. *Zenith International Journal of Multidisciplinary Research,* (4), 170-180.

Kimbell, L. (2015). *Rethinking Design Thinking: Part I Thinking: Part I.* doi:10.2752/175470811X13071166525216

Kim, N., Woo, H., & Ramkumar, B. (2020, July). The role of product history in consumer response to online second-hand clothing retail service based on circular fashion. *Journal of Retailing and Consumer Services, 60*, 102457. doi:10.1016/j.jretconser.2021.102457

Kioskeridis, I., & Margaris, N. (1996, February). Loss minimization in induction motor adjustable-speed drives. *IEEE Transactions on Industrial Electronics, 43*(1), 226–231. doi:10.1109/41.481429

Korber, S., & McNaughton, R. (2018). *Resilience and Entrepreneurship: A Systematic Literature Review.* https://papers.ssrn.com/sol3/papers.cfm?abstract_id=3993485

Kothari, S. P. (2001). *Capital market research in accounting*. Paper presented to JAR Rochester Conference. 10.1016/S0165-4101(01)00030-1

Kouvara, T., Karachristos, C., Karasoula, S., Orphanoudakis, T., Lacapele, A., Dupont, B., & Batsi, Z. (2022). Integrating Digital Pedagogies in the Era of the Inclusive Education: Needs Analysis and Use Cases from the Perspective of the "Visitor" Project. In *Inclusive Digital Education* (pp. 159–174). Springer International Publishing. doi:10.1007/978-3-031-14775-3_10

Krishnan, A. (2022, May 16). *Watch: Shocked by the viral video, he quit his job to make plastic-free bamboo packaging*. The Better India. Retrieved September 15, 2022, from https://www.thebetterindia.com/285540/plastic-free-packaging-bambrew-bengaluru-eco-friendly-startup/

Krishnan, G. V., & Parsons, L. M. (2008). Getting to the bottom line: An exploration of gender and earnings quality. *Journal of Business Ethics, 78*(1/2), 65–76. doi:10.100710551-006-9314-z

Krupakar, H., & Jayakumar, A. (2016). *A Review of Intelligent Practices for Irrigation Prediction.* arXiv preprint arXiv:1612.02893.

Kuckertz, A., Brändle, L., Gaudig, A., Hinderer, S., Reyes-Aldasoro, C. C., Prochotta, A., ... Berger, E. S. (2021). Startups in times of crisis–A rapid response to the COVID-19 pandemic. *Journal of Business Venturing Insights, 15*, e00200.

Kuhl, J., & Kazén, M. (1999). Volitional facilitation of difficult intentions: Joint activation of intention memory and positive affect removes Stroop interference. *Journal of Experimental Psychology. General, 128*(3), 382–399. doi:10.1037/0096-3445.128.3.382

Kumar & Jain. (2010). Survival Skills of Business Management Graduates: A Study With Reference to Retail and Banking. *Far East Journal of Psychology and Business, 1*(1).

Kumar, B., & Rani, A. (2018). Loss Minimization in Induction Motor Drive using Grey Wolf Optimization. In *2018 International Conference on Computing, Power and Communication Technologies (GUCON)* (pp. 770-774). IEEE.

Kumar, D., Tu, D., Zhu, N., Hou, D., & Zhang, H. (2017). In-line acoustic device inspection of leakage in water distribution pipes based on wavelet and neural network. *Journal of Sensors, 2017*, 2017. doi:10.1155/2017/5789510

Kumar, M. S., & Revankar, S. T. (2017). Development scheme and key technology of an electric vehicle: An overview. *Renewable & Sustainable Energy Reviews, 70*, 1266–1285. doi:10.1016/j.rser.2016.12.027

Kuratko, D., Hornsby, J., & Naffziger, D. W. (1997). *An Examination of Owner's Goals in Sustaining Entrepreneurship*. https://www.semanticscholar.org/paper/An-Examination-of-Owner%27s-Goals-in-Sustaining-Kuratko-Hornsby/d08fb48489400903e66f25cf8df5ea0eec38cf25

Kurdyś-Kujawska, A., Strzelecka, A., & Zawadzka, D. (2021). The Impact of Crop Diversification on the Economic Efficiency of Small Farms in Poland. *Agriculture, 11*(3), 250. doi:10.3390/agriculture11030250

Kyaw, K., Olugbode, M., & Petracci, B. (2015). Does gender diverse board mean less earnings management? *Finance Research Letters, 14*, 135–141. doi:10.1016/j.frl.2015.05.006

Kyro. (2001). *Annual Report 2001 - Euroland*. https://www.yumpu.com/en/document/view/19569465/annual-report-2001-euroland

Lafuente, E., Vaillant, Y., Vendrell-Herrero, F., & Gomes, E. (2018). Bouncing Back from Failure: Entrepreneurial Resilience and the Internationalisation of Subsequent Ventures Created by Serial Entrepreneurs. *Applied Psychology, 68*(4), 658–694. doi:10.1111/apps.12175

Lamberton, C. P., & Rose, R. L. (2012). When is ours better than mine? A framework for understanding and altering participation in commercial sharing systems. *Journal of Marketing, 76*(4), 109–125. doi:10.1509/jm.10.0368

Lang, L., Stulz, R., & Walkling, R. (1989). Managerial performance, Tobin's q, and the gains from successful tender offers. *Journal of Financial Economics, 1*(24), 137–154. doi:10.1016/0304-405X(89)90075-5

Larson, A. L., & Yarime, M. (2020). Revisiting the literature on inclusive innovation: A perspective from innovation studies. *Journal of Cleaner Production, 273*, 123015.

Leach, M., Rockström, J., Raskin, P., Scoones, I., Stirling, A. C., Smith, A., Thompson, J., Millstone, E., Ely, A., Arond, E., & Folke, C. (2012). *Transforming Innovation for Sustainability*. Academic Press.

Leick, Assadi, & Vinogradov. (2021). Digital Entrepreneurship and the Sharing Economy. Taylor & Francis.

Leiponen, A., & Srivastava, S. (2021). Inclusive innovation: Lessons from the COVID-19 pandemic. *Research Policy*, *50*(10), 104178.

Leon, N. De, Sun, Q., Utriainen, T., Nordberg, M., & Jones, R. (2018). *Future states: Design and science for sustainability*. Academic Press.

Lessig, L. (2008). *Remix: Making art and commerce thrive in the hybrid economy*. Penguin. doi:10.5040/9781849662505

Lieberman, M. B., & Montgomery, D. B. (1998). First-mover (dis)advantages: Retrospective and link with the resource-based view. *Strategic Management Journal*, *19*(12), 1111–1125. doi:10.1002/(SICI)1097-0266(1998120)19:12<1111::AID-SMJ21>3.0.CO;2-W

Liem, M. C. (2016). Corporate governance in Banking Industry: An explanatory study. *Research Journal of Finance and Accounting*, *7*(6), 30–48.

Lim, S., & Nam, K. (2004). Loss-minimising control scheme for induction motors. *IEE Proceedings. Electric Power Applications*, *151*(4), 385–397. doi:10.1049/ip-epa:20040384

Lim, W. M. (2017). Inside the sustainable consumption theoretical toolbox: Critical concepts for sustainability, consumption, and marketing. *Journal of Business Research*, *78*, 69–80. doi:10.1016/j.jbusres.2017.05.001

Lim, W. M. (2020). The sharing economy: A marketing perspective. *Australasian Marketing Journal*, *28*(3), 4–13. doi:10.1016/j.ausmj.2020.06.007

Lipton, M., & Lorsch, J. W. (1992). A modest proposal for improved corporate governance. *Business Lawyer*, *48*(1), 59–77.

Liu, J., Zang, D., Liu, C., Ma, Y., & Fu, M. (2019). A leak detection method for oil pipeline based on markov feature and two-stage decision scheme. *Measurement*, *138*, 433–445. doi:10.1016/j.measurement.2019.01.029

Local, L. (n.d.). Retrieved November 13, 2022, from https://www.littlelocal.in/pages/about-us

Locke, E. A., & Latham, G. P. (2002). Building a practically useful theory of goal setting and task motivation: A 35-year odyssey. *The American Psychologist*, *57*(9), 705–717. doi:10.1037/0003-066X.57.9.705 PMID:12237980

Loorbach, D., van Bake, J. C., Whiteman, G., & Rotmans, J. (2010). Business strategies for transitions towards sustainable systems. *Business Strategy and the Environment*, *19*(2), 133–146. doi:10.1002/bse.645

Lubabah, M., & Bawa, A. (2013). Board composition, executive duality and performance of banks in the post consolidated era in Nigeria. *International Journal of Academic Research in Economics and Management Sciences*, *2*(1).

Lumpkin, G. T., & Dess, G. G. (1996). Clarifying the Entrepreneurial Orientation Construct and Linking It To Performance. *Academy of Management Review*, *21*(1), 135–172. doi:10.2307/258632

Luo, J. H., Xiang, Y., & Huang, Z. (2017). Female directors and real activities manipulation: Evidence from China. *China Journal of Accounting Research*, *10*(2), 141–166. doi:10.1016/j.cjar.2016.12.004

Maher, M., & Andersson, T. (1999). Corporate governance: Effects on firm performance and economic growth. OECD.

Maher, R., Maher, M., Mann, S., & McAlpine, C. A. (2018). Integrating design thinking with sustainability science: A Research through Design approach. *Sustainability Science*, *13*(6), 1565–1587. doi:10.100711625-018-0618-6 PMID:30546488

Maignan, I., & Ferrell, O. (2000). Measuring corporate citizenship in two countries: The case of the United States and France. *Journal of Business Ethics*, *23*(3), 283–297. doi:10.1023/A:1006262325211

Malaya, M. F. (2006). *A Gender-based Analysis of Performance of Small and Medium Printing Firms in Metro Manila*. https://www.semanticscholar.org/paper/A-Gender-based-Analysis-of-Performance-of-Small-and-Malaya/6f470562a24185cf7be018b dd5371394fdb88ac0

Malgorzata, B. (2010). Diffusion of Innovations in the Systems Thinking Approach. *Management Business Innovation*, *6*(6), 16–24.

Mallin, C. A. (2007). Corporate governance (2nd Ed.). Oxford.

Mangla, S. K., Kumar, A., & Rana, N. P. (2020). Exploring the impact of blockchain technology on supply chain sustainability: A conceptual framework and research agenda. *Journal of Cleaner Production*, *272*, 122638.

Mangla, S. K., Rana, N. P., & Dwivedi, Y. K. (2021). Blockchain for smart and sustainable cities: A comprehensive review, synthesis, and future research directions. *Renewable & Sustainable Energy Reviews*, *139*, 110654.

Maresch, D., Harms, R., Kailer, N., & Wimmer-Wurm, B. (2020). Sustainable entrepreneurship and innovation in SMEs: Exploring the factors that facilitate or hamper innovation for sustainability. *Journal of Cleaner Production*, *244*, 118715.

Marilyn, K. (2013). *Ex-post facto research: Dissertation and scholarly research, Recipes for success*. Dissertation Success LLC. http://www.dissertationrecipes.com/wpcontent/uploads/2011/04 /

Marshall, R. E., & Farahbakhsh, K. (2013). Systems approaches to integrated solid waste management in developing countries. *Waste Management (New York, N.Y.)*, *33*(4), 988–1003. doi:10.1016/j.wasman.2012.12.023 PMID:23360772

Martin, C. J. (2016). The sharing economy: A pathway to sustainability or a nightmarish form of neoliberal capitalism? *Ecological Economics*, *121*, 149–159. doi:10.1016/j.ecolecon.2015.11.027

Martin, S., Brannigan, J., Hall, A., Martin, S., Brannigan, J., Sustainability, A. H., Martin, S., Brannigan, J., & Hall, A. (2007). Sustainability, Systems Thinking and Professional Practice Sustainability. *Systems Thinking and Professional Practice.*, *8265*. Advance online publication. doi:10.1080/03098260500030389

Massari, S., Principato, L., Antonelli, M., & Pratesi, C. A. (2022). Learning from and designing after pandemics. CEASE: A design thinking approach to maintaining food consumer behaviour and achieving zero waste. *Socio-Economic Planning Sciences*, *82*, 101143. doi:10.1016/j.seps.2021.101143

Masten, A. S., & Wright, M. O. (2010). Resilience over the lifespan: Developmental perspectives on resistance, recovery, and transformation. In J. W. Reich, A. J. Zautra, & J. S. Hall (Eds.), *Handbook of adult resilience* (pp. 213–237). The Guilford Press.

Mayer, C. (1997). Corporate Governance, Competition, and Performance. *Journal of Law and Society*, *24*(1), 152–176. doi:10.1111/1467-6478.00041

Mazzucato, M. (2018). Mission-oriented innovation policies: Challenges and opportunities. *Industrial and Corporate Change*, *27*(5), 803–815. doi:10.1093/icc/dty034

Mazzucato, M., & Semieniuk, G. (2020). COVID-19 and the need for a new approach to innovation. *The Lancet Digital Health*, *2*(7), e349–e351.

McClelland, E., Swail, J., Bell, J., & Ibbotson, P. (2005). *Following the Pathway of Female Entrepreneurs: A Six-Country Investigation.* https://papers.ssrn.com/sol3/papers.cfm?abstract_id=1500896

McConnell, J. J., & Servaes, H. (1990). Additional evidence on equity ownership and corporate value. *Journal of Financial Economics*, *27*(2), 595–613. doi:10.1016/0304-405X(90)90069-C

McGowan, P., Redeker, C. L., Cooper, S. Y., & Greenan, K. (2012). Female entrepreneurship and the management of business and domestic roles: Motivations, expectations and realities. *Entrepreneurship and Regional Development*, *24*(1-2), 53–72. doi:10.1080/08985626.2012.637351

McKay, S. (2001). Between Flexibility and Regulation: Rights, Equality and Protection at Work. *British Journal of Industrial Relations*, *39*(2), 285–303. doi:10.1111/1467-8543.00200

McLean, S. (2015). The rise of the sharing economy. *Computers & Law Magazine of SCL*, *26*(1), 26–28.

Micheli, P., Wilner, S. J. S., Bhatti, S. H., Mura, M., & Beverland, M. B. (2019). *Doing Design Thinking: Conceptual Review, Synthesis, and Research Agenda.* doi:10.1111/jpim.12466

Miliopoulou, G., & Kapareliotis, I. (2021). The toll of success: Female leaders in the "women-friendly" Greek advertising agencies. *Gender, Work and Organization*, *28*(5), 1741–1765. Advance online publication. doi:10.1111/gwao.12636

Minniti, M., & Bygrave, W. D. (2003). *Global Entrepreneurship Monitor (Gem) - National Entrepreneurship Assessment United States of America - 2003 Executive Report*. https://papers.ssrn.com/sol3/papers.cfm?abstract_id=1509254

Möhlmann, M. (2015). Collaborative consumption: Determinants of satisfaction and the likelihood of using a sharing economy option again. *Journal of Consumer Behaviour*, *14*(3), 193–207. doi:10.1002/cb.1512

Morabito, V. (2022). *Digital Entrepreneurship Management, Systems and Practice*. Cambridge University Press.

Morozova, I., & Letyagina, I. (2020). Sustainable development and social innovation: Theoretical approaches and practical implications. *Journal of Cleaner Production*, *266*, 121957.

Moser, G., Paal, S. G., & Smith, I. F. (2018). Leak detection of water supply networks using error-domain model falsification. *Journal of Computing in Civil Engineering*, *32*(2), 04017077. doi:10.1061/(ASCE)CP.1943-5487.0000729

Mugadza, G. (2015). Systems Thinking and Design Thinking: Complimentary Approaches. *Systems Thinking World Journal. Reflection in Action*, *4*(February), 1–7.

Mumford, M. D., Zaccaro, S. J., Harding, F. D., Jacobs, T. O., & Fleishman, E. A. (2000). Leadership skills for a changing world: Solving complex social problems. *The Leadership Quarterly*, *11*(1), 11–36. doi:10.1016/S1048-9843(99)00041-7

Muna, K. H., Kareema, A. J., & Wisam, H. A. (2021). Impact of corporate social responsibility on financial performance: Applied research in Iraqi commercial banks. *International Journal of Innovation, Creativity, and Change*, *12*(1). www.ijicc.net

Muñoz, P., Kimmitt, J., Kibler, E., & Farny, S. (2019). Living on the slopes: Entrepreneurial preparedness in a context under continuous threat. *Entrepreneurship and Regional Development*, *31*(5-6), 413–434. doi:10.1080/08985626.2018.1541591

Mustapha, M., & Subramaniam, P. A. (2016). Challenges and Success Factors of Female Entrepreneurs: Evidence from a Developing Country. *International Review of Management and Marketing*, *6*(4S), 224–231. https://econjournals.com/index.php/irmm/article/view/2492

Nambisan, S. (2018). Digital entrepreneurship: Toward a digital technology perspective of entrepreneurship. *Entrepreneurship Theory and Practice*, *42*(6), 1019–1039.

Narwal, K. P., & Jindal, S. (2015). The impact of corporate governance on the profitability: An empirical study of the Indian Textile Industry. *International Journal of Research in Management, Sciences, and Technology*, *3*(2), 81–85.

Nasir, M. (2020). The Influence of Social Presence on Students' Satisfaction toward Online Course. *Open Praxis*, *12*(4), 485. doi:10.5944/openpraxis.12.4.1141

Nawang, W. M. Z. W., Mamat, I., & Sa'at, N. H. (2018). The Relationship between Predictor Factors and Career Inclination of Entrepreneurship among Program Tunas Niaga Members. *Akademika.*, *88*, 19–31.

Nelson, J. (1996). *Feminism, Objectivity and Economics*. Routledge.

Nguyen, N. C., & Bosch, O. J. H. (2013). *A Systems Thinking Approach to identify Leverage Points for Sustainability: A Case Study in the Cat Ba Biosphere Reserve, Vietnam.* Academic Press.

Nidumolu, R., Prahalad, C. K., & Rangaswami, M. R. (2009). *Why Sustainability Is Now the Key Driver of Innovation.* Academic Press.

Nieman, G. (2014). *Entrepreneurship: A SouthAfrican Perspective* (3rd ed.). Van Schaik.

Nor, Z. M., & Ramli, Z. (2016). A Glimpse at Women Entrepreneurs in Penang. *Akademika,* (86), 79-86. 1 doi:0.17576/akad-2016-8602-06

Nripinder, K., & Vikramjit, S. (2021). Empirically examining the impact of corporate social responsibility on financial performance: Evidence from the Indian steel industry. *Asian Journal of Accounting Research*, *6*(2), 134–151. doi:10.1108/AJAR-07-2020-0061

NSDC. (n.d.). *Schemes and Initiatives*. Retrieved December 14, 2022 from https://nsdcindia.org

Nwaoga, C. T., & Omeke, F. C. (2012). Entrepreneurship and Employability Among Nigerian Graduates. *Mediterranean Journal of Social Sciences*, *3*(16), 68.

Odiwo, W. O., Chukwuma, C. S., & Kifordu, A. A. (2013). The impact of corporate governance on the performance of manufacturing firms in Nigeria. *International Journal of Scientific Research (Ahmedabad, India)*, *5*(9), 924–933.

OECD. (2010). *Global corporate governance forum, background document*. https://www.oecd.org/dataoecd/63/60/46435512.pdf

Okolie, U. C., Igwe, P. A., Ayoola, A. A., Nwosu, H. E., Kanu, C., & Mong, I. K. (2021). Entrepreneurial competencies of undergraduate students: The case of universities in Nigeria. *International Journal of Management Education*, *19*(1), 100452. doi:10.1016/j.ijme.2021.100452

Olayinka, M. U. (2010). The impact of board structure on corporate financial performance in Nigeria. *International Journal of Business and Management*, *5*(10), 45–827.

Olumuyiwa, Y., & Babalola, Y. A. (2012). Impact of corporate governance on capital structure decision of Nigerian Firms. *Research Journal in Organizational Psychology and Educational Studies*, *1*(2), 121–128.

Ong'olo, P. B. (2012). Relationship between corporate social responsibility practices and market share among supermarkets in Kisumu town [Unpublished MBA Research project]. University of Nairobi.

Osisioma, C. B., Egbunike, A. P., & Adeaga, J. C. (2015). Investigating the impact of corporate governance on banks' performance in Nigeria: A field experiment. *International Journal of Economics and Business Administration, 1*(2), 98–112.

Osundina, J. A., Olayinka, I. M. & Chukwuma, J. U. (2016). Corporate governance and financial performance of selected manufacturing companies in Nigeria. *International Journal of Advanced Academic Research/Social and Management Sciences, 2*(10), 29 – 43.

Overbeke, K. K., Bilimoria, D., & Somers, T. (2015). Shared vision between fathers and daughters in family businesses: The determining factor that transforms daughters into successors. *Frontiers in Psychology, 6*. Advance online publication. doi:10.3389/fpsyg.2015.00625 PMID:26074830

Padmini. (2012). Education Vs Employability-The Need to Bridge the Skills Gap among the Engineering and Management Graduates in Andhra Pradesh. *International Journal of Management & Business Studies, 2*(3).

Palmberg, I., Hofman-bergholm, M., Jeronen, E., & Yli-panula, E. (2017). *education sciences Systems Thinking for Understanding Sustainability? Nordic Student Teachers' Views on the Relationship between Species Identification, Biodiversity and Sustainable Development.* doi:10.3390/educsci7030072

Pandey. (2012). Awareness of Life Skills for Job Sustainability amongst Management Students. *Tripude's National Journal of Business Research, 4*(1).

Pant, N., & Mishra, M. (2015). *Bridging the Gap: Driving Scale and Impact in Skill Development and Employability through Corporate Social Responsibility*. IICA and Sattva.

Paranjpe, I., Fuster, V., Lala, A., Russak, A. J., Glicksberg, B. S., Levin, M. A., Charney, A. W., Narula, J., Fayad, Z. A., Bagiella, E., Zhao, S., & Nadkarni, G. N. (2020). Association of treatment dose anticoagulation with in-hospital survival among hospitalized patients with COVID-19. *Journal of the American College of Cardiology, 76*(1), 122–124. doi:10.1016/j.jacc.2020.05.001 PMID:32387623

Patil, P., & Deshpande, Y. (2019). Why Women Enter into Entrepreneurship? An Exploratory Study. *Journal of Organisational Studies and Innovation,* (6), 30-40. https://www.researchgate.net/publication/334389192_Why_Women_Enter_Into_ Entrepreneurship_An_Exploratory_Study#fullTextFileContentiv

Patterson, J. M. (2002). Understanding family resilience. *Journal of Clinical Psychology, 58*(3), 233–246. doi:10.1002/jclp.10019 PMID:11836706

Paulrajan, R. (2011). Employability Skills in Chennai Retail Market, India. Acta Universitatis Danubius, 7(5).

Pawłowski, A. (2008). How many dimensions does sustainable development have? *Sustainable Development, 16*(2), 81–90. doi:10.1002d.339

Pearce, D. W., & Warford, J. J. (1993). In *World without end: economics, environment, and sustainable development*. Oxford University Press.

Pérez-López, M. C., González-López, M. J., & Rodríguez-Ariza, L. (2016). Competencies for entrepreneurship as a career option in a challenging employment environment. *Career Development International*, *21*(3), 214–229. doi:10.1108/CDI-07-2015-0102

Perifanis, N. A., & Kitsios, F. (2023). Investigating the Influence of Artificial Intelligence on Business Value in the Digital Era of Strategy: A Literature Review. *Information*, *14*(2), 85. doi:10.3390/info14020085

Perlines, F. H., Ariza-Montes, A., & Blanco-González-Tejero, C. (2022). Intrapreneurship research: A comprehensive literature review. *Journal of Business Research*, *153*, 428–444. doi:10.1016/j.jbusres.2022.08.015

Pfeffer, J., & Fong, C. T. (2002). The end of business schools? Less success than meets the eye. *Academy of Management Learning & Education*, *1*(1), 78–95. doi:10.5465/amle.2002.7373679

Ping, Z., & Wing, C. W. (2011). Corporate governance: A summary review of different theoretical approaches. *International Research Journal of Finance and Economics*, 68.

Placet, M., Anderson, R., Fowler, K. M., Placet, M., Anderson, R., & Fowler, K. M. (2015). *Strategies for Sustainability*. doi:10.1080/08956308.2005.11657336

Porter, T. (2009). *Three Views of Systems Theories and their Implications for Sustainability Education*. Academic Press.

Pradhan, R. P., Arvin, M. B., Nair, M. S., Hall, J. H., & Bennett, S. E. (2021). Sustainable economic development in India: The dynamics between financial inclusion, ICT development, and economic growth. *Technological Forecasting and Social Change*, *169*, 120758. doi:10.1016/j.techfore.2021.120758

PwC. (2015). Consumer intelligence series 'The sharing economy.' PricewaterhouseCoopers.

Qureshi, M. A. (2007). System dynamics modeling of firm value. *Journal of Modelling in Management*, *2*(1), 24–39. doi:10.1108/17465660710733031

Radwan, M. B., Patsiaouras, G., & Saren, M. (2019). To own or to access? An exploration of sharing and access practices by Arab millennials. In *Handbook of the Sharing Economy*. Edward Elgar Publishing. doi:10.4337/9781788110549.00012

Raei, E., Shafiee, M. E., Nikoo, M. R., & Berglund, E. (2019). Placing an ensemble of pressure sensors for leak detection in water distribution networks under measurement uncertainty. *Journal of Hydroinformatics*, *21*(2), 223–239. doi:10.2166/hydro.2018.032

Rajeswaran, A., Narasimhan, S., & Narasimhan, S. (2018). A graph partitioning algorithm for leak detection in water distribution networks. *Computers & Chemical Engineering*, *108*, 11–23. doi:10.1016/j.compchemeng.2017.08.007

Ramadani, V., Hisrich, R. D., & Rashiti, S. G. (2015). Female entrepreneurs in transition economies: Insights from Albania, Macedonia and Kosovo. *World Review of Entrepreneurship, Management and Sustainable Development*, *11*(4), 391. doi:10.1504/WREMSD.2015.072066

Rao, K. N., & Reddy, G. V. K. (2012). Green Entrepreneurship- A Paradigm Shift towards Environment Consciousness. *Asia Pacific Journal of Management and Entrepreneurship Research, 1*(3), 112–118.

Rathi, D. (2018). India's backbone is break bone. *International Journal of Basic and Applied Research, 8*(6), 622–627.

Rauch, A., & Frese, M. (2000). Psychological approaches to entrepreneurial success. *International Review of Industrial and Organizational Psychology*, 101–142. https://research.rug.nl/en/publications/psychological-approaches-to-entrepreneurial-success

Revlon, W. (2020). *Corporate social responsibility and financial performance of U.S. manufacturing and service small- and medium-sized enterprises*. Walden University.

Rezvani, M. L. (2018). Organisational entrepreneurial alertness framework in opportunity discovery. *Academy of Entrepreneurship Journal.*

Rhee & White. (2017). The relationship between the emotional intelligence of entrepreneurs and the new venture creation: The role of age, gender and motive. *Arab Economic and Business Journal, 12*(2), 99–108. doi:10.1016/j.aebj.2017.10.002

Rimon, E., Aiman, R., & Sandy, K. (2014). The effect of corporate governance on firm performance: Evidence from Egypt. *Asian Economic and Financial Review, 4*(12), 1865–1877.

Rojek, I., & Studzinski, J. (2019). Detection and localization of water leaks in water nets supported by an ICT system with artificial intelligence methods as a way forward for smart cities. *Sustainability, 11*(2), 518. doi:10.3390u11020518

Rosti, L., & Chelli, F. (2005). Gender Discrimination, Entrepreneurial Talent and Self-Employment. *Small Business Economics, 24*(2), 131–142. doi:10.100711187-003-3804-5

Salisu, A. A., Sikiru, A. A., & Vo, X. V. (2020). *Pandemics and the emerging stock markets.* Borsa Istanbul Review. doi:10.1016/j.bir.2020.11.004

Samira, I. R., Noor, N. B., & Muhammed, H. (2018). 'Impact of CSR on firm's financial performance: A study on some selected agribusiness industries of Bangladesh. *American Journal of Economics, Finance, and Management, 4*(3), 74–85.

Sanda, A. U., Mukaila, A. S., & Garba, T. (2005). *Corporate governance mechanisms and firm financial performance in Nigeria.* Final Report Presented to the Biannual Research Workshop of the AERC, Nairobi, Kenya.

Sanda, A. U., Mukaila, A. S., & Garba, T. (2011). *Board independence and firm financial performance: Evidence from Nigeria.* African Economic Research Consortium (AERC) Research Paper 213.

Santi, R., Sossini, L., Italia, M., D'Ambrosio, S., Zurlo, F., & Del Curto, B. (2022). Materials for SDGs: A Synergy Towards Sustainable Development. *DIID*, *76*(76). Advance online publication. doi:10.30682/diid7622i

Sarasvathy, S. D. (2001). Causation and Effectuation: Toward a Theoretical Shift from Economic Inevitability to Entrepreneurial Contingency. *Academy of Management Review*, *26*(2), 243–263. doi:10.2307/259121

Saremi, S., Mirjalili, S., & Lewis, A. (2017). Grasshopper optimisation algorithm: Theory and application. *Advances in Engineering Software*, *105*, 30–47. doi:10.1016/j.advengsoft.2017.01.004

Satalkina, L. (2020). *Digital Entrepreneurship and its Role in Innovation Systems: A Systematic Literature Review as a Basis*. Academic Press.

Sawhney, M., & Evans, D. (2020). Innovation's new world order. *Harvard Business Review*, *98*(4), 66–74.

Schaltegger, S., Lüdeke-Freund, F., & Hansen, E. G. (2016). Business models for sustainability: A co-evolutionary analysis of sustainable entrepreneurship, innovation, and transformation. *Organization & Environment*, *29*(3), 264–289. doi:10.1177/1086026616633272

Schor, J. B., & Cansoy, M. (2019). The sharing economy. The Oxford Handbook of Consumption, 51.

Schumpeter, J., & Opie, R. (1934). *The theory of economic development; an inquiry into profits, capital, credit, interest, and the business cycle*. Harvard University Press.

Scott, J. W. (1986). Gender: A Useful Category of Historical Analysis. *The American Historical Review*, *91*(5), 1053–1075. doi:10.2307/1864376

Seadon, J. K. (2010). Sustainable waste management systems. *Journal of Cleaner Production*, *18*(16–17), 1639–1651. doi:10.1016/j.jclepro.2010.07.009

Senin, S. F., Jaafar, M. S., & Hamid, R. (2019). Locating Underground Water Pipe Leakages Via Interpretation of Ground Penetrating Radar Signals. *IACSIT International Journal of Engineering and Technology*, *8*(2), 72–77.

Shah, K. K., Modi, B., Pandey, H. P., Subedi, A., Aryal, G., Pandey, M., & Shrestha, J. (2021). Diversified Crop Rotation: An Approach for Sustainable Agriculture Production. *Advances in Agriculture*.

Shane, S., & Venkataraman, S. (2000). The Promise of Enterpreneurship as a Field of Research. *Academy of Management Review*, *25*(1), 217–226. doi:10.2307/259271

Sharma, B. R., Sharma, A., Ali, S., & Dadhich, J. (2021). Corporate social responsibility and financial performance: Evidence from manufacturing and service industry. *Academic Journal of Interdisciplinary Studies*, *10*(3), 301–307. doi:10.36941/ajis-2021-0085

Sharma, N. K., & Kushwaha, G. S. (2015). Emerging Green Market as an Opportunity for Green Entrepreneurs and Sustainable Development in India. *J Entrepren Organiz Manag*, *4*(2), 134.

Shukla, S., & Singh, B. (2018). Solar powered sensorless induction motor drive with improved efficiency for water pumping. IET Power Electronics, 11(3), 416-426. doi:10.1049/iet-pel.2017.0452

Shukla, D. (2012). Employability Skill among Professionals – Chagrin of HR Executives in Indian Labor Market: A Study on Engineering Graduates of Bhopal City. *VSRD International Journal of Business & Mngt. Research*, *2*(8).

Singh, R., Gehlot, A., Ranjit, P. S., & Sharma, D. (Eds.). (2022). *Futuristic Sustainable Energy & Technology: Proceedings of the International Conference on Futuristic Sustainable Energy &Technology (ICFSE, 2021), 19-20 September, 2021*. CRC Press. 10.1201/9781003272328

Singh, N., Ogunseitan, O. A., & Tang, Y. (2021). Medical waste: Current challenges and future opportunities for sustainable management. *Critical Reviews in Environmental Science and Technology*, *0*(0), 1–23. doi:10.1080/10643389.2021.1885325

Smith, J., Chae, J., Learn, S., Hugo, R., & Park, S. (2018, September). Pipeline rupture detection using real-time transient modelling and convolutional neural networks. In *International Pipeline Conference* (*Vol. 51883*, p. V003T04A016). American Society of Mechanical Engineers. 10.1115/IPC2018-78426

Soldevila, A., Blesa, J., Fernandez-Canti, R. M., Tornil-Sin, S., & Puig, V. (2019). Data-driven approach for leak localization in water distribution networks using pressure sensors and spatial interpolation. *Water (Basel)*, *11*(7), 1500. doi:10.3390/w11071500

Soldevila, A., Fernandez-Canti, R. M., Blesa, J., Tornil-Sin, S., & Puig, V. (2017). Leak localization in water distribution networks using Bayesian classifiers. *Journal of Process Control*, *55*, 1–9. doi:10.1016/j.jprocont.2017.03.015

Soltanifar, M., & Smailhodžić, E. (2021). Developing a digital entrepreneurial mindset for data-driven, cloud-enabled, and platform-centric business activities: practical implications and the impact on society. *Digital Entrepreneurship, 3*.

Southwick, S. M., Bonanno, G. A., Masten, A. S., Panter-Brick, C., & Yehuda, R. (2014). Resilience definitions, theory, and challenges: Interdisciplinary Perspectives. *European Journal of Psychotraumatology*, *5*(1), 25338. doi:10.3402/ejpt.v5.25338 PMID:25317257

Sreejeth, M., Singh, M., & Kumar, P. (2019). Efficiency enhancement for indirect vector-*controlled induction motor drive. International Journal of Electronics*, *106*(9), 1281–1294. doi:10.1080/00207217.2019.1584921

Sridharan, S., & Krein, P. T. (2016). Minimization of system-level losses in VSI-based induction motor drives: Offline strategies. *IEEE Transactions on Industry Applications*, *53*(2), 1096–1105. doi:10.1109/TIA.2016.2631513

Srivastava & Shah. (2014). A Study on Factors Affecting Employability Skills of Management Students. *International Journal of Management and Development Studies, 3*(2).

St-Arnaud, L., & Giguère, É. (2018). Women entrepreneurs, individual and collective work–family interface strategies and emancipation. *International Journal of Gender and Entrepreneurship, 10*(4), 198–223. doi:10.1108/IJGE-09-2017-0058

Startienė, G., & Remeikienė, R. (2008). Gender Gap in Entrepreneurship. *The Engineering Economist, 60*(5). https://inzeko.ktu.lt/index.php/EE/article/view/11596

Statistica. (2020). *Statistica.* Retrieved from https://www.statista.com/topics/1164/social-networks/

Stephens, W. D. (2021). *Arranging Resilience: The role of social actors in preventing violent extremism.* https://research.vu.nl/en/publications/arranging-resilience-the-role-of-social-actors-in-preventing-viol

Sterbenk, Y., Champlin, S., Windels, K., & Shelton, S. (2021). Is Femvertising the New Greenwashing? Examining Corporate Commitment to Gender Equality. *Journal of Business Ethics.* Advance online publication. doi:10.100710551-021-04755-x

Strandberg, R. (2001). Corporate governance and firm performance: Evidence from Pakistan. *Pakistan Development Review, 45*(4), 231–244.

Suchek, N., Fernandes, C. I., Kraus, S., Filser, M., & Sjögrén, H. (2021). Innovation and the circular economy: A systematic literature review. *Business Strategy and the Environment, 30*(8), 3686–3702. doi:10.1002/bse.2834

Sun, C., Parellada, B., Puig, V., & Cembrano, G. (2020). Leak localization in water distribution networks using pressure and data-driven classifier approach. *Water (Basel), 12*(1), 54. doi:10.3390/w12010054

Sustainable development and - India budget. (n.d.). Retrieved August 26, 2022, from https://www.indiabudget.gov.in/budget2019-20/economicsurvey/doc/vol2chapter/echap05_vol2.pdf

Sustainable Packaging Solutions: Bengaluru. (n.d.). Retrieved September 10, 2022, from https://www.bambrew.in/

Sustainable products for happy humans ! (2022, August 23). Retrieved September 3, 2022, from https://www.ecoright.com/

Sutherland, W., & Jarrahi, M. H. (2018). The sharing economy and digital platforms: A review and research agenda. *International Journal of Information Management, 43*, 328–341. doi:10.1016/j.ijinfomgt.2018.07.004

Tariq, I., & Naveed, M. (2016). Effects of board & ownership structure on firm financial performance: An economic value added perspective. *Developing Country Studies, 6*(8), 1–9.

Ter Huurne, M., Ronteltap, A., Corten, R., & Buskens, V. (2017). Antecedents of trust in the sharing economy: A systematic review. *Journal of Consumer Behaviour, 16*(6), 485–498. doi:10.1002/cb.1667

Thiruvadi, S., & Huang, H. (2011). Audit committee gender differences and earnings management. *Gender in Management*, *26*(7), 483–498. doi:10.1108/17542411111175469

This startup aims to eliminate 1 million plastic bottles in 2022 by refilling homecare liquids. (2022, July 19). Retrieved July 23, 2022, from https://www.indiatimes.com/news/india/refillable-mumbai-startup-offering-refilling-homecare-liquids-at-doorstep-575115.html#:~:text=Conceived%20in%202019%20during%20the,2020%20just%20by%20offering%20refills

Thuraisingam, R. (2013). The effects of corporate governance on company performance: Evidence from Sri Lankan Financial Services Industry. *Journal of Economics and Sustainable Development*, *4*(17), 103–109.

Tobin, J. (1969). A general equilibrium approach to monetary theory. *Journal of Money, Credit and Banking*, *1*(1), 15–29. doi:10.2307/1991374

Trapp, C. T., & Kanbach, D. K. (2021). Green entrepreneurship and business models: Deriving green technology business model archetypes. *Journal of Cleaner Production*, *297*, 126694. doi:10.1016/j.jclepro.2021.126694

Tripathi, B. (2018, June). 40% of Indians will have no access to drinking water by 2030: NITI Aayog. *Business Standard*. Retrieved 24th Nov., 2020 from https://www.business-standard.com/article/current-affairs/40-of-indians-will-have-no-access-to-drinking-water-by-2030-niti-aayog-118062500074_1.html

Tripoli, A. M. (1998). Planning and allocating: Strategies for managing priorities in complex jobs. *European Journal of Work and Organizational Psychology*, *7*(4), 455–476. doi:10.1080/135943298398501

Tschimmel, K. (2012). Design Thinking as an effective Toolkit. *Proceedings of the XXIII Conference: Action for Innovation: Innovation from Experience*, 1–20.

Tunn, V., & Dekoninck, E. (2016). *How Does Sustainability Help or Hinder Innovation? A Study of Successful Companies Founded on Sustainability Principles*. doi:10.1007/978-3-319-32098-4

Turi, A. N. (2020). *Technologies for Modern Digital Entrepreneurship*. Apress Publisher. doi:10.1007/978-1-4842-6005-0

Udeh, F. N., Abiahu, M. F. C., & Tambou, L. E. (2017). Impact of corporate governance on firm's financial performance: A Study of Quoted Banks in Nigeria. *The Nigerian Accountant*, *2*(50), 54–62.

Umoren, A. O., Ogbari, M. E., & Atolagbe, T. M. (2016). Corporate social responsibility and firm performance: A study of listed firms in Nigeria. *ICAN 2nd Annual International Academic Conference on Accounting and Finance*.

Ungar, M. (2013). Resilience, Trauma, Context, and Culture. *Trauma, Violence & Abuse*, *14*(3), 255–266. doi:10.1177/1524838013487805 PMID:23645297

Vaidya, P. N., & Honagannavar, D. V. (2017). Green Entrepreneurship towards Sustainable Environment. *International Journal of Commerce and Management Research, 3*(1), 88–91.

Value and Supply Chain Development. (2007). European Economic and Social Committee.

Van Praag, M., & Versloot, P. H. (2008). *The Economic Benefits and Costs of Entrepreneurship: A Review of the Research*. https://papers.ssrn.com/sol3/papers.cfm?abstract_id=1625828

Vardhini, H., & Janardhana Raju, G. (2020). Design of Internet of Things Based Smart and Efficient Water Distribution System for Urban and Agriculture Areas. *Journal of Computational and Theoretical Nanoscience, 17*(9-10), 4688–4691. doi:10.1166/jctn.2020.9301

Verheul, I., van Stel, A., & Thurik, R. (2004, February 1). *Explaining female and male entrepreneurship across 29 countries*. https://ideas.repec.org/p/esi/egpdis/2004-08.html

Verheul, I., & Thurik, R. (2001). Start-Up Capital: "Does Gender Matter? *Small Business Economics, 16*(4), 329–346. doi:10.1023/A:1011178629240

Vig, A. (2020, September 6). *5 startups by 'green entrepreneurs' whose products are environmentally sustainable*. Retrieved September 2, 2022, from https://yourstory.com/socialstory/2020/09/startups-green-entrepreneurs-eco-friendly-products

Vineela, G. S. (2018). *Digital Entrepreneurship*. Academic Press.

Wahid, A. S. (2018). The effects and the mechanisms of board gender diversity: Evidence from financial manipulation. *Journal of Business Ethics, 159*(3), 1–21.

Wahla, K. U. R., Shah, S. Z. A., & Hussain, Z. (2012). Impact of Ownership Structure on Firm Performance: Evidence from Non-Financial Listed Companies at Karachi Stock Exchange. *International Research Journal of Finance and Economics, 84*(1), 613.

Wang, L. (2009). Corporate governance, industry clustering, and corporate performance. The Business Review, 12(1).

Watson, T. J. (2002). Reviews. *Management Learning, 33*(3), 407–410. doi:10.1177/1350507602333009

WECD. (1987). *Our Common Future*. Report of the World Commission on Environment and Development. www.un-documents.net/our- common-future.pdf/

Weisman, V. L. (2000). The impact of facilitative leadership: Multi-rater measurement of behavioral outcomes of managerial leaders. *Proceedings of the Academy of Human Resource Development*, 20-28.

Welsh, D. H. B., Kaciak, E., & Shamah, R. (2018). Determinants of women entrepreneurs' firm performance in a hostile environment. *Journal of Business Research, 88*, 481–491. doi:10.1016/j.jbusres.2017.12.015

Wernerfelt, B., & Montgomery, C. A. (1988). Tobin's q and the importance of focus in firm performance. *The American Economic Review*, *78*(1), 246–250.

Wilkerson, B., & Trellevik, L.-K. L. (2021). Sustainability-oriented innovation: Improving problem definition through combined design thinking and systems mapping approaches. *Thinking Skills and Creativity*, *42*, 100932. doi:10.1016/j.tsc.2021.100932

Williams, A., Sagen, S., & Ahlstr, H. (2020). *Enhancing systems thinking in corporate sustainability through a transdisciplinary research process.* doi:10.1016/j.jclepro.2020.120691

Williams, A., Kennedy, S., Philipp, F., & Whiteman, G. (2017). Systems thinking: A review of sustainability management research. *Journal of Cleaner Production*, *148*, 866–881. doi:10.1016/j.jclepro.2017.02.002

WIN. (2015). Semantics, Analytics, Visualization. Enhancing Scholarly Data.

Wogu, I. A. P., Sanjay Misra, J., Assibong, P. A., Adewumi, A., Maskeliunas, R., & Damasevicius, R. (2018). A Critical Review of the Politics of Artificial Intelligent Machines, Alienation and the Existential Risk Threat to America's Labour Force. In *Computational Science and Its Applications – ICCSA 2018. Lecture Notes in Computer Science* (vol. 10963). Springer. https://rdcu.be/5XTm https://link.springer.com/chapter/10.1007/978-3-319-95171-3_18

Wogu, I. A., Njie, S. N., Ezennwa, E. O., Chukwuedo, C. N., Ukagba, G. U., Misra, S., Uniamikogbo, E., & Olu-Owolabi, E. F. (2021). The Politics of Climate Change and the Rising Demand for Global Energy in the 21st Century: Implications for Human and Economic Development. *International Journal of Energy Optimization and Engineering*, *10*(3), 1–23. doi:10.4018/IJEOE.2021070101

Wogu, I. A., Njie, S. N., Katende, J. O., Ukagba, G. U., Edogiawerie, M. O., & Misra, S. (2020). The Social Media, Politics of Disinformation in Established Hegemonies, and the Role of Technological Innovations in 21st Century Elections: The Road Map to US 2020 Presidential Elections. *International Journal of Electronic Government Research*, *16*(3), 65–84. doi:10.4018/IJEGR.2020070104

Wolfe, J., & Sauaia, A. C. A. (2003). The Tobin q as a Company Performance Indicator. *Developments in Business Simulation and Experiential Learning, 30.*

Wong, L., Deo, R., Rathnayaka, S., Shannon, B., Zhang, C., Chiu, W. K., & Widyastuti, H. (2018). Leak detection in water pipes using submersible optical optic-based pressure sensor. *Sensors (Basel)*, *18*(12), 4192. doi:10.339018124192 PMID:30513585

Wooi, H. C., & Ming, T. C. (2009). *Directors' Pay-Performance: A Study on Malaysian Government Linked Companies.* CenPRIS Working Paper No. 110/09, Universiti Sains Malaysia.

Xavier, M. S., Shukla, J., Oduor, J., & Mbabazize, M. (2015). Effect of corporate governance on the financial performance of the Banking Industry in Rwanda: A case study - Commercial Banks in Rwanda. *International Journal of Small Business and Entrepreneurship Research*, *3*(6), 29–43.

Xiaolin, X. (2019). *The impact of corporate social responsibilities on financial performance in China. International master of environmental policy. Nicholas School of Environment & Sanford School of Policy*, Duke University.

Yang, S., Talbot, R. W., Frish, M. B., Golston, L. M., Aubut, N. F., Zondlo, M. A., & McSpiritt, J. (2018). Natural gas fugitive leak detection using an unmanned aerial vehicle: Measurement system description and mass balance approach. *Atmosphere*, *9*(10), 383. doi:10.3390/atmos9100383

Yin, S., Meng, D., Diao, L., Li, Y., & Dong, K. (2019). Improved hybrid loss control with optimized flux for traction induction motor under light load. *IEEJ Transactions on Electrical and Electronic Engineering*, *14*(3), 485–492. doi:10.1002/tee.22830

Young, G. (2010). *Design thinking and sustainability*. Academic Press.

Zabri, S. M., Ahmad, K., & Wah, K. K. (2016). Corporate governance practices and firm performance: Evidence from top 100 public listed companies in Malaysia. *Procedia Economics and Finance*, *35*, 287–296. doi:10.1016/S2212-5671(16)00036-8

Zaman, A. U., & Lehmann, S. (2013). The zero waste index: A performance measurement tool for waste management systems in a ‘zero waste city’. *Journal of Cleaner Production*, *50*, 123–132. doi:10.1016/j.jclepro.2012.11.041

Zaman, A., & Newman, P. (2021). Plastics: Are they part of the zero-waste agenda or the toxic-waste agenda? *Sustainable Earth*, *4*(1), 4. doi:10.118642055-021-00043-8

Zenko, Z., & Sardi, V. (2014). Systemic thinking for socially responsible innovations in social tourism for people with disabilities. *Kybernetes*, *43*(3), 652–666. doi:10.1108/K-09-2013-0211

Zhang, J., Lindsey, A. R., Peters, R. S., Heraty, J. M., Hopper, K. R., Werren, J. H., Martinson, E. O., Woolley, J. B., Yoder, M. J., & Krogmann, L. (2020). Conflicting signal in transcriptomic markers leads to a poorly resolved backbone phylogeny of chalcidoid wasps. *Systematic Entomology*, *45*(4), 783–802. doi:10.1111yen.12427

Zhang, T. C., Gu, H., & Jahromi, M. F. (2019). What makes the sharing economy successful? An empirical examination of competitive customer value propositions. *Computers in Human Behavior*, *95*, 275–283. doi:10.1016/j.chb.2018.03.019

Zhou, X., Tang, Z., Xu, W., Meng, F., Chu, X., Xin, K., & Fu, G. (2019). Deep learning identifies accurate burst locations in water distribution networks. *Water Research*, *166*, 115058. doi:10.1016/j.watres.2019.115058 PMID:31536886

Zikmund, W. G., Babin, B. J., Carr, J. C., & Griffin, M. (2013). *Business Research Methods*. Cengage Learning.

About the Contributors

Sanjay Misra , a Sr. member of IEEE and ACM Distinguished Lecturer, is a Senior Scientist at the Institute of Energy Technology(IFE), Halden, Norway. Before joining IFE, he was associated with the Computer Science and Communication department of Østfold University College, Halden, Norway. He holds a PhD. in Information & Knowledge Engg (Software Engg) from the University of Alcala, Spain & M.Tech.(Software Engg) from MLN National Institute of Tech, India. His expertise is in the area of Applied Informatics (Cyber Security, Health Informatics, Software Engineering Applications, and Intelligent systems using AI and computational techniques) and has been the publishing (- around 150 JCR/SCIE) in top journals like Computers and Security, Information Processing and Management, Engineering Applications of Artificial Intelligence, Expert Systems, and Applications, etc. He has been amongst the top 2% of scientists in the world (published by Stanford University) for the last three consecutive years, ranked no 2 in the whole of Africa in computer science (as per Elsevier: Scival analysis during 2017-2022) and also got several awards for outstanding publications (2014 IET Software Premium Award (UK)), TUBITAK-Turkish Higher Education, and Atilim University). He is Editor in Chief of Int J of Human Capital & Inf Technology Professionals(IGI), IT Personnel and Project Management(IGI), and editor in various SCIE journals(Nature: Scientific Report((Impact Factor: 4.996), Elsevier: Alex. Engineering((Impact Factor: 6.626, Q1 7/92)), edited several special issues and 80 books from Springer(65 LNCSs, 4 LNEEs, 3 LNNSs, 3 CCISs) , 10 IEEE proceedings and several books. He delivered more than 100 keynotes, invited talks and public lectures at reputed conferences and institutes (he traveled to more than 60 countries).

Amit Jain is currently President of Amity University Rajasthan. Prior to this Prof. Amit served the university as Pro-Vice Chancellor, Dean Faculty of Management, and Director, Amity Business School. Prof. Jain has held senior positions with several organizations including Director-International Collaborations, Director-School of Hotel Management with Manipal University Jaipur, JK Lakshmipat University, etc. Prof. Amit has been a Visiting Professor with University of Technology (UTS),

Sydney, Australia, Szechenyi Istvan University, Hungary & Selye Janos University, Slovakia. Prof. Amit holds a Ph.D. from Sardar Patel University and has completed FDP from IIM Ahmedabad. Prof. Amit is actively involved in administration, teaching, training and research. He is associated with various management and training institutes as a guest faculty such as Bank of Baroda Staff College, Staff College Union Bank, Sardar Patel University, NCHMCT, etc to name a few. Prof. Amit has Designed and conducted training programmes/sessions for executives of various organizations including IDBI Bank, Bank of Baroda, BKT Tyres, JK Tyre, JK Paper, JK Lakshmi Cement, Claris Life Sciences, Veeda Clinical Research, Natraj Foods, Trimurti Foodtech, E-mall Infotech, Euro India Foods, Fenner India, Gravita India, ECGC, GAIL, etc., on topics related to Marketing Orientation, Effective Selling Skills, Customer Relationship Management, Managerial Effectiveness, Leadership and Communication Skills. He has several publications to his credit and has presented research papers at National and International conferences organized by institutes like Singapore Management University (SMU), University of Technology, Sydney, IIM, and IIT. He has also received award for three research papers at National and International Conferences. His professional associations include Life Membership of Indian Society for Training and Development (ISTD) and currently holds position of National Council Member. He is a Member of All India Management Association and IIM Ahmedabad Alumni Association. Dr Amit is Reviewer and Committee Member with several Journals and Conferences. He is an Editorial Board Member of Indian Journal of Training and Development and Chief Editor of Amity Management Review. His area of interest for Research, Training and Consultancy includes Marketing Strategy, Sales Management, Marketing Communications, Digital Marketing and Entrepreneurship.

Manju Kaushik is presently working as a Professor-AIIT, President, IIC, Amity University Rajasthan. Deputy director Amity Innovation Incubator, E-Cell,IEEE, ACM Branch Counselor &Coordinator Tech. Clubs, AUR. She has more than 17 years of experience in the field of teaching & research. She was awarded Ph.D. from the Mohan Lal Sukhadia University, Udaipur, Raj. Her research papers have been published in various journals and conferences of National and International repute like IEEE, springer, Elsevier, and Scopus indexed. She has organized international conference and more than 60 events (workshop, webinars, FDPs, awareness programs) two research scholars have successfully awarded with Ph.D. under her supervision. Currently She is Guiding 06 Ph.D scholars, Guided more than 100 PG Level students (MCA, M.tech.). She has appointed as paper setter and an external examiner for the viva-voce exams of post graduate students, Ph.D Students of various Universities. She is an active reviewer of different indexed journals. Presently, she is the executive member at Rajasthan sub-section of IEEE & Member of ACM, life member of ISTE and CSI. She has published 02 Patents & editor of 02 Books.

Chitreshh Banerjee Associate Professor, Amity Institute of Information Technology, Amity University Rajasthan, A Science Graduate (B.Sc.), he holds a Masters Degree in Computer Science (M.Tech.), Masters Degree in Computer Applications (MCA) with GNIIT (3 years) program from NIIT Ltd. He is Ph.D. CS. He has a rich academic experience of about 21+ years in the field of Computer Science and IT. He is currently working as Associate Professor in Amity Institute of Information Technology, Amity University, Jaipur, Rajasthan. He is the Vice President of Institute Innovation Council (IIC, an initiative of MHRD, India), Amity University Rajasthan. He is also a member in 21 International Societies/Associations. He has been awarded Best Researcher in Online Award Ceremony organized by Institute of Technical and Scientific Research, Jaipur, India during the year 2020. Under the Institute-Industry linkage programme, he delivers expert lectures on varied themes pertaining to CS and IT. As a prolific writer in the arena of Computer Sciences and Information Technology, he penned down a number of books/learning material on Multimedia Systems, Information Technology, Software Engineering, E-banking Security Transactions, System Analysis and Design, Web Technologies, etc. He has contributed 75 research papers/chapters/articles in the conferences / journals / seminar / publications of international and national repute. He also provides consultancy in the area of software and project management to a no. of IT companies. He has acted as Editor in five International Journals and in two International Convention of Climate Change and Water (during 2012 & 2013). He has acted as an organizing member in 9 National and International Conferences. He is also Reviewer of 7 International Journals. He is Guest Editor in 6 International Journal and Books of Inderscience Publisher, IGI Global, and Springer. His area of interest includes software security, software engineering, IoT, smart systems, intelligent systems and e-systems.

* * *

Arpita Banerjee, a Commerce Graduate (B.Com. Honours) from M.D.S. Univ., Ajmer, holds a Master's Degree in Information Technology (M.Sc. IT) from Rajasthan University, Jaipur and M.Tech CS from Jagannath University, Jaipur, and Ph.D. (CS) from Mody University, Laxmangarh, Sikar. She has a good academic and industry experience in the field of Computer Science & Application / IT. As a prolific writer in the arena of Computer Sciences and Information Technology, she has contributed some chapters in books on Multimedia Systems and E-banking Security Transactions. She has taken a step further in the field of research in software security and has 45 research papers in journal & conference of international and national repute. She is member of Machine Intelligence Learning (MIR) Labs, USA. Her area of interest includes topics related to Software Engineering and Security and related areas.

Chitreshh Banerjee, a Science Graduate (B.Sc.), holds a Masters Degree in Computer Applications (MCA) with GNIIT (3 years) program from NIIT Ltd. He is Ph.D. CS from Pacific University, Udaipur, Rajasthan, India. He has a rich academic experience of about 24+ years in the field of Computer Applications / Science / IT. He is currently working as Assistant Professor (AP-III), Amity Institute of Information Technology, Amity University, Jaipur. He has also worked as Executive Officer in the Board of Studies, The Institute of Chartered Accountants of India (Set up by an Act of Parliament), New Delhi. He was also a member of management committee of Jaipur Chapter of CSI (Computer Society of India) for the year 2011-12 & 2012-13. In addition, he is also member in 21 International Societies/Associations. He has been awarded Best Researcher in Online Award Ceremony organized by Institute of Technical and Scientific Research, Jaipur, India on 13 th Sep., 2020. He has an excellent academic background with a very sound academic and research experience. Under the Institute-Industry linkage programme, he delivers expert lectures on varied themes pertaining to IT. As a prolific writer in the arena of Computer Sciences and Information Technology, he penned down a number of books/learning material on Multimedia Systems, Information Technology, Software Engineering, E-banking Security Transactions, System Analysis and Design, Web Technologies, etc. He has contributed 75 research papers/chapters/ articles in the conferences / journals / seminar / publications of international and national repute. He also provides consultancy in the area of software and project management to a no. of IT companies. He has acted as Editor in five International Journals and in two International Convention of Climate Change and Water (during 2012 & 2013). He has acted as organizing member in 9 National and International Conference. He is also Reviewer of 7 International Journals. He is Guest Editor in 6 International Journal and Books of Inderscience Publisher, IGI Global, and Springer. His area of interest includes software security, software engineering, IoT, smart systems and e-systems.

Hemant Bhanawat is an Assistant Professor in Amity Business School, Amity University, Rajasthan in the area of Finance & Accounting. Prior to this, he worked at Birla School of Commerce, Birla Glibal University India MLS University, India and Eternal University, India. He is familiar with the subjects like Basic and Advanced Accounting, Financial Management, and Direct & Indirect Taxation. He has many research papers cum book chapters to his credit in various reputed (SCOPUS/UGC) indexed journals and in books. He has been appointed as the referee for peer review of research papers of Asia-Pacific Financial Markets Journal (Springer).

Hridaya Raj Bharti is the Assistant Professor in Institute of Commerce, Nirma University. Prior to joining Nirma University, Dr. Bharti was pursuing his Post-Doctoral from Indian Council of Social Science Research with the University College of Commerce and Management Studies (U.C.C.M.S), Mohanlal Sukhadia University (M.L.S.U). Dr. Bharti has completed his PhD. From U.C.C.M.S, M.L.S.U and been a 'Visiting Faculty' at the U.C.C.M.S. His areas of interest include International Business, Banking and Financial System. In addition, he has published and presented several papers at national and international conferences.

Narender Singh Bhati is presently working as Associate Professor in Department of Business Administration, Manipal University Jaipur. He has gained a total experience of about than 14 years, including more than 13 years in academics having specialization in the field of Quantitative Techniques, Operations Management, and Business Research Methods at various prestigious management institutions. His area of research is Marketing, Service Quality Management and E-commerce. He has more than 30 research papers, conferences, workshops, FDP attended. Additionally, he has 16 research publication (all in referred journals) including 7 Scopus and Elsevier publication, others in UGC listed journals. He has edited two book and has 15 books chapters published in books with ISBN. In addition to this, he has been awarded and recognised in the field of academics and research by Best Faculty Award, Gold medal, Best research papers awards, etc.

Yudhveer Chahal has served as Associate Professor in the department of Amity Institute of Information Technology, Amity University Rajasthan. He has more than 15 years rich and illustrious teaching experience at undergraduate and postgraduate levels. He has published more than 35 papers in good indexed International Journal and serves as reviewer and editor in renowned international journals of repute along with He has presented more than 20 research papers in national and international conferences. He has supervised 3 research scholars for Ph.D. degree and his specialization area is special function, Fractional Calculus, Integral equation, Integral Transform and its applications.

Abhishek Choudhary is currently a research scholar at Amity Business School, Amity University Jaipur. He is working as an Assistant Professor at the Department of Fashion & Clothing, Indian Institute of Crafts & Design, Jaipur.

Toolika Gupta is the Director of the Indian Institute of Crafts and Design, Jaipur, since 2017. She has taught at NIFT New Delhi as an Associate Professor and Centre Coordinator of the Fashion Design Department. She has taught part-time at NID, NIFT, and Pearl. She is a researcher and an educator in the field of clothing, textiles, crafts, and design. She has a PhD in History of Arts (Dress and Textiles) from the University of Glasgow, UK; M.Sc. in Textiles and Clothing from Lady Irwin College, New Delhi, India; and has been associated as a PhD fellow with the Centre for Textile Research, Copenhagen, Denmark. Realizing the need for the promotion of indigenous research and bringing it closer to interested people, she along with many like-minded people, set up the TCRC, Textiles and Clothing Research Centre, New Delhi in 2016. She is currently also the secretary of TCRC and Dean (Design Skills) at the Rajasthan ILD Skills University. She has authored and presented many papers at national and international conferences.

Madhu Kaushik, with a solid academic background of 15 plus years, is actively researching the subject of Organizational Behaviour and Human Resources. She was recently awarded the Degree of Doctoral of Philosophy in Human Resources from Vivekananda Global University, Jaipur.

Bhavnesh Kumar is an Assistant Professor in the area power electronics & drives at Division of Instrumentation & Control Engineering, NSIT Delhi. He holds Bacheclor of Technology in Electrical & Electronics from Uttar Pradesh Technical University, Lucknow and Master of Technology in Control & Instrumentation from Motilal Nehru National Institute of Technology, Allahabad. He holds a Ph.D from Gautam Buddha University, Greater Noida in the area of artificial intelligent controllers for induction motor drives. With a teaching experience of more than five years he had served GBU, Greater Noida, Airports Authority of India, KNGD Modi Engineering College, Modinagar. He has published various research papers in journals and conferences. He has presented his research work in many international conferences. He is a member of various professional bodies such as Institute of Electrical and Electronics Engineers (IEEE), International Association of Computer Science and Information Technology (IACSIT).

Manish Kumar is an enthusiastic and dedicated research scholar in the department of Instrumentation & Control Engineering of Netaji Subhas Institute of Technology, University of Delhi. He is skilled in electric vehicle motor control algorithm with strong knowledge in drives and power electronic control. His focus is on developing an intelligent electric vehicle controller. He has a strong publication record related to motor control -based techniques within electric motor drives. He has obtained his

Master of Technology from Jamia Millia Islamia University, Delhi and Bachelor of Technology from Mahatma Jyotibha Phule Rohilkhand University, Bareilly.

Diliza L. Madikiza is based in the Research Administration division of the University of South Africa. His research interests are in sustainable business practices, media, and communications. He holds postgraduate degrees in communications and business management.

Pallavi Mishra is serving as an Associate Professor at Amity School of Communication, Amity University Rajasthan, Jaipur, India. Awarded with the Junior Research Fellowship by the University Grant Commission, Government of India. Awarded with a meritorious award of Second Topper in Master of Mass Communication from the University of Lucknow. With over a decade of experience in academics and industry her work has centred around Print Journalism, Creative Writing, Radio, TV, Communication, Research and Digital Media. Digital Media has a diverse set of unconventional career opportunities which are riding the crest of the wave in all facets of the media industry. With a rigorous thinking and thorough understanding of academics cultivated student's involvement through capturing their interest in training, support, and guidance and Awarded with Asian Education Awards 2021 for the Contribution to Student Development and Excellence in Education. Awarded with Best Paper Award for her Research Paper Award. She has served in renowned organizations like Banasthali Vidyapith, Rajasthan, University of Lucknow, Lucknow, Hindustan Times, Lucknow. Apart from the Academic contribution she is the Convener of Amity's Institution's Innovation Council and Entrepreneurship cell wherein she train budding entrepreneurs to develop their business models and groom their entrepreneurship skills.

Asha Rani received her B.Tech. in Electrical Engineering from Regional Engineering College (Now NIT), Hamirpur, Himachal Pradesh in 1998. She received M.E. degree in Electrical Engineering from IIT Roorkee in 2000 and Ph.D in 2013from University of Delhi, Delhi. She joined as lecturer in Instrumentation and Control Engineering Division at Netaji Subhas University of Technology, New Delhi in 2001 and currently she is a Professor in the organisation. She has published many papers in international journals and conferences. More than 28 M.Tech. and 6 Ph.D. thesis are completed under her guidance. Currently 3 Ph.D. students are working under her supervision. Her areas of research are Renewable Energy, Intelligent Control, Adaptive Control, Softcomputing based Adaptive Control, Biomedical Signal Processing and Robotic manipulator. She is the senior member of IEEE and IETE.

Amit Kumar Singh is currently working as an Assistant Professor in a renowned university. He is a MTech in computer science & engineering with specialisation in security, MCA, PGDCA and B.Sc. (Maths). He currently pursuing the PhD in the field of malware analysis. He is a certified ethical hacker, digital forensic expert and certified network security specialist. He has more than 8 years of training & teaching experiences. His areas of research are Malware Analysis, Intrusion Detection system, Cryptography, Blockchain. He has published research papers in national and international journals of repute and indexing agency. He has published two patents. Besides these he also associates as a Chief Editor, Guest Editor, and Reviewer of various International and National Journal of repute.

Ambar Srivastava is currently working as Assistant Professor in the Department of Commerce at Eternal University Himachal Pradesh India. Mr. Srivastave completed his M.Com from Jai Narayan Vyas University, Jodhpur and also cleared Group I of Chartered Accountant final course.

Swapnesh Taterh is currently serving as Professor & Head, Amity Institute of Information Technology, Amity University Rajasthan, Jaipur, India. In an academic career spanning over 20 years, he had served with various responsibilities Departmental Coordinator, Program Coordinator, Library Faculty In-charge, Mentor and Member of various committees like – Research Committee, Board of Studies, Academic Council, Examination Committee, Discipline Committee, Technical Program Committee and others. As an ingenious researcher, had presented several research papers at national and international conferences and published more than 45 research papers in international journals. His doctoral thesis work focuses on software security. He holds two master degrees in computer science and a bachelor degree in science. His current and prospective research & academic interests include Information Security and Open Source software. He had Filled Patents and published research paper in reputed Indexed journals with Impact Factor 13.473, ranking it 2 out of 162 in Computer Science Journal, SCIE, 2021. Besides these he also participated in UGC sponsored Orientation & Refresher Course, Awarded with A+ Grade. He associates as a Chief Editor, Guest Editor, and Reviewer of International and National Journal of repute including IGI and InderScience.

Anadi Trikha is a strong education professional and currently pursuing a Doctoral of Philosophy in Consumer Behavior from Rajasthan Technical University.

Emmanuel Uniamikogbo is an Associate Professor of Accounting at the Department of Accounting, Rhema University, Nigeria. He is a researcher with research interest in corporate reporting, taxation, international accounting, petroleum accounting, public sector accounting, accounting theory, auditing, forensic accounting, etc. He reviews articles for reputable international and local journals. He possessed skills in diverse fields of study outside accounting and auditing.

Ikedinachi Ayodele Power Wogu (PhD) has authored or co-authored over 93 publications comprising Journal articles, Books, Book Chapters, Book Review, Editorial Reviews Keynote addresses, Monographs, and Peer-reviewed Conference Proceedings/papers, with indexing in reputable indexing bodies like IEEE, Thomson Reuters, Scopus, ISI, Springer, Tailor and Francis, Web of Science and Google scholar, to mention but a few. His Google scholar citation currently stands at 252. He currently serves as an editor /Ad Hoch editor of the International Journal of Human Capital and Information Technology Professionals (IJHCITP), Educational Research Journal (ERJ); A Book of chapters: Handbook of Research on the Role of Human Factors in IT Project Management; Journal of International and Global Studies (JIGS); International Journal of Political Science and Development (IJPSD) and an IGI Global Book of Chapters: Recent Applications of Financial Risk Modelling and Portfolio Management. He currently teaches and conducts research in the Department of Political Science and Administration, Rhema University Nigeria, Aba, Abia State.

Index

www.ingramcontent.com/pod-product-compliance
Lightning Source LLC
LaVergne TN
LVHW061537290926
849162LV00004B/823